Pro PHP and jQuery

Second Edition

Jason Lengstorf

Keith Wald

Apress®

Pro PHP and jQuery

ISBN-13 (pbk): 978-1-4842-1231-8

ISBN-13 (electronic): 978-1-4842-1230-1

Managing Director: Welmoed Spahr
Lead Editor: Steve Anglin
Technical Reviewer: Tri Phan
Editorial Board: Steve Anglin, Pramila Balan, Louise Corrigan, Jonathan Gennick, Robert Hutchinson, Celestin Suresh John, Michelle Lowman, James Markham, Susan McDermott, Matthew Moodie, Jeffrey Pepper, Douglas Pundick, Ben Renow-Clarke, Gwenan Spearing
Coordinating Editor: Mark Powers
Copy Editor: Mary Behr
Compositor: SPi Global
Indexer: SPi Global
Artist: SPi Global

Distributed to the book trade worldwide by Springer Science+Business Media New York, 233 Spring Street, 6th Floor, New York, NY 10013. Phone 1-800-SPRINGER, fax (201) 348-4505, e-mail orders-ny@springer-sbm.com, or visit www.springeronline.com. Apress Media, LLC is a California LLC and the sole member (owner) is Springer Science + Business Media Finance Inc (SSBM Finance Inc). SSBM Finance Inc is a Delaware corporation.

For information on translations, please e-mail rights@apress.com, or visit www.apress.com.

Apress and friends of ED books may be purchased in bulk for academic, corporate, or promotional use. eBook versions and licenses are also available for most titles. For more information, reference our Special Bulk Sales–eBook Licensing web page at www.apress.com/bulk-sales.

Any source code or other supplementary materials referenced by the author in this text is available to readers at www.apress.com/9781484212318. For detailed information about how to locate your book's source code, go to www.apress.com/source-code/. Readers can also access source code at SpringerLink in the Supplementary Material section for each chapter.

Contents at a Glance

Contents

About the Authors

Jason Lengstorf is a web designer and developer based in Big Sky country. He specializes in content management software using PHP, MySQL, AJAX, and web standards.

   He spends most of his time running Ennui Design: a collection of web designers and developers from all over the world specializing in premium custom websites. In his off hours, he runs a clothing company called Humblecock™ and tries to make time for hobbies including golf, travel, and hunting down new beers.

Keith Wald is an instructor at UC Santa Cruz Extension, an experienced web developer and PHP, JavaScript, Python, and Perl coder.

   He has worked for many years in the chip design industry, and does consulting in a variety of fields including firmware and software development. Originally, he intended to pursue a career as a musician, but then went back to school to get his PhD in physics from UC Berkeley, and has been doing mostly technical work ever since.

About the Technical Reviewer

Tri Phan is the founder of the Programming Learning Channel on YouTube. He has over seven years of experience in the software industry. Specifically, he has worked for many outsourcing companies and has written applications in a variety of programming languages such as PHP, Java, and C#. In addition, he has over six years of experience in teaching at international and technological centers such as Aptech, NIIT, and Kent College.

PART 1

Getting Comfortable with jQuery

In the first part of this book, you'll be getting familiar with the history and basic capabilities of jQuery. By the end of this section, you will have a general grasp on the overarching concepts behind jQuery, and—after you've revisited object-oriented PHP in Part 2—you'll be ready to tackle the exercises in Part 3 (where you actually start building a real-world project with jQuery and PHP).

CHAPTER 1

■ ■ ■

Introducing jQuery

To fully understand jQuery and its applications in modern web programming, it's important to take a moment and look back at where jQuery came from, what needs it was built to fulfill, and what programming in JavaScript was like before jQuery came around.

In this chapter, you'll learn about JavaScript libraries and the needs they seek to fulfill, as well as why jQuery is the library of choice for the majority of web developers. You'll also learn the basics of jQuery, including how to make the library available for use in your applications and how the core of jQuery—its powerful selector engine—works.

Choosing jQuery Over JavaScript

The JavaScript language has a very mixed reputation in the software development community. Much of the syntax superficially resembles that of familiar languages, such as C or Java. But the *semantics* of JavaScript code can be very different, which tends to frustrate the uninitiated. (Noted software architect Douglas Crockford has written and spoken extensively about this, and it is certainly worth looking up his material on the Web if you want to dig deeper.)

The browser adds yet another, even more serious, layer of complication to the web development process. Different browsers provide (in general) different implementations of the JavaScript interpreter. And you have virtually no control over the browser that your end user will be running, or what support it may have for the features you rely on. But the situation is not really as bleak as it might appear; the web development community has stepped up to help.

Understanding JavaScript Libraries

The steep learning curve and the browser support issues associated with JavaScript have been sore spots for developers for years, and as frustrations grew, several ambitious developers started building JavaScript **libraries**, also referred to as JavaScript **frameworks**.

These libraries aimed to simplify the use of JavaScript and make its power more accessible to both new and existing developers by creating easy-to-use control functions that remove some of the heavy lifting from everyday JavaScript tasks. Libraries are especially useful in the realm of AJAX (a term originally derived from Asynchronous JavaScript and XML). As you will see later, AJAX is the key to making web applications more responsive by asynchronously performing needed requests to the server (often without the user even noticing).

JavaScript libraries provide a simpler syntax for common tasks, which translates to a faster workflow for developers and a less intimidating learning curve for beginners. They also eliminate some of the headache involved in coding cross-browser JavaScript by doing all the compatibility checks for you within their built-in methods, which is a *huge* time-saver when coding.

3

▓ **Note** The difference between using jQuery's AJAX tools versus the straight JavaScript method will be explored in Chapter 2.

A good number of JavaScript libraries are available. Several of the most popular currently in use are Prototype (`www.prototypejs.org`), MooTools (`http://mootools.net`), Yahoo! UI Library (`http://developer.yahoo.com/yui`), AngularJS (`https://angularjs.org/`), and Dojo (`https://dojotoolkit.org/`), among others. Many of them provide very different functionality for a variety of purposes, but we will focus on the most popular library targeted specifically at facilitating the most common interactions with the web browser: jQuery.

Understanding the Benefits of jQuery

Every JavaScript framework has its own benefits. jQuery is no exception, providing the following benefits:

- Small file size (approximately 80KB as of version 2.1.4)

- Extremely simple syntax

- Chainable methods

- Easy plug-in architecture for extending the framework

- A huge online community

- Great documentation at `http://api.jquery.com`

- Optional extensions of jQuery for added functionality, such as jQueryUI

Understanding the History of jQuery

The brain child of developer John Resig, jQuery was first announced at BarCamp NYC in early 2006 (for more on BarCamp, see `http://barcamp.org`). Resig noted on his web site that he created jQuery because he was unhappy with the currently available libraries and felt that they could be vastly improved by reducing "syntactic fluff" and adding specific controls for common actions (`http://ejohn.org/blog/selectors-in-javascript/`).

jQuery was a big hit in the development community and quickly gained momentum. Other developers came on to help refine the library, ultimately resulting in the first stable release of jQuery, version 1.0, on August 26, 2006.

Since then, jQuery has progressed to version 2.1.4 (at the time of this writing) and has seen a huge influx of plug-ins from the development community. A **plug-in** is an extension of jQuery that isn't part of the core library. You'll learn more about (and build) jQuery plug-ins in Chapter 10.

Setting Up a Testing Environment

Because there's no better way to understand a new language than to just get your hands dirty, you'll need a testing environment to try out some introductory exercises with jQuery. Fortunately, setting up this testing environment is a simple two-step process: install Firefox, and install Firebug.

Throughout this book, all exercises will assume that you are using the Firefox browser with the Firebug plug-in due to its excellent JavaScript testing console.

Installing Firefox

To get Firefox up and running on your computer, navigate to `http://firefox.com` and download the latest version of Firefox (version 42.0 at the time of this writing), available at `www.mozilla.org/en-US/firefox/products/`.

Installing Firebug

To install Firebug, use Firefox to navigate to `http://getfirebug.com/downloads`, and click the Download link for the latest version (2.0.13 as of this writing). This takes you to the Firefox add-ons directory entry for Firebug. Once there, click the "Add to Firefox" button, which will bring up the installation dialog in the browser (see Figure 1-1). Click the Install button, and wait for the add-on to install.

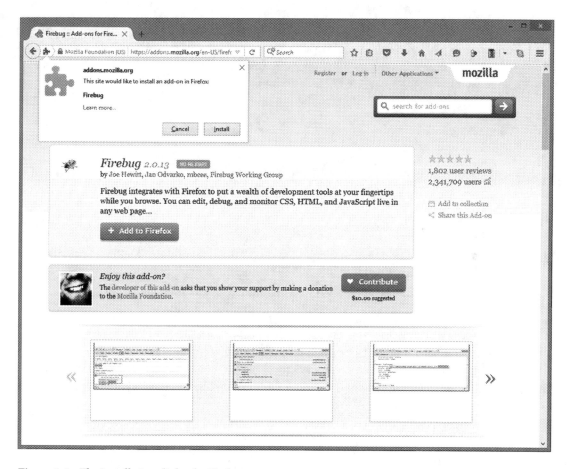

Figure 1-1. *The installation dialog for Firebug*

After the installer completes, an icon will appear in the status bar that looks like a lightning bug. Clicking that icon will bring up the Firebug controls, starting with the console (see Figure 1-2).

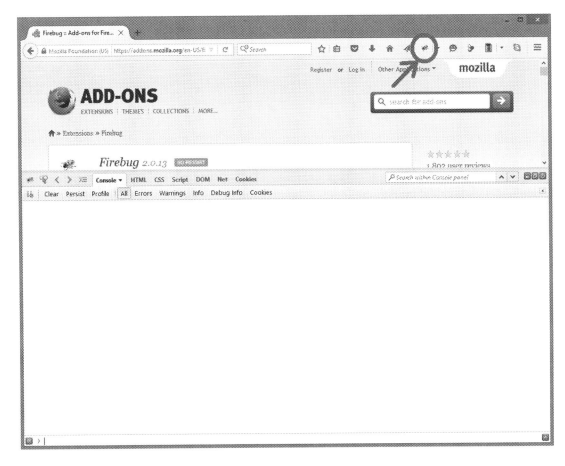

Figure 1-2. *The Firebug add-on opens to the console panel*

▓ **Note** Firebug is useful for much more than JavaScript debugging. It's an invaluable addition to any web developer's arsenal. To learn more, visit `http://getfirebug.com`.

SETTING UP A LOCAL TESTING ENVIRONMENT

Although setting up a local testing environment is not required for the exercises presented in this book, doing so is a good development practice. Testing locally allows for quicker, more secure development and is generally easier than trying to develop on a remote server.

Installing XAMPP

To quickly and easily set up a local development environment on your computer, download and install XAMPP using the following steps.

1. Visit www.apachefriends.org/en/xampp.html, and download the latest version of XAMPP for your operating system (7.0.1 as of this writing). Throughout this book, PHP version 7.x will be assumed; this will become important starting with Chapter 3.

2. Open the downloaded file. For a PC, run the EXE file, select a directory, and install. For a Mac, mount the DMG, and drag the XAMPP folder into your Applications folder.

3. Open the XAMPP Control Panel in the XAMPP folder, and start Apache.

4. Navigate to http://localhost/ to ensure than XAMPP is working. If so, the XAMPP home page will let you know.

In addition to the Windows and Mac versions of XAMPP, there are distributions for Linux and Solaris. Each operating system has quirks when installing XAMPP, so refer to the help section for additional information on getting a local testing environment running on your machine.

Including jQuery in Web Pages

To use jQuery in a project, the library needs to be loaded in your HTML document to give your script access to the library's methods. If the library is not loaded first, any scripts using jQuery syntax will likely result in JavaScript errors. Fortunately, loading jQuery is very simple, and there are a couple of options available to developers to do so.

Including a Downloaded Copy of the jQuery Library

The first option for including jQuery in a project is to save a copy of the library within your project's file structure and include it just like any other JavaScript file:

```
<script src="js/jquery-2.1.4.min.js"></script>
```

7

Including a Remotely Hosted Copy of the jQuery Library

The second option is to include a copy of the jQuery library hosted by Google. This is done in the hopes that visitors to your web site will have a copy of the library already cached from another site including the same file, which decreases load time for your site's users.

The remote copy is included just like the downloaded copy:

```
<script src=" https://ajax.googleapis.com/ajax/libs/jquery/2.1.4/jquery.min.js">
</script>
```

Setting up a Test File

Now that your testing environment is set up, create a new folder in the htdocs folder within your XAMPP installation called testing, and create a new file inside it called index.html. In the editor of your choice, insert the following HTML markup:

```
<!DOCTYPE html>
<html>
<head>
    <title>Testing jQuery</title>
</head>
<body>
    <p>Hello World!</p>
    <p class="foo">Another paragraph, but this one has a class.</p>
    <p><span>This is a span inside a paragraph.</span></p>
    <p id="bar">Paragraph with an id.
        <span class="foo">And this sentence is in a span.</span>
    </p>

    <script src="https://ajax.googleapis.com/ajax/libs/jquery/2.1.4/jquery.min.js">
    </script>
</body>
</html>
```

▓ **Note** Loading the JavaScript right before the closing body tag (</body>) is done to keep the scripts from blocking other page elements, such as images, from loading. Doing so also prevents JavaScript from running before the elements are fully loaded on the page, which can result in unexpected behavior or JavaScript errors.

Save this file and navigate to http://localhost/testing/ in Firefox (see Figure 1-3).

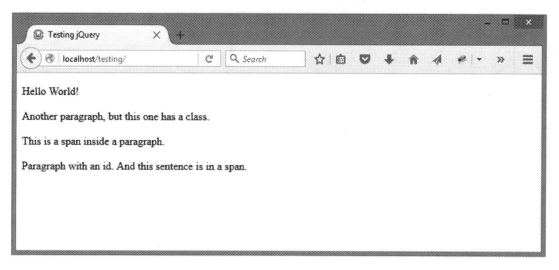

Figure 1-3. *The test file loaded in Firefox*

You'll be using this file to get your feet wet with the basic operations of jQuery.

Introducing the jQuery Function

At the core of jQuery is the jQuery function. This function is the heart and soul of jQuery and is used in every instance where jQuery is implemented. In most implementations of jQuery, the shortcut $() is used instead of jQuery() to keep the code concise.

We won't get too deep into the programming theory that makes this function tick, but basically it creates a jQuery object and evaluates the expression passed as its parameters. It then determines how it should respond and modifies itself accordingly.

■ **Caution**   Certain other JavaScript libraries also use the $() function, so conflicts may occur when attempting to use multiple libraries simultaneously. jQuery provides a fix for this situation with jQuery.noConflict(). For more information, see http://docs.jquery.com/Core/jQuery.noConflict.

Selecting DOM Elements Using CSS Syntax

Everything in jQuery revolves around its incredibly powerful selector engine. The rest of this chapter teaches you the different methods with which you can select elements from the Document Object Model (DOM) using jQuery.

▓ **Note**   The DOM is a collection of objects and nodes that make up HTML, XHTML, and XML documents. It is platform-and language-independent; this essentially means that developers can use a variety of programming languages (such as JavaScript) to access and modify DOM information on multiple platforms (such as web browsers) without compatibility issues.

One of the strongest and most alluring features of jQuery is the ease with which a developer is able to select elements within the DOM. The use of pseudo-CSS selectors[1] adds an incredible level of power to jQuery. Pseudo-CSS allows a developer to target specific instances of elements in his HTML. This is especially helpful to anyone with prior experience with CSS due to the nearly identical syntax. Essentially, using the same CSS syntax you would use to set up style rules, you're able to select elements in the following ways:

- Basic selectors
- Hierarchy selectors
- Filters
  - Basic filters
  - Content filters
  - Visibility filters
  - Attribute filters
  - Child filters
- Form filters

Basic Selectors

The basic selectors allow developers to select elements by tag type, class name, ID, or any combination thereof. While viewing `http://localhost/testing/`, launch the Firebug dialog, and click the Console tab (see Figure 1-4). If the Console panel is disabled, click the Console tab, and select Enabled. You will be using this console for all examples in this chapter.

---

[1] www.w3schools.com/CSS/css_pseudo_classes.asp.

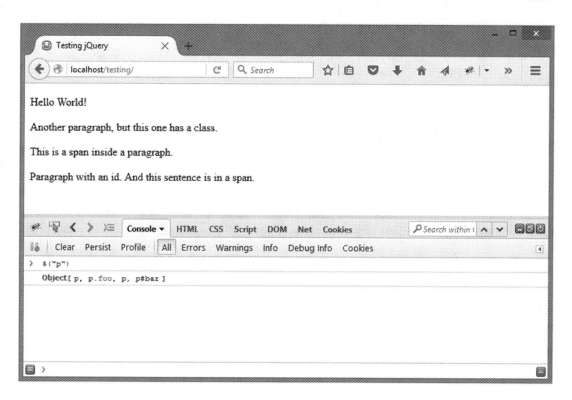

Figure 1-4. *The Firebug console after executing a command*

▨ **Note**   If you're familiar with CSS, you will be able to skim this section, because the selectors behave the same as their CSS counterparts.

Selecting Elements by Tag Type

To select an element by tag type, simply use the name of the tag (such as p, div, or span) as your selector:

element

To select all paragraph (<p>) tags in your test document, enter the following snippet at the bottom of the console:

$("p");

Press Enter and the code will execute. The following results will be displayed in the console (see Figure 1-4):

```
> $("p");
Object[ p, p.foo, p, p#bar ]
```

The first line shows the command that was executed, and the second line shows what was returned from the code. There are four paragraph tags in your test document: two without class or ID attributes, one with a class foo, and one with an ID bar (you'll learn about this syntax in the next sections). When you pass the tag name to the jQuery function, all instances are found and added to the jQuery object.

Selecting Tags by Class Name

Just as quickly as you can select by tag type, you can select elements by their assigned class or classes. The syntax for this is the use the class name preceded by a period (.):

```
.class
```

Select all the elements with the class foo by executing the following snippet in the console:

```
$(".foo");
```

After execution, the following will show up in the console:

```
> $(".foo");
Object[ p.foo, span.foo ]
```

Both a paragraph tag and a span are returned, since they both have the class foo.

Selecting Elements by ID

To select an element by its ID attribute, the CSS syntax of the ID preceded by a hash sign (#) is used:

```
#id
```

Match all elements with an ID of bar with the following:

```
$("#bar");
```

Only one paragraph in your document has an ID of "bar", as you can see in the result:

```
> $("#bar");
Object[ p#bar ]
```

Combining Selectors for More Precise Selection

In some situations, it may be necessary to isolate only certain tags that correspond to a class, which is easy to do by combining tag type and class in your selector.

Enter the following in the console to select only paragraph tags with the class foo:

```
$("p.foo");
```

The results in the console confirm that the span was ignored, even though it has the class foo:

```
> $("p.foo");
Object[p.foo]
```

Using Multiple Selectors

In the event that you need to access multiple elements, multiple selectors can be used to access all of those elements at once. For instance, if you want to select any paragraph tag with a class of foo or any element with an ID of bar, you can use the following:

```
$("p.foo,#bar");
```

This returns elements that match *at least one* selector specified in the string:

```
> $("p.foo,#bar");
Object[ p.foo, p#bar ]
```

Hierarchy Selectors

Sometimes, it's not enough to be able to select by element, class, or ID. There are points at which you'll need to access elements contained within, next to, or after another element, such as removing an active class from all menu items except the one that was just clicked, grabbing all the list items out of the selected unordered list, or changing attributes on the wrapper element when a form item is selected.

Selecting Descendant Elements

Selecting descendant elements, which are elements contained within other elements, is done using the ancestor selector followed by a space and the descendant selector, like so:

```
ancestor descendent
```

To select descendant spans in your test document, execute the following command in the Firebug console:

```
$("body span");
```

This will find all spans contained within the body tag (<body>) of the document, even though the spans are also inside paragraph tags:

```
> $("body span");
Object[ span, span.foo ]
```

13

Selecting Child Elements

Child elements are a more specific style of descendant selector. Only the very next level of element is considered for matching. To select a child element, use the parent element followed by a greater than (>) symbol, followed by the child element to match:

```
parent>child
```

In your test file, try to select any spans that are child elements of the body element by entering the following command in the console:

```
$("body>span");
```

Because there are no spans directly contained within the body element, the console will output the following:

```
> $("body>span");
Object[ ]
```

Next, filter all span elements that are direct children of a paragraph element:

```
$("p>span");
```

The resulting output looks like this:

```
> $("p>span");
Object[ span, span.foo ]
```

Selecting Next Elements

Occasionally in a script you'll need to select the next element in the DOM. This is accomplished by providing an identifier for the starting element (any selector pattern works here), followed by a plus sign (+), followed by the selector to match the next instance, like so:

```
start+next
```

Try this in the console by typing the following command:

```
$(".foo+p");
```

There is only one element with the class foo, so only one paragraph element is returned:

```
> $('.foo+p');
Object[ p ]
```

Next, use a more general query, and select the next paragraph element after any paragraph element:

```
$('p+p');
```

There are four paragraphs in the markup, and all of them but the last have a next paragraph, so the console will display three elements in the result:

```
> $('p+p');
Object[ p.foo, p, p#bar ]
```

This result set is the second, third, and fourth paragraphs from the HTML markup.

Selecting Sibling Elements

Sibling elements are any elements contained within the same element. Selecting sibling elements works similarly to selecting next elements, except the sibling selector will match *all* sibling elements after the starting element, rather than just the next one.

To select sibling elements, use the starting element selector, followed by an equivalency sign (~), and the selector to match sibling elements with, like so:

```
start~siblings
```

To match all siblings after the paragraph with class foo, execute the following command in the console:

```
$(".foo~p");
```

The result set will look like the following:

```
> $(".foo~p");
Object[ p, p#bar ]
```

Basic Filters

Filters are another very powerful method of accessing elements in the DOM. Instead of relying on element types, classes, or IDs, you're able to find elements based on their position, current state, or other variables.

The basic syntax of a filter is a colon (:) followed by the filter name:

```
:filter
```

In some filters, a parameter can be passed in parentheses:

```
:filter(parameter)
```

The most common and useful filters are covered in the next few sections.

■ **Note** Not all available filters are covered here for the sake of getting into actual development quickly. For a complete listing of available filters, see the jQuery documentation.

Selecting First or Last Elements

One of the most common uses of filters is to determine if an element is the first or last element in a set. With filters, finding the first or last element is incredibly simple. You just append the filter :first or :last to any selector, like so:

```
$("p:last");
```

This returns the following when executed in the console:

```
> $("p:last");
Object[ p#bar ]
```

Selecting Elements That Do Not Match a Selector

If you need to find all elements that *don't* match a selector, the :not() filter is the easiest way to go about it. Append this filter to your selector along with a selector as its parameter, and the result set will return any elements that match the original selector, but not the selector passed as a parameter to :not().

For example,

```
$("p:not(.foo)");
```

will return the following result set:

```
> $("p:not(.foo)");
Object[ p, p, p#bar ]
```

Selecting Even or Odd Elements

Similar to :first and :last, the :even and :odd filters are syntactically simple and return exactly what you might expect, the even or odd elements from a result set, respectively:

```
$("p:odd");
```

Executing the preceding line in the console will result in the following output:

```
> $("p:odd");
Object [ p.foo, p#bar ]
```

Selecting Elements by Index

In the event that you need to grab a particular element by its index, the :eq() filter allows you to specify which element is needed by passing an index as the filter's parameter:

```
$("p:eq(3)");
```

This outputs the following:

```
> $("p:eq(3)"); ,
Object[ p#bar ]
```

> ▓ **Note** An element's **index** refers to its position among other elements in the set. Counting in programming starts at zero (0), so the first element is at index 0, the second is at index 1, and so on.

Content Filters

Filters are also available to select elements based on their content. These can range from containing certain text to surrounding a given element.

Selecting Elements That Contain Certain Text

To select only elements that contain certain text, use the :contains() filter, where the text to be matched is passed as a parameter to the filter:

```
$("p:contains(Another)");
```

When executed in the console, the preceding line will return the following:

```
> $("p:contains(Another)");
Object[ p.foo ]
```

> ▓ **Note** The :contains() filter is case sensitive, meaning capitalization matters for matching text. A case-insensitive version of the filter has been added to the comments of the :contains() entry on the API documentation by a member of the development community. For more on this filter, see http://api.jquery.com/contains-selector.

Selecting Elements That Contain a Certain Element

If you need to select only elements that contain another element, you can use the :has() filter. This works similarly to :contains(), except it accepts an element name instead of a string of text:

```
$("p:has(span)");
```

When executed in the console, this outputs the following:

```
> $("p:has(span)");
Object[ p, p#bar ]
```

Only paragraphs containing span elements are returned.

Selecting Elements That Are Parents

The opposite of :empty, :parent will only match elements that contain children, which can be either other elements, text, or both.

Select all paragraphs that are parents using the following:

```
$("p:parent");
```

Because all paragraphs in your sample HTML document contain text (and other elements in some cases), all paragraphs are returned in the result set:

```
> $("p:parent");
Object[ p, p.foo, p, p#bar ]
```

Visibility Filters

Visibility filters, :hidden and :visible, will select elements that are, respectively, hidden and visible. Select all visible paragraphs like so:

```
$("p:visible");
```

Because none of the elements in your HTML example are currently hidden, this returns the following result set:

```
> $("p:visible");
Object[ p, p.foo, p, p#bar ]
```

Attribute Filters

Element attributes are also a great way to select elements. An **attribute** is anything in the element that further defines it (this includes the class, href, ID, or title attributes). For the following examples, you'll be accessing the class attribute.

▦ **Note**   Please bear in mind that it is faster (and better practice) to use ID (#id) and class (.class) selectors in production scripts whenever possible; the examples below are just to demonstrate the capabilities of the filter.

Selecting Elements That Match an Attribute and Value

To match elements that have a given attribute and value, enclose the attribute-value pair in square brackets ([ ]):

```
[attribute=value]
```

To select all elements with a class attribute of foo, execute the following in the console:

```
$("[class=foo]");
```

This returns the following:

```
> $("[class=foo]");
Object[ p.foo, span.foo ]
```

Selecting Elements That Don't Have the Attribute or Don't Match the Attribute Value

Inversely, to select elements that *do not* match an attribute-value pair, insert an exclamation point (!) before the equals sign between the attribute and value:

```
[attribute!=value]
```

Select all paragraphs without the class foo by running the following command:

```
$("p[class!=foo]");
```

This results in the following:

```
> $("p[class!=foo]");
Object[ p, p, p#bar ]
```

Child Filters

Child filters add an alternative to the use of :even, :odd, or :eq(). The main difference is that this set of filters starts indexing at 1 instead of 0 (like :eq() does).

Selecting Even or Odd Parameters or Parameters by Index or Equation

One of the more versatile filters, :nth-child() provides four different options to pass as a parameter when selecting elements: even, odd, index, or an equation.

Like other child filters, this one starts indexing at 1 instead of 0, so the first element is at index 1, the second element at 2, and so on.

Using :odd, the result set contained the paragraphs with a class of foo and an ID of foo; select odd paragraphs using :nth-child() to see the difference in how the filters handle by executing the following command:

```
$("p:nth-child(odd)");
```

The results display as follows in the console:

```
> $("p:nth-child(odd)");
Object[ p, p ]
```

Although this output may seem strange, the mismatched results are a product of the difference in how the elements index.

Selecting First or Last Child Elements

While very similar to :first and :last, :first-child and :last-child differ in that the returned element set can contain more than one match. For instance, to find the last span that is a child of a paragraph element, you might use

```
$("p span:last");
```

which returns the following in the console:

```
> $("p span:last");
Object[ span.foo ]
```

However, if you needed to find *every* span that was the last child of a paragraph element, you would use :last-child instead:

```
$("p span:last-child");
```

This uses each parent as a reference instead of the DOM as a whole, so the results are different:

```
> $("p span:last-child");
Object[ span, span.foo ]
```

Form Filters

Forms are a huge part of web sites these days, and their major role inspired a set of filters specifically geared toward forms.

Because your HTML example does not have any form elements in it, you'll need to append the file with some new markup for the following examples. In index.html, add the following HTML between the last paragraph tag and the first script tag:

```
<form action="#" method="post">
    <fieldset>
        <legend>Sign Up Form</legend>
        <label for="name">Name</label><br />
        <input name="name" id="name" type="text" /><br />
        <label for="password">Password</label><br />
        <input name="password" id="password"
            type="password" /><br /><br />
        <label>
            <input type="radio" name="loc" />
            I'm on my computer
        </label><br />
        <label>
            <input type="radio" name="loc" checked="checked" />
            I'm on a shared computer
        </label><br /><br />
```

```
        <input type="submit" value="Log In" /><br />
        <label>
            <input type="checkbox" name="notify"
                    disabled="true" />
            Keep me signed in on this computer
        </label><br />
    </fieldset>
</form>
```

After saving, reload the page in your browser at http://localhost/testing/ to see the form for testing (see Figure 1-5).

Figure 1-5. *The form as it appears after editing index.html*

> ▨ **Note** Because this page includes a password field, and you are running in plain (non-secure) mode, you will likely see security warnings as in Figure 1-5. Configuring your apache setup to run securely would take you too far afield here, but of course production applications should be run in secure (https) mode. See the docs at `https://httpd.apache.org/docs/2.4/ssl/` for more info.

Matching by Form Element Type

The most common form-specific filters simply match form element types. The available filters are `:button`, `:checkbox`, `:file`, `:image`, `:input`, `:password`, `:radio`, `:submit`, and `:text`.

To select all radio inputs, use the following code:

```
$("input:radio");
```

This outputs the following in the console:

```
> $("input:radio");
Object[ input property value = "on" attribute value = "null", input property value = "on"
attribute value = "null" ]
```

These filters are particularly useful because all of the provided types are input elements, so matching certain types of inputs only without these filters would be a little more difficult.

Selecting Only Enabled or Disabled Form Elements

Additionally, filters to select enabled or disabled form elements are available using `:enabled` and `:disabled`. To select all disabled form elements, use the following code:

```
$(":disabled");
```

This outputs the following in the console:

```
> $(":disabled");
Object[ input property value = "on" attribute value = "null" ]
```

The "Keep me signed in on this computer" check box is disabled, and therefore returned, by the `:disabled` filter.

Selecting Checked or Selected Form Elements

Radio and check box inputs have a `checked` state, and select inputs have a `selected` state. Filters are provided to retrieve the form elements that are in either state using `:checked` or `:selected`, respectively.

To select the currently checked radio button in your HTML example, execute the following code in the console:

```
$(":checked");
```

This returns the radio input that is currently selected in the console:

```
> $(":checked");
Object[ input property value = "on" attribute value = "null" ]
```

Summary

In this chapter you learned what jQuery is, why it was created, and the basics of how it works. You also set up a development environment using XAMPP, Firefox, and the Firebug plug-in.

At this point, you should feel comfortable selecting elements from the DOM using jQuery's powerful selector engine. This chapter was a tad dry, but it's important that you fully understand the *how* of jQuery before moving on to heavier bits of coding.

In the next chapter, you'll learn how to traverse, access, and manipulate the DOM using jQuery's built-in methods.

CHAPTER 2

Common jQuery Actions and Methods

Now that you understand how element selection works, you can start learning the basics of how jQuery simplifies interaction with web pages. In this chapter, you'll get your hands dirty with the most common and useful aspects of jQuery.

This chapter will read more like a reference and may be a bit dry at times, but it's definitely in your best interest to work through the examples presented within. Having a basic understanding of how these methods work and what they do will prove invaluable as you start building the example project later on in this book.

Understanding the Basic Behavior of jQuery Scripts

One of the most convenient features of jQuery is the fact that nearly all its methods are **chainable**, which means methods can be executed one right after the other. This leads to clear, concise code that is easy to follow, like

```
$('p')
    .addClass('new-class')
    .text("I'm a paragraph!")
    .appendTo('body');
```

Chainable methods are possible because each method returns the jQuery object itself after modification. At first, this concept may seem difficult to understand, but as you work through the examples in this chapter, it should become clearer.

Understanding jQuery Methods

jQuery attempts to make several common programming tasks easier. At a glance, it simplifies JavaScript development by providing the following powerful tools:

- DOM element selection using CSS syntax (which you learned in Chapter 1)
- Simple traversal and modification of the DOM
- Easy syntax for handling browser events (such as clicks and mouse-overs)

- Access to all attributes of an element, including CSS and styling properties, and the ability to modify them

- Animation and other effects

- Simple AJAX controls

▓ **Note**   The preceding list is only a partial list of jQuery's features and capabilities. As you continue on through the projects in this book, other helpful features will be explored. As always, for a complete reference, visit the documentation at `http://api.jquery.com`.

Traversing DOM Elements

Traversal in jQuery is the act of moving from one DOM element to another; traversal is essentially another form of filtering performed *after* the initial selection has been made. This is useful because it allows developers to complete an action and then move to another part of the DOM without needing to perform another search by selector.

It also aids developers in affecting the elements immediately surrounding an element that is being manipulated or otherwise utilized by a script. This can range from adding a class to parent elements to indicate activity to disabling all inactive form elements to any number of other useful tasks.

▓ **Note**   You will be using the HTML test file from Chapter 1 for the examples in this chapter as well. If you're using XAMPP to test locally, point your browser to `http://localhost/testing/` to load this file. Make sure the Firebug console is open and active (see Chapter 1 for a refresher on using the Firebug console).

.eq()

If a set of elements needs to be narrowed down to just one element identified by its index, then you can use the `.eq()` method. This method accepts one argument: an index for the desired element. For `.eq()`, indices start at 0.

```
$("p").eq(1);
```

When executed in the Firebug console, the following returns:

```
> $("p").eq(1);
Object[ p.foo ]
```

Additionally, a negative number can be supplied to `.eq()` to count backward from the end of the selection set (e.g., passing -2 will return the second-to-last element from the set).

To select the same paragraph as the preceding example by counting backward from the end of the result set, use the following code:

```
$("p").eq(-3);
```

This returns the same paragraph in the console:

```
> $("p").eq(-3);
Object[ p.foo ]
```

.filter() and .not()

To use a whole new selector within a set of elements, the `.filter()` method comes in handy. It accepts any selector that can be used in the jQuery function, but it applies only to the subset of elements contained within the jQuery object.

For instance, to select all paragraphs and then filter out all but the ones with class foo, use the following:

```
$("p").filter(".foo");
```

The result in the console will read as follows:

```
> $("p").filter(".foo");
Object[ p.foo ]
```

The inverse of `.find()` is `.not()`, which will return all elements from a result set that *do not* match the given selector. For instance, to select all paragraphs and then limit the selection to paragraphs that do not have the class foo, use the following:

```
$("p").not(".foo");
```

This results in the following:

```
> $("p").not(".foo");
Object[ p, p, p#bar ]
```

.first() and .last()

The `.first()` and `.last()` methods work identically to `.eq(0)` and `.eq(-1)`, respectively. To select the last paragraph from a set of all paragraphs on the page, use the following:

```
$("p").last();
```

This results in the following:

```
> $("p").last();
Object[ p#bar ]
```

.has()

To select an element that contains elements matching a certain pattern, you can use the .has() method. For instance, use the following to select all paragraphs and filter the results to only paragraphs that contain a span element:

```
$("p").has("span");
```

This outputs the following:

```
> $("p").has("span");
Object[ p, p#bar ]
```

.is()

The .is() method is a little different from other methods in that it *does not return* the jQuery object. It evaluates a result set without modifying it, which makes it ideal for use in callback functions or functions executed after the successful execution of a function or method.

You'll learn more about practical uses of .is() in later examples of this book; right now, select all paragraphs in your test document and then check if one has the class foo:

```
$("p").is(".foo");
```

The result is a Boolean (true or false) answer:

```
> $("p").is(".foo");
true
```

.slice()

To select a subset of elements based on its index, the .slice() method comes into play. It accepts two arguments: the first is a starting index from which to generate the subset, and the second is an optional ending point. If the second parameter isn't supplied, the subset will continue until the end of the selection is reached.

░ **Note**   The index passed in the second parameter *will not be included* in the result set. Therefore, if you need the second through the fourth elements in a set (indices 1 to 3), your parameters need to be 1 and 4.

Additionally, like with .eq(), a negative index can be used. This can be applied to the start and/or end point.

To select all paragraphs and then limit the selection to the second and third paragraphs, use the following code:

```
$("p").slice(1,3);
```

The result in the console reads as follows:

```
> $("p").slice(1,3);
Object[ p.foo, p ]
```

To select the last two elements from the paragraph set, use the following:

```
$("p").slice(-2);
```

This generates the following result:

```
> $("p").slice(-2);
Object[ p, p#bar ]
```

.children()

Oftentimes it becomes necessary to drill down in a result set to find child elements. This is accomplished using the .children() method, which accepts one optional parameter: a selector to match child elements against.

To select all paragraphs and then change the selection to match all child elements of the paragraphs, execute the following code:

```
$("p").children();
```

This outputs the following:

```
> $("p").children();
Object[ span, span.foo ]
```

If you need a more specific set of children than that, you can pass an optional selector to the .children() method. To select all paragraphs and then find all children with a class foo, use the following:

```
$("p").children(".foo");
```

This produces the following results:

```
> $("p").children(".foo");
Object[ span.foo ]
```

.closest()

The `.closest()` method is an easy way to find elements up the **DOM tree**, which is the nesting order of elements (a DOM tree relationship in this example is the span within a paragraph within the body element).

For example, to find the closest paragraph to the span with class foo, run the following code snippet in the console:

```
$("span.foo").closest("p");
```

This outputs the following:

```
> $("span.foo").closest("p");
Object[ p#bar ]
```

.find()

Similar to the `.children()` method, the `.find()` method matches descendants of elements within the current set. The main difference between `.find()` and `.children()` is that `.children()` only checks one level down in the DOM tree, whereas `.find()` doesn't care how deep the matched elements are.

To demonstrate, select the body tag and then find any contained span elements using the following:

```
$("body").find("span");
```

This results in both spans being returned:

```
> $("body").find("span");
Object[ span, span.foo ]
```

However, if you try the same thing using `.children()`, an empty result set is returned:

```
> $("body").children("span");
Object[ ]
```

.next(), .nextAll(), and .nextUntil()

A trio of useful methods for finding the next sibling elements in a set is provided in `.next()`, `.nextAll()`, and `.nextUntil()`.

The `.next()` method will find the next sibling element in the set for each of the elements in the original result set. To select a paragraph with class foo and then traverse to the next sibling element, execute the following code in the console:

```
$("p.foo").next();
```

This generates the following output:

```
> $("p.foo").next();
Object[ p ]
```

A selector can be passed to .next() as well, which allows developers to determine *which type* of next sibling element should be matched:

```
$("p.foo").next("#bar");
```

This returns an empty result set, since the next element does not have an ID of bar:

```
> $("p.foo").next("#bar");
Object[ ]
```

Because .next() returns only one element, a companion method was created that returns all next sibling elements, .nextAll(). To select all paragraphs after the paragraph with the class foo, use the following code:

```
$(".foo").nextAll("p");
```

This returns the following result:

```
> $(".foo").nextAll("p");
Object[ p, p#bar ]
```

▓ **Note**   The selector is optional in .nextAll(), as it is in .next().

The third method available for selecting next sibling elements is the .nextUntil() method. As its name suggests, this method will return all next elements until a selector is matched. It's important to note that the element matched by the selector *will not be included in the result set*.

To demonstrate this, select the paragraph with the class foo and use .nextUntil() with a selector of "#bar":

```
$(".foo").nextUntil("#bar");
```

Only one paragraph is returned in the result set, and the paragraph with the ID of bar is not included:

```
> $(".foo").nextUntil("#bar");
Object[ p ]
```

To include the paragraph with an ID of bar, you need to look at the element immediately following, which is the form element in this case. Try the selector again using this updated code:

```
$(".foo").nextUntil("form");
```

Now both following paragraphs are returned:

```
> $(".foo").nextUntil("form");
Object[ p, p#bar ]
```

.prev(), .prevAll(), and .prevUntil()

The .prev(), .prevAll(), and .prevUntil() functions work exactly like .next(), .nextAll(), and .nextUntil(), except they look at previous sibling elements rather than next sibling elements:

```
> $("#bar").prev();
Object[ p ]

> $("#bar").prevAll();
Object[ p, p.foo, p ]

> $("#bar").prevUntil(".foo");
Object[ p ]
```

.siblings()

To select sibling elements on both sides of an element, use the .siblings() method. This accepts a selector as an argument to limit what types of elements are returned. To match all sibling paragraph elements to the paragraph with ID bar, execute the following code:

```
$("#bar").siblings("p");
```

The results will look as follows:

```
> $("#bar").siblings("p");
Object[ p, p.foo, p ]
```

.parent()

The .parent() method returns a set of the immediate parent elements of the current selection. For instance, to select all parent elements of any elements with the class foo, use the following:

```
$(".foo").parent();
```

This returns the following:

```
> $(".foo").parent();
Object[ body, p#bar ]
```

To match only paragraph elements that are parents of elements with class foo, modify the code to the following:

```
$(".foo").parent("p");
```

This narrows the result set:

```
> $(".foo").parent("p");
Object[ p#bar ]
```

.parents() and .parentsUntil()

Unlike .parent(), .parents() will return all parent elements, with an optional selector passed to filter the results.

To select all parent elements of the check box in the form on the example page, use the following code:

```
$(":checkbox").parents();
```

This finds every parent element, all the way out to the html element:

```
> $(":checkbox").parents();
Object[ label, fieldset, form #, body, html ]
```

To filter the results so that only the parent form element is returned, modify the code as follows:

```
$(":checkbox").parents("form");
```

This returns only the parent form element:

```
> $(":checkbox").parents("form");
Object[ form # ]
```

Finally, to select a range of parents until a selector is matched, similar to .nextUntil() or .prevUntil(), use .parentsUntil():

```
$(":checkbox").parentsUntil("form");
```

This returns all parent elements until the form element is encountered:

```
> $(":checkbox").parentsUntil("form");
Object[ label, fieldset ]
```

.add()

The `.add()` method is versatile and, therefore, a bit more complicated. Essentially, it allows you to add additional elements to the existing jQuery object using a selector or a string of HTML.

To select all paragraphs and then add the span with class `foo` to the object, use the following:

```
$("p").add("span.foo");
```

This outputs the following:

```
> $("p").add("span.foo");
Object[ p, p.foo, p, p#bar, span.foo ]
```

The `.add()` method also allows you to create elements on the fly, like so:

```
$("p").add('<span id="bat">This is a new span</span>');
```

Executing the preceding code will output this:

```
> $("p").add('<span id="bat">This is a new span</span>');
Object[ p, p.foo, p, p#bar, span#bat ]
```

▓ **Note** Notice that the element `span#bat` is faded in the console output. This happens because, while the element exists in the jQuery object, it has not been appended to the DOM and, therefore, does not display on the page. You'll learn how to add new elements to the DOM in the next section, "Creating and Inserting DOM Elements."

.andSelf()

If you're using a traversal method, you may want to keep the original matched set of elements as well. The c provides this ability by allowing the original set to be recalled and appended to the new set.

For instance, to match all paragraph elements and then find child spans, use the following code:

```
$("p").find("span");
```

This returns the spans in the document, but you've lost the paragraphs:

```
> $("p").find("span");
Object[ span, span.foo ]
```

To keep the paragraphs *and* match the spans, add a call to `.andSelf()` to the end of the code:

```
$("p").find("span").andSelf();
```

This results in the desired output:

```
> $("p").find("span").andSelf();
Object[ p, p.foo, p, span, p#bar, span.foo ]
```

.contents()``

The .contents() method works similarly to the .children() method, except .contents() returns *text nodes* as well, which are simply the character data contained within an element (the actual text displayed by an element).[1]

To find all contents of the span with class foo, use the following:

```
$("span.foo").contents();
```

This results in the following output:

```
> $("span.foo").contents();
Object[ <TextNode textContent="And this sentence is in a span."> ]
```

.end()

At times in jQuery scripts you will find it necessary to back up to the last set of elements stored in the jQuery object. The .end() method does exactly this: it reverts the jQuery object to the state immediately preceding the last filtering action in the current jQuery object chain.

To select all paragraphs and then find all spans, the original set of paragraphs is no longer available:

```
> $("p").find("span");
Object[ span, span.foo ]
```

To revert back to the set of paragraphs, add .end() to the chain:

```
> $("p").find("span").end();
Object[ p, p.foo, p, p#bar ]
```

---

[1]www.w3.org/TR/DOM-Level-3-Core/core.html#ID-1312295772

Creating and Inserting DOM Elements

The first thing you'll learn that actually *changes* the DOM, rather than simply selects elements from it, is how to create new elements and insert them into the DOM. Luckily in jQuery, this is pretty straightforward.

This section of the book starts using more involved code snippets, and will therefore require a minor adjustment to your Firebug console. At the bottom right of the console is a round button with an arrow pointing upward (see Figure 2-1).

Figure 2-1. *The button to activate the multiline console test area*

Click this button to activate the multiline testing area, where you'll be able to enter commands across multiple lines, making them easier to read and allowing for more advanced examples (see Figure 2-2).

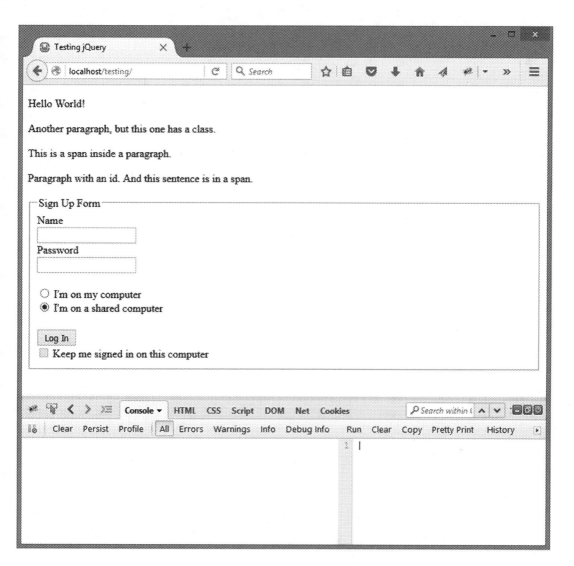

Figure 2-2. *The multiline testing area (shown at the right-hand side of the console)*

With the multiline testing area, you now need to click the Run button at the bottom to execute the code. Pressing Enter, as with the single-line test console, will now break to a new line.

Creating New DOM Elements

To create a new DOM element, jQuery only needs the tag to be created. For instance, to create a new paragraph element, use the following:

```
$("<p>");
```

To add attributes and text to this element, you can simply write it out as plain HTML:

```
$('<p class="bat">This is a new paragraph!</p>');
```

▓ **Note**   The preceding example uses single quotation marks to enclose the string of HTML rather than double ones. This has no effect on the jQuery function; it merely eliminates the need to escape the double quotes used in the class attribute (e.g., `class=\"bat\"`).

You can also add attributes to this new element by passing a second argument as JavaScript Object Notation (JSON)[2]:

```
$("<p>", {
    "class":"bat",
    "text":"This is a new paragraph!"
});
```

This code results in the following:

```
> $("<p>", { "class":"bat", "text":"This is a new paragraph!" });
Object[ p.bat ]
```

Because this is only creating the element, it hasn't been attached to the DOM yet and, therefore, isn't visible in the browser window. You'll learn to insert new elements in the next section, "Inserting New Elements into the DOM."

▓ **Note**   At its simplest, JSON is a key-value pairing where both the key and value are surrounded by quotation marks and all key-value pairs are comma-separated and enclosed in curly braces ({}). A sample of JSON data is { "key":"value" } or { "key1":"value1", "key2":"value2" }.

---

[2]http://en.wikipedia.org/wiki/Json

Inserting New Elements into the DOM

Now that you have a basic understanding of how to create new elements, you can begin learning how to insert them into the DOM. jQuery provides several methods for handling this, which you'll explore in this section.

An important note to make here is that the modification of the DOM is temporary, meaning that any changes made will be reset back to the original HTML document once the page is refreshed. This happens because JavaScript is a *client-side* language, which means it isn't modifying the actual files from the server, but the browser's individual interpretation of the file.

Changes made with JavaScript can be saved on the server through the use of AJAX (which you'll learn about later in this chapter), which allows JavaScript to interface with server-side languages such as PHP.

■ **Note**   After performing the examples in each of the following sections, refresh your page so each new example is starting with a fresh copy of the example HTML file.

.append( ) and .prepend( )

The `.append()` and `.prepend()` functions will attach the elements passed as arguments to the jQuery object to which they are chained. The only difference is that `.append()` attaches the elements at the end and `.prepend()` attaches at the beginning.

The content will be appended or prepended *inside* the matched elements, meaning if you match all paragraphs on the page and append a new sentence, "This was added by jQuery", it will be appended *inside the closing paragraph tag* (`</p>`).

Try this out by entering the following code into your console:

```
$("p").append(" This was added by jQuery.");
```

Executing the code will add this sentence to the end of each paragraph inside the closing paragraph tag. This is evident because the text is not knocked to the next line, as it would be if it were outside the closing tag.

INSPECTING HTML USING THE ELEMENT INSPECTOR IN FIREBUG

You can also see this by using the element inspection tool provided by Firebug. Near the top left of the console, there's a button that looks like a mouse cursor over a rectangle (see Figure 2-3). Click it to activate the element inspector.

Figure 2-3. *The button to activate the element inspector*

After the inspector is active, you can hover over different elements in the browser, and they'll highlight with a blue outline. Hover over one of the paragraphs you just appended text to, and click it. This brings up the HTML panel of Firebug with the current element collapsed and highlighted, and a tab to expand the element (see Figure 2-4).

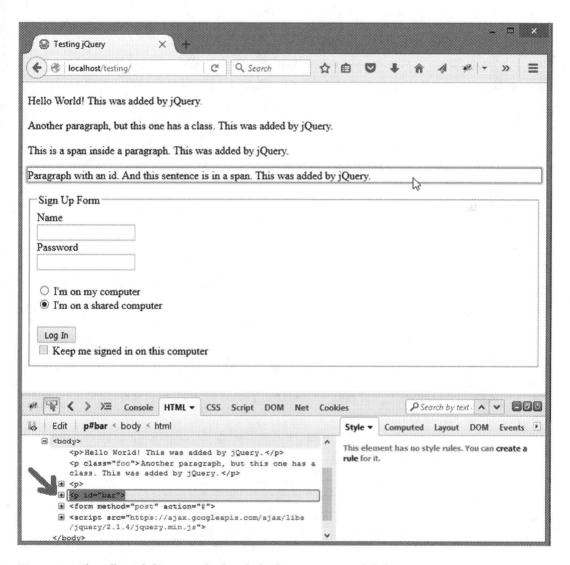

Figure 2-4. *The collapsed element as displayed after hovering over and clicking it*

Click the tab to expand the element, and you can see the contents, including the appended text, which is contained within the paragraph element (see Figure 2-5).

Figure 2-5. *The expanded element, including the dynamically added text*

You can use this technique throughout the rest of the exercises in this book to see where content and elements are being added to the DOM.

Using `.append()` and `.prepend()`, you can also add new elements to the DOM. For instance, to add a new paragraph at the top of the browser page, prepend a new element to the body using this code:

```
var para = $("<p>", {
        "text":"I'm a new paragraph!",
        "css":{"background":"yellow"}
    });
$("body").prepend(para);
```

▧ **Note**   This example uses a variable to store the new element before prepending it to the body. This is done to increase the legibility of the script. You'll be using this technique often throughout this book.

After executing the preceding code in your console, a new paragraph with a yellow background appears at the top of your browser window (see Figure 2-6).

Figure 2-6. *The new paragraph as it appears after prepending it to the body element*

.appendTo( ) and .prependTo( )

In the last example, you had to create an element, store it, and then select the element to which it was appended. This can be a somewhat roundabout approach, but fortunately, jQuery provides `.appendTo()` and `.prependTo()`, which chain instead to the object to be appended and accept the selector of the element to which you wish to append.

Using the last example as a starting point, to add the same paragraph element to the body using `.prependTo()`, your code would simplify thusly:

```
$("<p>", {
        "text":"I'm a new paragraph!",
        "css":{"background":"yellow"}
})
        .prependTo("body");
```

This produces an identical result with a much more concise snippet of code.

.after( ) and .before( )

The `.after()` and `.before()` methods are similar to `.append()` and `.prepend()`, except they add the content *outside* the element either before or after it, instead of inside the element at the beginning or end.

To add a new paragraph after the paragraph with class foo, use the following snippet:

```
$("p.foo").after("<p>A new paragraph.</p>");
```

Executing the code results in a new paragraph insertion just below the paragraph with class foo (see Figure 2-7).

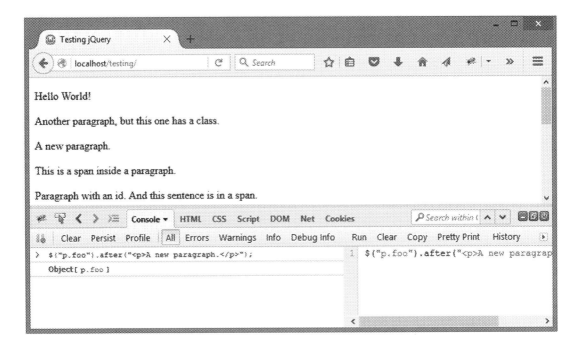

Figure 2-7. *A new paragraph inserted after the paragraph with class foo*

.insertAfter( ) and .insertBefore( )

The same way that .appendTo() and .prependTo() allow for more concise addition of new elements to the DOM, .insertAfter() and .insertBefore() offer the same alternative for .after() and .before().

To repeat the example from the previous section using .insertAfter(), alter the code to read as follows:

```
$("<p>", {
        "text":"A new paragraph."
    })
    .insertAfter("p.foo");
```

This duplicates the result from before (see Figure 2-7).

.wrap( )

The .wrap() method allows developers to enclose existing elements with one or more new elements quickly and easily.

The argument accepted by .wrap() can either be a collection of one or more tags to wrap around the selected elements, or a callback function to generate the tags.

First, wrap all the spans in the example document with a strong tag using the following:

```
$("span").wrap("<strong />");
```

This results in the text of the two spans becoming bold (see Figure 2-8).

Figure 2-8. *The spans appear bold after wrapping them with strong tags*

The syntax used for the wrapping element is relatively forgiving, and the output shown in Figure 2-8 could have been accomplished using either "`<strong />`", "`<strong>`", or "`<strong></strong>`".

Additionally, multiple tags can be wrapped around elements by passing a nested set of tags to the `.wrap()` method:

```
$("span").wrap("<strong><em></em></strong>");
```

After executing the preceding line, the text in the spans will appear bold and italicized (see Figure 2-9).

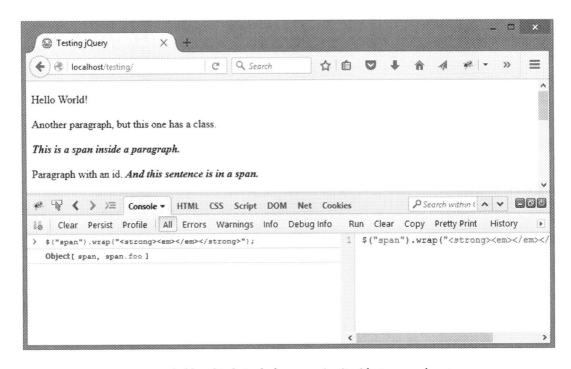

Figure 2-9. *Span text appears bold and italicized after wrapping it with strong and em tags*

To use a callback function to generate the desired HTML tag to wrap an element with, you must return a tag from the callback. For instance, to wrap all spans with the class `foo` in `strong` tags and all other spans in `em` tags, execute the following code:

```
$("span").wrap(function(){
        return $(this).is(".foo") ? "<strong>" : "<em>";
    });
```

After executing this snippet, the browser shows one span in italics, and the other (the one with class foo) in bold (see Figure 2-10).

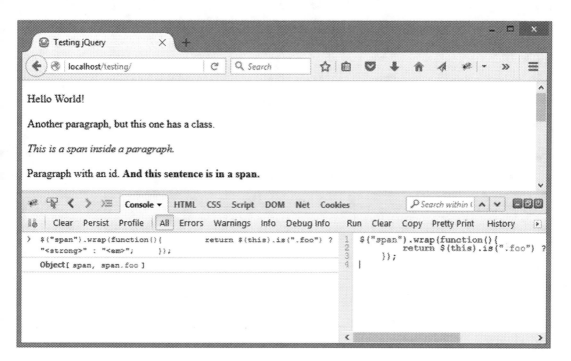

Figure 2-10. *Use a callback function to conditionally wrap certain elements*

.unwrap( )

The inverse of .wrap(), .unwrap() will remove tags that surround a given element. It does not accept any arguments; it simply finds the immediate parent element and removes it.

To unwrap the span elements in the example file, execute this code:

```
$("span").unwrap();
```

This removes the parent elements (but leaves the text nodes intact), which alters the layout (see Figure 2-11).

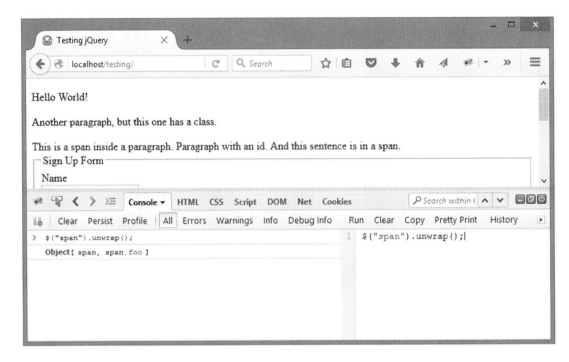

Figure 2-11. *After unwrapping the span elements, the document layout changes*

.wrapAll( )

If an entire set of elements needs to be wrapped in a new tag, `.wrapAll()` is used. Instead of individually wrapping each selected element with a new tag, it groups all selected elements and creates one wrapper around the whole group.

To wrap a `div` element with a yellow background around all paragraphs on the page, use the following code:

```
var div = $("<div>", {
        "css":{"background-color":"yellow"}
    });
$("p").wrapAll(div);
```

After executing this code, the new `div` is in place, and all paragraphs appear within its yellow background (see Figure 2-12).

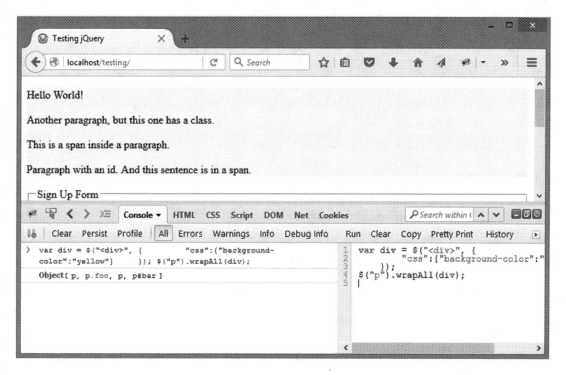

Figure 2-12. *The yellow background shows the div successfully wrapped all paragraphs*

There's one important note about `.wrapAll()`: it will move elements in the DOM to group them. To demonstrate this, use `.wrapAll()` to add a `strong` tag around all spans in the document:

```
$("span").wrapAll("<strong />");
```

After executing the command, note that the second span in the document was moved next to the first one so they could be wrapped in the same tag (see Figure 2-13).

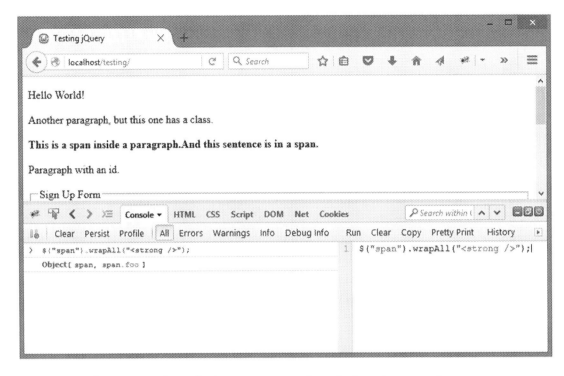

Figure 2-13. *The spans are relocated to be next to one another so both can be wrapped*

.wrapInner( )

In some cases, it's desirable to wrap the content of an element but not the tag itself. A good example of this is making an entire paragraph bold: to wrap `strong` tags around a paragraph is not valid HTML and, therefore, isn't a desirable solution. Fortunately, jQuery provides `.wrapInner()`, which wraps everything contained within an element in a new tag.

To italicize all text in the paragraphs on the test page, use the following code:

```
$("p").wrapInner("<em />");
```

After execution, all the text on the page is italicized and the markup is validly nested (see Figure 2-14).

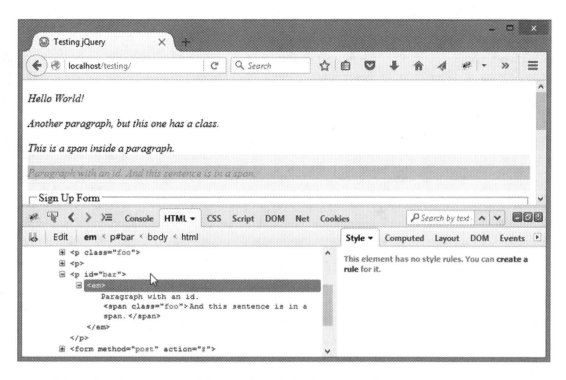

Figure 2-14. *All text is italicized, and the em tags are inside the paragraph tags*

.remove() and .detach()

To remove an element from the DOM entirely, the .remove() and .detach() methods are used. Both methods remove selected elements from the DOM, but the .detach() method keeps jQuery data for the element intact, which makes it ideal for situations in which an element will be reattached to the DOM at some point.

Both .remove() and .detach() accept an optional selector to filter the elements being removed. In your example, remove all paragraphs with class foo using the following:

```
$("p").remove(".foo");
```

When the code is run, the paragraph with class foo is removed from view and is no longer part of the DOM.

To demonstrate the difference between .remove() and .detach(), you'll have to jump ahead a bit and use a method called .data(), which allows developers to attach information to an element without adding additional tags or attributes. Note that .data() will be covered more thoroughly in the next section.

First, add some data to the first paragraph in the DOM. Then, with the data added, remove the element from the DOM using .detach(), reattach it, and attempt to read the data:

```
$("p:first").data("test","This is some data.");
var p = $("p:first").detach();
console.log("Data stored: "+p.data("test"));
```

> ▓ **Note** You're using a Firebug-specific object, `console`, and its `.log()` method to output specific information to the Firebug console. This is especially useful for debugging, but it needs to be removed before a project goes live to avoid JavaScript errors on computers that don't have Firebug installed.

After running this code, the `.data()` method attaches some information to the first paragraph and gets removed from the DOM and stored in a variable; then the script attempts to output the value of the information stored with `.data()`. The console will output the following:

```
> console.log("Data stored: "+p.data("test"));
Data stored: This is some data.
```

Now, run the same test, but use `.remove()` instead of `.detach()`:

```
$("p:first").data("test","This is some data.");
var p = $("p:first").remove();
console.log("Data stored: "+p.data("test"));
```

The output shows that the data was lost when the element was removed:

```
> console.log("Data stored: "+p.data("test"));
Data stored: undefined
```

Accessing and Modifying CSS and Attributes

Previously, when you were creating DOM elements, you were able to define attributes such as CSS styles, the text contained within, and more. To access and modify this information for existing elements, jQuery has a set of built-in methods.

.attr()

For most element attributes, the `.attr()` method is used. This method has two purposes. The first is to read a given attribute, which is accomplished by supplying the name of the desired attribute as the first argument to the method with no other arguments. The second is to set an attribute by passing the name of the attribute to be set as the first argument and the value to which it is to be set as the second.

First, retrieve the ID of the last paragraph using the following:

```
$("p:eq(3)").attr("id");
```

In the console, this produces the following output:

```
> $("p:eq(3)").attr("id");
"bar"
```

Next, change the ID attribute of the last paragraph to "bat" using this code:

```
$("#bar").attr("id", "bat");
```

After execution, the following displays in the console:

```
> $("#bar").attr("id", "bat");
Object[ p#bat ]
```

Now, if you try to select elements with an ID of bar, an empty result set is returned:

```
> $("#bar");
Object[ ]
```

However, you can now select a paragraph element with an ID of bat:

```
> $("#bat");
Object[ p#bat ]
```

Additionally, multiple attributes can be set using JSON format:

```
$("p:eq(3)").attr({
        "id":"baz",
        "title":"A captivating paragraph, isn't it?"
    });
```

After executing this code, the HTML panel of Firebug reveals that the paragraph's markup has been changed:

```
<p id="baz" title="A captivating paragraph, isn't it?">
```

.removeAttr()

To remove an attribute, simply call .removeAttr() on the element from which you wish to remove the attribute and pass the attribute's name.

Enable the check box in the sample form by removing the disabled attribute:

```
$(":checkbox").removeAttr("disabled");
```

After executing this code, the check box can now be checked and unchecked at will.

.css()

The .css() method works just like .attr(), except it applies to styling rules. To return a value, pass the name of the value as the only argument to the method; to set a value, pass both an attribute name and a new value for it. Like .attr(), multiple values can be set using JSON format.

To change all elements with class foo to have red text and a yellow background, use the following:

```
$(".foo").css({
        "color":"red",
        "background-color":"yellow"
    });
```

This code, once executed, adds new style rules to the selected elements (see Figure 2-15).

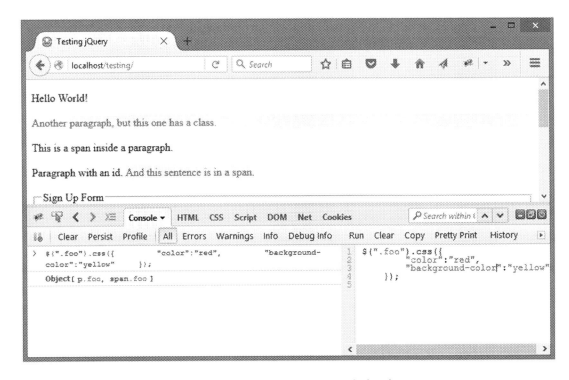

Figure 2-15. *The document after adding CSS styling to elements with class foo*

Before reloading the page, retrieve the background value from elements with class foo using the following code:

```
$(".foo").css("background-color");
```

This will return the following:

```
> $(".foo").css("background-color");
"rgb(255, 255, 0)"
```

▓ **Tip** The values returned are CSS shorthand properties.[3] An added bonus of jQuery is the ability to set CSS properties using CSS shorthand, which doesn't work using basic JavaScript.

.text( ) and .html( )

When dealing with the contents of an element, the .text() and .html() methods are used. The difference between the two is that .html() will allow you to read out and insert new HTML tags into an element, where .text() is for reading and writing text only.

If either of these methods is called on an element set with no arguments, the contents of the element are returned. When a value is passed to the method, the existing value is overwritten, and the new one put in its place.

To read the text out of the paragraph with ID bar, run the following code in the console:

```
$("#bar").text();
```

This captures all text (including whitespace) but ignores the span tag. The following is output:

```
> $("#bar").text();
"Paragraph with an id.
        And this sentence is in a span.
    "
```

To read everything out of the paragraph, including the span tag, use the following code:

```
$("#bar").html();
```

This results in the following:

```
> $("#bar").html();
"Paragraph with an id.
        <span class="foo">And this sentence is in a span.</span>
    "
```

Now, change the text by passing a value to the .text() method:

```
$("#bar").text("This is new text.");
```

The previous content of the paragraph is removed, and the new text is inserted. Note that the span tag was removed as well; *all contents* of an element are replaced when using .text() and .html().

---

[3]www.456bereastreet.com/archive/200502/efficient_css_with_shorthand_properties/

55

To insert HTML into the paragraph, replace its contents again with the following snippet:

```
$("#bar").html("This is some <strong>HTML</strong> text.");
```

After execution, the new text appears in the paragraph and the word "HTML" appears in bold (see Figure 2-16).

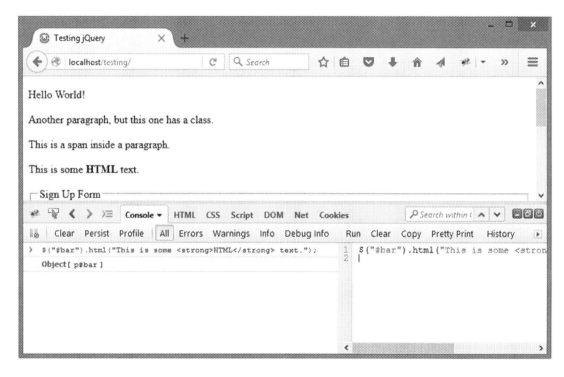

Figure 2-16. *The browser after inserting text and HTML tags*

.val()

Accessing and modifying the content of form elements is accomplished through the `.val()` method. This method returns the value of an input, or if a value is supplied, sets the value of an input.

Retrieve the value of the submit button in your test form by using

```
$(":submit").val();
```

which outputs

```
> $(":submit").val();
"Log In"
```

Now, update the value of the submit input to read "Sign In" using this code:

```
$(":submit").val("Sign In");
```

The submit button is called Sign In after running the preceding code snippet.

.data()

Previously, you used the .data() method to store information for a test of .remove() and .detach(). The .data() method does exactly that: it allows you to store information about an element within the jQuery object in a safe, easy manner.

To give the first two paragraphs in the test document nicknames, store the information using .data() and then log it in the console:

```
$("p:first")
    .data("nickname", "Pookie")
    .next("p")
        .data("nickname", "Shnookums");
console.log("My nickname: "+$("p:first").data("nickname"));
console.log("My nickname: "+$("p:eq(1)").data("nickname"));
```

After executing this script, the following will be logged in the console:

```
> $("p:first") .data("nick…name: "+$("p:eq(1)").data("nickname"));
My nickname: Pookie
My nickname: Shnookums
```

Data can be added to an element *en masse* as in JSON format as well:

```
$("p.foo").data({
    "nickname":"Wubby",
    "favorite":{
        "movie":"Pretty Woman",
        "music":"Sade",
        "color":"pink"
    }
});
console.log("Nickname: "+$("p.foo").data("nickname"));
console.log("Favorite Movie: "+$("p.foo").data("favorite").movie);
```

The preceding will produce the following output when executed:

```
> $("p.foo").data({ "nickname":"Wubby",....data("favorite").movie);
Nickname: Wubby
Favorite Movie: Pretty Woman
```

This can also be simplified by caching the data in a variable, like so:

```
$("p.foo").data({
    "nickname":"Wubby",
    "favorite":{
        "movie":"Pretty Woman",
        "music":"Sade",
        "color":"pink"
    }
});
var info = $("p.foo").data(); // cache the data object in a variable
console.log("Nickname: "+info.nickname);
console.log("Favorite Movie: "+info.favorite.movie);
```

This produces an identical result to the previous example, but performs a little better and is a bit easier to read.

.addClass(), .removeClass(), and .toggleClass()

A trio of shortcut methods was written for dealing with classes, since their use is so integral to modern web design. The first two methods, .addClass() and .removeClass(), simply add or remove a class attribute, respectively:

```
$("p:first").addClass("bat");
console.log("Text: "+$(".bat").text());
$("p:first").removeClass("bat");
console.log("Text: "+$(".bat").text());
```

The preceding snippet outputs the following in the console:

```
> $("p:first").addClass("bat"…le.log("Text: "+$(".bat").text());
Text: Hello World!
Text:
```

The third method, .toggleClass(), accepts a class name or names and then either adds the class if it doesn't already exist for the element or removes it if the class already exists.

Add the class baz and remove the class foo from the second paragraph in the example page using the following code:

```
$("p.foo").toggleClass("foo baz");
```

Upon execution, the paragraph is modified and appears with the old class removed and the new one added (see Figure 2-17).

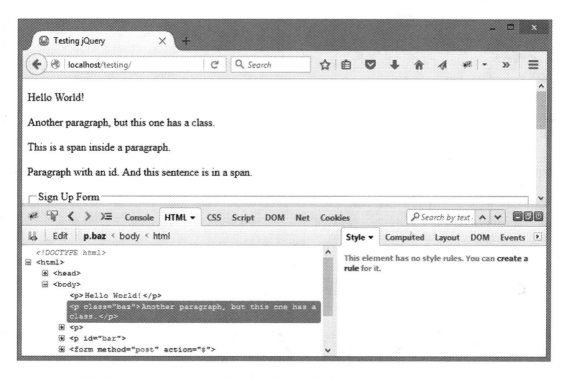

Figure 2-17. *The foo class is removed, and the baz class is added*

To revert to the original class of foo and remove baz, select the paragraph, and apply .toggleClass() again:

```
$("p.baz").toggleClass("foo baz");
```

This results in the paragraph going back to having only one class: foo.

.hasClass()

The .hasClass() method works similarly to the .is() method in that it determines if a class exists on a selected element and then returns either true or false. This makes it ideal for callback functions.

Check if the first paragraph has class foo and conditionally output a message using the following:

```
var msg = $("p:eq(1)").hasClass("foo") ? "Found!" : "Nope!";
console.log("Class? "+msg);
```

.height() and .width()

To obtain the height or width of an element, the .height() and .width() methods are handy. Both return a value without units, meaning the value returned is an integer (if the element is 68 pixels high, .height() will return 68). This differs from .css(), which will return the units of measure as well.

Get the height of the form by running the following code:

```
console.log("Form height: "+$("form").height()+"px");
```

This outputs the following in the console:

```
> console.log("Form height: "+$("form").height()+"px");
Form height: 252px
```

Note   The actual height returned may vary on your browser depending on which operating system you're using.

By passing a value to `.height()` or `.width()`, a new value is set. Make all paragraphs on the page 100 pixels high with a yellow background using the following code:

```
$("p").height(100).css("background-color","yellow");
```

Upon execution, all paragraph heights change and their backgrounds become yellow (see Figure 2-18).

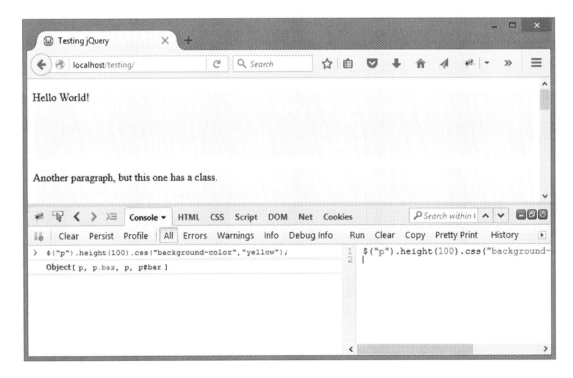

Figure 2-18. *The modified height and backgrounds of all document paragraphs*

.innerHeight(), .innerWidth(), .outerHeight(), and .outerWidth()

The inner height and width of an element is the width or height not counting borders or margins. You can access this information using the .innerHeight() and .innerWidth() methods.

If you wish to include the borders in the height or width of the element, use .outerHeight() or .outerWidth(). To include margins as well, use .outerHeight(true) or .outerWidth(true).

Add a margin and border to the paragraph with class foo and then log its different widths and heights:

```
var el = $("p.foo");
el.css({
        "margin":"20px",
        "border":"2px solid black"
    });
console.log("Inner width: "+el.innerWidth()+"px");
console.log("Inner height: "+el.innerHeight()+"px");
console.log("Outer width: "+el.outerWidth()+"px");
console.log("Outer height: "+el.outerHeight()+"px");
console.log("Outer width with margins: "+el.outerWidth(true)+"px");
console.log("Outer height with margins: "+el.outerHeight(true)+"px");
```

This outputs the following in the console:

```
> var el = $("p.foo"); el.c…rgins: "+el.outerHeight(true)+"px");
Inner width: 840px
Inner height: 20px
Outer width: 844px
Outer height: 24px
Outer width with margins: 884px
Outer height with margins: 64px
```

▓ **Note** Again, your results may vary depending on what operating system you're using.

Affecting Result Sets

To process a set of elements, you need a set of methods that allows you to affect each element in the set.

.map() and .each()

The .map() and .each() methods allow developers to apply a function individually to each element in a set using a callback function that has two arguments: the current element index and the current DOM element.

The difference between the two is that .map() returns a new object containing the returned values of the callback, whereas .each() will return the original object with the changes performed by the callback included. This means that .each() is chainable, while .map() is not.

To loop through each paragraph and element with class foo and append the tag name and element index, use the following code:

```
$("p,.foo").map(function(index, ele){
        $(this).append(" "+ele.tagName+" #"+index);
    });
```

This adds the element's tag name and the index number to the end of each matched element (see Figure 2-19).

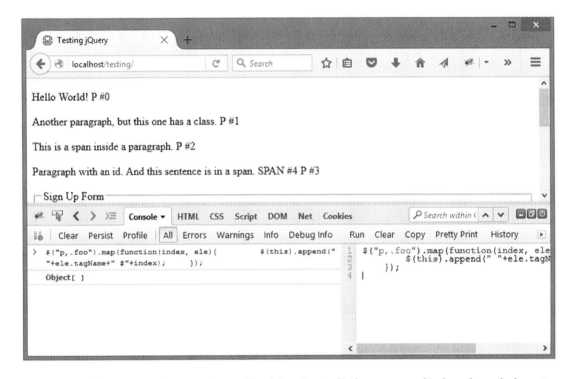

Figure 2-19. *The test page after mapping a callback function to display names and indexes for each element*

To accomplish the same thing with `.each()`, simply swap out the call to `.map()`:

```
$("p,.foo").each(function(index, ele){
        $(this).append(" "+ele.tagName+" #"+index);
    });
```

This produces an identical result.

The difference comes into play if you need to perform further processing *after* the call to .map() or .each(). For instance, if you want to append the tag name and index to each paragraph and the span with class foo as previously illustrated and then filter to just the span with class foo and change its background and text colors, you can try the following:

```
$("p,.foo").map(function(index, ele){
    $(this).append(" "+ele.tagName+" #"+index);
})
    .find("span.foo")
    .css({
        "color":"red",
        "background":"yellow"
    });
```

After execution, the tag names and indices are appended, but the span doesn't have any style changes applied. This happens because the elements are no longer referenced by the object returned from .map().

To get the preceding snippet to perform as expected, you must swap out the call to .map() for a call to .each():

```
$("p,.foo").each(function(index, ele){
    $(this).append(" "+ele.tagName+" #"+index);
})
    .find("span.foo")
    .css({
        "color":"red",
        "background":"yellow"
    });
```

Now running the code produces the desired result (see Figure 2-20).

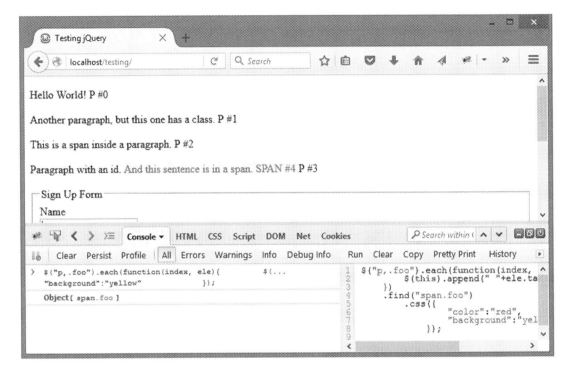

Figure 2-20. *Using .each(), the expected results are produced*

Using Animation and Other Effects

One of the most exciting features of jQuery is its library of methods that allow for animation and special effects, which are all possible with plain JavaScript but are *incredibly* easy using jQuery. A traditional JavaScript approach is tricky and much more involved.

░ **Note** Because it's difficult to show animations as static images, you'll need to rely on your browser for an illustration of how these examples should look. For live demonstrations of the different animation effects, visit the jQuery API at `http://api.jquery.com`, and look up the individual method you wish to see demonstrated.

.show() and .hide()

The most basic effects functions are `.show()` and `.hide()`. When fired without a parameter, they simply add or remove `display:none;` from the element's style attribute.

Hide the paragraph with ID `bar` using the following:

```
$("#bar").hide();
```

The paragraph disappears from the browser window but is still visible in the DOM using the element inspector. To bring it back into view, call .show():

```
$("#bar").show();
```

The element comes back as it was before.

To make the hiding and showing of elements animated, the duration (in milliseconds) can be passed, as well as an optional callback to be fired after the animation is complete. To demonstrate, add a background and border to the paragraph with ID bar and then hide it with a duration of 2 seconds and a callback function that will log a message in the console:

```
$("#bar")
    .css({
        "background":"yellow",
        "border":"1px solid black"
    })
    .hide(2000,function(){
        console.log("Animation complete!");
    });
```

Upon execution, the CSS styles are added to the element, and the .hide() method fires. This causes the element to shrink horizontally and vertically, as well as fading its opacity. After two seconds it will finish disappearing and the callback function logs the "Animation complete!" message in the console.

■ **Note** The callback function will be fired for each element in a set that is animated.

.fadeIn(), .fadeOut(), and .fadeTo()

To fade an element in or out (using opacity), use .fadeIn() and .fadeOut(). When called, these methods adjust the opacity of the elements either from 0 to 1 in .fadeIn() or 1 to 0 in .fadeOut(). When an element is faded out, display:none; is applied to the element as well. When faded in, display:none; is removed from the element if it exists.

Both methods accept optional parameters for the duration of the animation (the default is 400 milliseconds) and a callback to be fired when the animation completes. The duration has two shortcut strings, "fast" and "slow", which translate to 200 and 600 milliseconds, respectively.

To fade out the form, log a message, fade it back in, and log another message, use the following:

```
$("form")
    .fadeOut(1000, function(){
        console.log("Faded out!");
    })
    .fadeIn(1000, function(){
        console.log("Faded in!");
    });
```

Alternatively, .fadeTo() allows you to specify the opacity to which the element should fade. This method requires two arguments: a duration and the opacity to which the element fades (a number between 0 and 1). An optional callback can be passed as the third argument as well.

Fade the form to 50 percent opacity and log a message using the following:

```
$("form")
    .fadeTo(1000, 0.5, function(){
            console.log("Faded to 50%!");
        });
```

.slideUp(), .slideDown(), and .slideToggle()

To hide an element by reducing its height to 0, `.slideUp()` is a shortcut method. It animates the reduction of the element's height until it reaches 0 and then sets `display:none;` to ensure the layout is no longer affected by the element. To reverse this, the `.slideDown()` method removes the `display:none;` and animates the height from 0 back to the original height of the element.

Just like `.fadeIn()` and `.fadeOut()`, two optional parameters are accepted: the duration and a callback function.

Slide up the paragraph with class foo, log a message, slide it back down, and log another message:

```
$("p.foo")
    .slideUp(1000, function(){
            console.log("Hidden!");
        })
    .slideDown(1000, function(){
            console.log("Shown!");
        });
```

The `.slideToggle()` method does the same thing as `.slideUp()` and `.slideDown()`, but it's smart enough to know if an element is hidden or shown and uses that information to determine which action to take.

To set up a display toggle for the paragraph with class foo, use the following:

```
$("p.foo")
    .slideToggle("slow", function(){
            console.log("Toggled!");
        });
```

Run this code multiple times to see the paragraph slide up and down in alternating fashion.

.animate()

The previously discussed animation methods are shortcuts that all call the `.animate()` method. This method will animate most visual CSS properties of an element and supports **easing**, which is one of any number of mathematical formulas that alter the way the animation operates. By default, `"linear"` and `"swing"` easing are supported, but an easy-to-include easing plug-in is available for jQuery (you'll learn about plug-ins later in this book).

The `.animate()` method accepts several arguments in two formats. In the first format, the method is passed a JSON-formatted set of CSS properties to animate as the first argument, an optional duration in milliseconds for the second argument, an optional easing formula as the third argument, and an optional callback as the fourth argument. The second format passes a JSON-formatted set of CSS properties as its first argument and a JSON-formatted set of options as its second.

CHAPTER 2 ▓ COMMON JQUERY ACTIONS AND METHODS

After setting a background and border style, to animate the height and width of the paragraph element with ID bar over the span of 5 seconds using the "swing" easing type and logging a message upon completion, use the following for the first format:

```
$("#bar")
    .css({
            "background":"yellow",
            "border":"1px solid black"
        })
    .animate({
            "width":"500px",
            "height":"100px"
        },
        5000,
        "swing",
        function(){
                console.log("Animation complete!");
        });
```

Upon completion, the paragraph is yellow with a black border and has changed its size to match the parameters passed (see Figure 2-21).

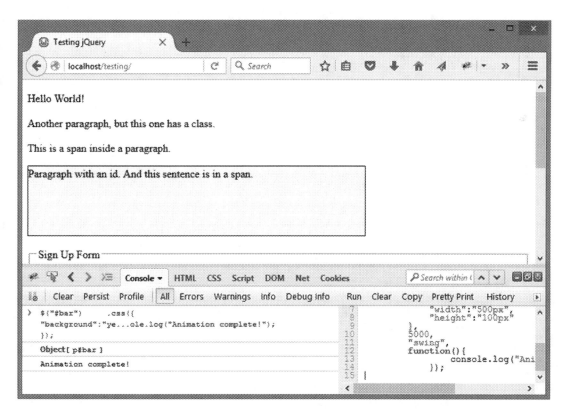

Figure 2-21. *The paragraph after animating its height and width*

Using the second format, the code would change as follows:

```
$("#bar")
    .css({
        "background":"yellow",
        "border":"1px solid black"
    })
    .animate({
        "width":"500px",
        "height":"100px"
    },
    {
        "duration":5000,
        "easing":"swing",
        "complete":function(){
            console.log("Animation complete!");
        }
    });
```

This produces an identical result. The second format of .animate() provides for additional options as well. To complete the same action using all available options, your code might look like this:

```
$("#bar")
    .css({
        "background":"yellow",
        "border":"1px solid black"
    })
    .animate({
        "width":"500px",
        "height":"100px"
    },
    {
        "duration":5000,
        "easing":"swing",
        "complete":function(){
            console.log("Animation complete!");
        },
        "step":function(){
            console.log("Step completed!");
        },
        "queue":true,
        "specialEasing":{
            "width":"linear"
        }
    });
```

The step option allows developers to create a callback function to be fired after each step of the animation. This is *each time the property is adjusted,* so the preceding example ends up outputting quite a few log messages of "Step completed!".

The queue option tells the animation whether or not it should be added to the current **queue**, that is, the order in which animations have been called. If multiple animations are called and queued, the first animation will complete before the second begins, the second will complete before the third begins, and so on.

The specialEasing option allows developers to attach different easing styles to each CSS property being animated.

.delay()

The .delay() method essentially allows developers to pause a script's execution for a given number of milliseconds. It provides the ability to run one animation and wait for a bit before starting the next animation.

To slide up the paragraph with ID bar, wait 3 seconds, and slide it back down, use the following code:

```
$("#bar")
    .css({
            "background":"yellow",
            "border":"1px solid black"
        })
    .slideUp(1000, function(){
            console.log("Animation completed!");
        })
    .delay(3000)
    .slideDown(1000, function(){
            console.log("Animation completed!");
        });
```

.stop()

To stop an animation, the .stop() method is used. This method accepts two Boolean arguments: one to determine whether the queue should be cleared and another to determine whether the animation should jump to the end. Both values default to false.

To start an animation, stop the animation, clear the queue, and jump to the end after 200 steps, use the following:

```
var count = 0; // Keep track of the current step count
$("#bar")
    .css({
            "background":"yellow",
            "border":"1px solid black"
        })
    .animate({
            "width":"500px"
        },
        {
            "duration":6000,
            "step":function(){
                    if(count++==200)
                    {
                        $(this).stop(true, true);
                    }
                }
        });
```

Handling Events

In many scripts, it's desirable to have certain actions occur when certain **events**, or browser actions, occur. Support is built into jQuery to handle browser events, which you'll learn in this section.

Browser Events

Browser events occur when the browser itself experiences a change or error.

.error()

If a browser error occurs, this event is triggered. One common instance of a browser error is an image tag that tries to load an image that does not exist. The .error() method allows developers to bind a **handler** (i.e., a function to be fired if the event occurs) to the event.

Create an image tag that tries to display an image that doesn't exist, and attach an error handler to the error event that outputs a message to the console:

```
$("<img />", {
        "src":"not/an/image.png",
        "alt":"This image does not exist"
    })
    .error(function(){
            console.log("The image cannot be loaded!");
        })
    .appendTo("body");
```

Upon execution of this code, the console will display something very much like the following:

```
> $("<img />", { "src":"not/an/image.png", …ot be loaded!"); }) .appendTo("body");
Object[ img not/an/image.png ]
"NetworkError: 404 Not Found - http://localhost/testing/not/an/image.png"
image.png
The image cannot be loaded!
```

.scroll( )

If the document is scrolled, the scroll event is fired. To bind a handler to this event, use the .scroll() method:

```
$(window)
    .scroll(function(){
            console.log("The window was scrolled!");
        });
```

After executing this code, scrolling the browser window will cause a message to be logged in the console.

Additionally, calling the `.scroll()` method without any parameters will trigger the `scroll` event to fire. After binding the preceding handler to the window, trigger the event by running the following:

```
$(window).scroll();
```

Executing this code will log the `scroll` event handler's message in the console.

Handling Document Loading Events

Often, JavaScript needs to wait until the document is ready before executing any scripts. Also, when users exit a page, sometimes it's desirable to fire a function to ensure they meant to navigate away from it.

.ready( )

The `.ready()` method is used in nearly every jQuery script as a safeguard against the script executing too early and, therefore, not performing properly. This method waits for the DOM to be ready for manipulation before firing its handler.

Common practice is to make the entire script a callback function to be fired by the `.ready()` handler:

```
$(document).ready(function(){
        // All jQuery functionality here
    });
```

Additionally, the `.ready()` method accepts a parameter to use as an alias for the jQuery function. This allows you to write failsafe jQuery scripts that will work as expected even if the $ alias is given back to another library using `jQuery.noConflict()` (which allows for multiple JavaScript libraries that use the $ alias to be used on the same project without issue).

You can guarantee the $ alias will work using the following:

```
jQuery.ready(function($){
        // All jQuery functionality here
        $("p").fadeOut();
    });
```

Technically, any alias can be passed here:

```
jQuery(document).ready(function(xTest){
        xTest("#bar").click(function(){console.log("Clicked!");});
    });
```

This performs as expected, with no errors. There aren't many cases in which this check would be necessary, but it illustrates how the alias works with the `.ready()` method.

Finally, the jQuery function itself can be used as an alias for `.ready()`:

```
jQuery(function($){
        // actions to perform after the DOM is ready
    });
```

71

.unload( )

The unload event is triggered whenever a user exits a page by clicking a link, reloading the page, using the forward or back buttons, or closing the window entirely. However, the handling of unload is not consistent across all browsers *and therefore should be tested in multiple browsers before being used in production scripts.* To create a link to Google and attach an alert to the unload event, use the following code:

```
$("<a>", {
        "href":"http://google.com",
        "text":"Go to Google!"
    })
    .appendTo("#bar");
$(window).unload(function(){
      alert("Bye! Google something neat!");
    });
```

Execute this code, and click the new link. The alert fires, and you're redirected to the Google home page.

Handling Event Attachment

There are a whole slew of browser events triggered by the user, and jQuery provides several methods to handle them easily. The available events are blur, focus, focusin, focusout, load, resize, scroll, unload, click, dblclick, mousedown, mouseup, mousemove, mouseover, mouseout, mouseenter, mouseleave, change, select, submit, keydown, keypress, keyup, and error.

.bind( ) and .unbind( )

To bind an event handler to an element, the .bind() method is used. It accepts an event as its first argument and a handler function as the second argument.

Multiple events can be bound using a space-separated list of events as the first argument. To bind different handlers to different events, a JSON-formatted object can be passed to .bind() as well.

To bind a console message log to the click event, use the following:

```
$("p")
    .bind("click", function(){
       console.log("Click happened!");
    });
```

Clicking a paragraph after running this code will result in a message being logged to the console.
To bind a handler to both the click and mouseover events, use the following:

```
$("p")
    .bind("click mouseover", function(){
          console.log("An event happened!");
      });
```

Now either clicking or hovering over a paragraph will log a message in the console.
If the handler needs to have data passed to it, an additional parameter is available. This is a JSON-formatted object containing variables to be used in the function. These variables are bound to the event object so that the values remain intact within the given handler.

Set a `click` handler for two paragraphs in the test document with identical functionality but different log messages using the following:

```
// Create a value for the notice variable
var notice = "I live in a variable!";
$("p.foo").bind("click", { n:notice }, function(event){
        console.log(event.data.n);
    });

// Change the value of the notice variable
var notice = "I live in a variable too!";
$("#bar").bind("click", { n:notice }, function(event){
        console.log(event.data.n);
    });
```

To bind different handlers to the `click` and `mouseover` events, use this code:

```
$("p")
    .bind({
            "click":function(){
                    console.log("Click happened!");
                },
            "mouseover":function(){
                    console.log("Mouseover happened!");
                }
        });
```

After execution, a different message will be logged to the console for each event when it occurs.

To remove an event, simply call the `.unbind()` method. If called with no parameters, all event bindings are removed from an element. To specify, the name of the event to unbind can be passed as the first argument. To further specify, the function to be removed from the event can be passed as a second argument.

To unbind all events from the paragraphs in your example, use the following:

```
$("p").unbind();
```

To only remove the `click` event handler, use this code:

```
$("p").unbind("click");
```

Or, if a specific function was bound to an element, it could be unbound like so:

```
var func1 = function(){
            console.log("An event was triggered!");
        },
    func2 = function(){
            console.log("Another handler!");
        };
```

```
$("#bar")
    .bind("click", func1)
    .bind("click", func2)
    .trigger("click") // fire the event once
    .unbind("click", func1);
```

The preceding code creates two functions (stored in the func1 and func2 variables), binds them to the click event for the paragraph with ID bar, triggers the event once (you'll learn about .trigger() later in this section), and unbinds the function stored in func1.

After running this code, clicking the paragraph will fire only the function stored in func2.

.live( ) and .die( )

Similar to .bind() and .unbind(), .live() and .die() will attach and remove event handlers from elements, respectively. The main difference is that .live() will attach handlers and JavaScript properties not only to existing events but to any new elements added to the DOM that match the selector afterward as well.

For instance, add a click event handler for any anchor elements using the following:

```
$("a")
    .live("click", function(){
        console.log("Link clicked!");
        return false; // prevent the link from firing
    });
```

Of course, there are not any links on the example page at the moment. Without reloading, add an anchor tag to the paragraph with ID bar using the following:

```
$("<a>", {
        "href":"http://google.com",
        "text":"Go to Google!"
    })
    .appendTo("#bar");
```

The new link appears, and even though the event was bound before any anchor tags existed in the DOM, clicking the link results in a message logged in the console and the link not firing.

Performing the previous action using .bind() does not work. Additionally, the click event handler bound with .live() cannot be removed with .unbind(); to remove the event, you must use .die(). The use of .die() is the same as that of .unbind().

.one( )

The function and use of the .one() method is identical to that of .bind(), except that the event handler is unbound after one occurrence of the event.

Add a new click event handler for the paragraph with ID bar that will only fire once using the following:

```
$("#bar").one("click", function(){
        console.log("This will only fire once.");
    });
```

After execution, clicking the paragraph with ID bar results in one message logged to the console, with subsequent clicks having no effect.

.toggle( )

The .toggle() function allows developers to bind two or more functions to the click event to be fired on alternating clicks. Alternatively, the function can be used to toggle visibility of elements (like toggling .show() and .hide()—similar to how .slideToggle() alternatively performs the functionality of .slideUp() and .slideDown() when called).

First, bind three different log messages to the click event for the paragraph with ID bar using the following:

```
$("#bar")
    .toggle(function(){
            console.log("Function 1");
        },
        function(){
            console.log("Function 2");
        },
        function(){
            console.log("Function 3");
        });
```

After execution, upon clicking the paragraph with ID bar, the three messages are logged in succession on consequent clicks.

Next, toggle the visibility of the paragraph with ID bar with the following code:

```
$("#bar").toggle();
```

Firing this function hides the paragraph. Firing it again brings it back. By adding the duration as the first argument, the method will animate the element as it's hidden or shown:

```
$("#bar").toggle(2000);
```

Last, a Boolean flag can be passed to determine whether all elements should be shown or hidden:

```
$("#bar").toggle(true);  // all elements will be shown
$("#bar").toggle(false); // all elements will be hidden
```

.trigger( )

To trigger an event, the .trigger() method is used. This method accepts an event to trigger and an optional array of arguments to be passed to the handler.

Bind a handler to the paragraph with ID bar, and trigger it using the following code:

```
$("#bar")
    .bind("click", function(){
            console.log("Clicked!");
        })
    .trigger("click");
```

To pass additional data, modify the code as follows:

```javascript
// create a variable
var note = "I was triggered!";
$("#bar")
    .bind("click", function(event, msg){ // allow a 2nd argument
            // If no msg variable is passed, a default message
            var log = msg || "I was clicked!";
            console.log(log);
        })
    .trigger("click", [ note ]); // array passed in square brackets
```

This outputs the message stored in the note variable to the console.

Shortcut Event Methods

Every event has a shortcut method that accepts the handler function as an argument. If passed without an argument, it calls .trigger() for its event type. The available shortcut functions are .blur(), .focus(), .focusin(), .focusout(), .load(), .resize(), .scroll(), .unload(), .click(), .dblclick(), .mousedown(), .mouseup(), .mousemove(), .mouseover(), .mouseout(), .mouseenter(), .mouseleave(), .change(), .select(), .submit(), .keydown(), .keypress(), .keyup(), and .error().

As an example, the following will bind a handler to the click event, and fire the event:

```javascript
$("#bar").click(function(){ console.log("Clicked!"); }).click();
```

Using AJAX Controls

The last set of jQuery methods we're going to cover are probably the most useful, and more than likely played a large role in the widespread adoption of jQuery. The methods providing AJAX [4] functionality are incredibly useful and, especially for anyone who has built AJAX scripts in plain JavaScript before, as easy as pie.

▓ **Note**   For further reading on AJAX, see the Wikipedia article at https://en.wikipedia.org/wiki/Ajax_(programming).

For this section, you'll need an external file to access using the AJAX controls. Create a new file in the testing folder called ajax.php. Inside, insert the following code:

```php
<?php

echo '<p class="ajax">This paragraph was loaded with AJAX.</p>',
            '<pre>GET variables: ', print_r($_GET, TRUE), '</pre>',
            '<pre>POST variables: ', print_r($_POST, TRUE), '</pre>';

?>
```

---

[4]https://en.wikipedia.org/wiki/Ajax_(programming)

This file will be called by the various AJAX methods available in jQuery. It will show you the data passed to the script for illustrative purposes.

$.ajax()

The **low-level,** or most basic, function for sending AJAX requests is $.ajax(). Notice that this function is called without a selector because it doesn't apply to the jQuery object. AJAX actions are global functions, carried out independently of the DOM.

The $.ajax() function accepts one argument: an object containing settings for the AJAX call. If called without any settings, the method will load the current page and do nothing with the result.

Quite a few settings are available for $.ajax(), not all of which are covered here or used in this book. See http://api.jquery.com/jQuery.ajax for a full list of available settings. The most common follow:

- data: This describes any data to be sent to the remote script, either as a query string (key1=val1&key2=val2) or as JSON ({"key1":"val1","key2":"val2"}).

- dataFilter(data, type): This callback allows prefiltering of data and is great for sanitizing data as it comes from the remote script.

- dataType: This describes the type of data expected from the request. jQuery makes an intelligent guess if this is left undefined. The available types are "xml", "html", "script", "json", "jsonp", and "text".

- error(XMLHttpRequest, textStatus, errorThrown): This callback is to be executed in the event of a request error. The XMLHttpRequest object, a string communicating the status of the request, and an error code are passed as arguments.

- success(data, textStatus, XMLHttpRequest): This callback is to be executed if the request completes successfully. The data returned from the remote script, a string communicating the status of the request, and the XMLHttpRequest object are passed as arguments.

- type: This is the type of request to send. The default is GET, but POST is also available. PUT and DELETE can be used but may not work properly in all browsers.

- url: This is the URL to which the request is to be sent.

To send a basic POST request to your sample script and load the results into the paragraph with ID bar, use the following:

```
$.ajax({
        "type":"POST",
        "url":"ajax.php",
        "data":"var1=val1&var2=val2",
        "success":function(data){
                $("#bar")
                    .css("background","yellow")
                    .html(data);
        }
    });
```

After executing this code, the contents of the paragraph are replaced with the loaded information (see Figure 2-22).

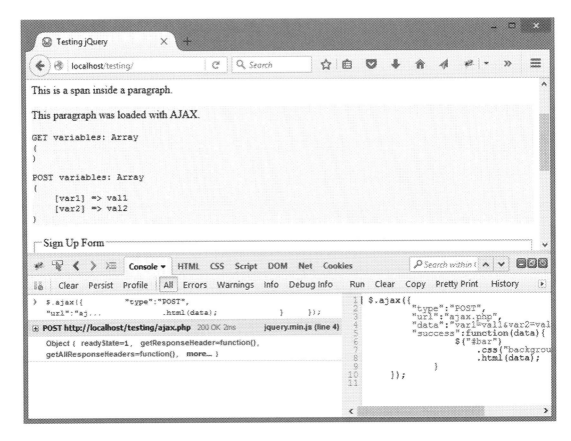

Figure 2-22. *The loaded AJAX information from ajax.php*

$.ajaxSetup()

To set default options for AJAX calls, the $.ajaxSetup() function is used. For instance, to specify that, by default, all AJAX requests should be sent to ajax.php using POST and then loaded into the paragraph with ID bar, use the following code:

```
$.ajaxSetup({
        "type":"POST",
        "url":"ajax.php",
        "success":function(data){
                $("#bar")
                        .css("background","yellow")
                        .html(data);
            }
    });
```

Now new AJAX requests can be made easily by simply passing new data:

```
$.ajax({
        "data":{
                "newvar1":"value1",
                "newvar2":"value2"
            }
    });
```

This results in the paragraph's contents being replaced with new content from ajax.php (see Figure 2-23).

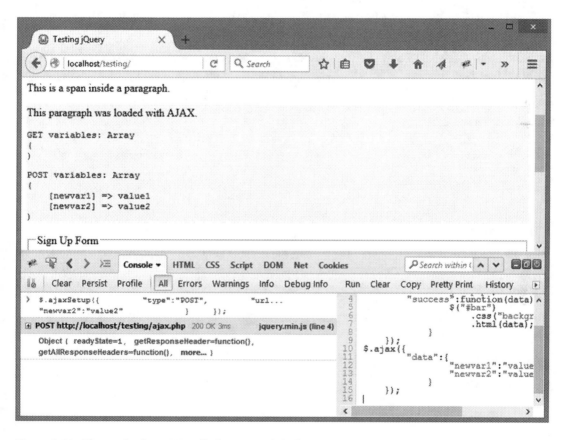

Figure 2-23. *The result of an AJAX call after setting default options*

These defaults can be overwritten in subsequent calls to `$.ajax()` by simply redefining the option in the new call:

```
$.ajax({
        "type":"GET",
        "data":{
                "newvar1":"value3",
                "newvar2":"value4"
            }
    });
```

This results in the data being sent using GET (see Figure 2-24).

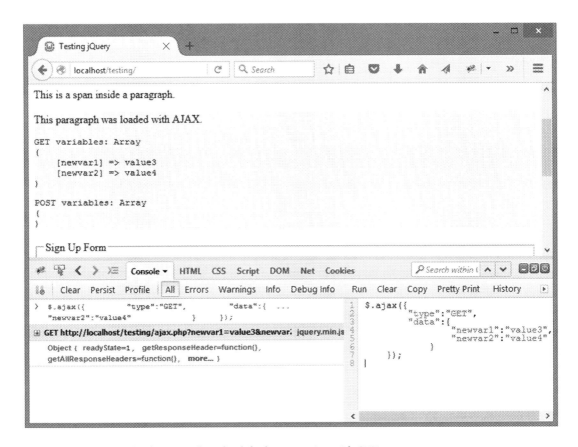

Figure 2-24. *The result after overriding the default type option with GET*

Using Shorthand AJAX Methods

There are several simple, one-use functions that are available for performing common AJAX tasks. In a nutshell, these shorthand methods are simply wrapper functions that call $.ajax() with some of the parameters already set.

Using these methods will incur a slight performance penalty, since you're essentially calling a method that sets up parameters and calls $.ajax() within itself. However, the convenience of using shorthand methods really speeds up development in many scripts.

$.get( ) and $.post( )

For standard GET and POST requests, the $.get() and $.post() functions are easy to use. Both take four arguments: the URL to which the request is to be sent, optional data to be sent to the remote script, an optional callback to be executed if the request is successful, and an optional dataType setting.

To load the result of ajax.php using GET with no data sent, use the following:

```
$.get("ajax.php", function(data){
        $("#bar")
            .css("background","yellow")
            .html(data);
    });
```

To send a request with data using POST, the following code could be used:

```
$.post("ajax.php", {"var1":"value"}, function(data){
        $("#bar")
            .css("background","yellow")
            .html(data);
    });
```

$.getJSON( )

When loading JSON data, $.getJSON() is a shortcut function. It accepts the URL to which requests are sent, optional data, and an optional callback function.

To run an example of this function, another test file needs to be created: create a new file called json.php in the testing folder, and insert the following JSON into it:

```
{"var1":"value1","var2":"value2"}
```

Now, load the contents of json.php and output the contents in the paragraph with ID bar:

```
$.getJSON("json.php",
        function(data){
                $("#bar")
                    .css("background","yellow")
                    .html(data.var1+", "+data.var2);
            });
```

Upon execution, the contents of the paragraph will be replaced with the string "value1, value2".

$.getScript()

To load external JavaScript, use the $.getScript() function. This accepts a URL to which the request is sent and an optional callback (which is generally not needed, as the script will execute automatically on a successful load).

Create a new file called script.php in the testing folder, and insert the following:

```
alert("This script was loaded by AJAX!");
```

Now, load this script by executing the following code in the console:

```
$.getScript("script.php");
```

Upon execution, the alert fires.

.load()

The .load() method works just like $.get() or $.post(), except it's a method instead of a global function. It has an implicit callback, which is to replace the HTML of the matched elements with the content returned from the remote file.

The method accepts the same three arguments: destination URL, optional data, and an optional callback (which fires *after* the element content has been replaced).

Load the contents of ajax.php in the paragraph with ID bar after sending some data using this code:

```
$("#bar").load("ajax.php", {"var1":"value1"});
```

After running this snippet, the content of the paragraph is replaced with the returned result.

Summary

This chapter was intense and covered an awful lot of ground. Remember to check the jQuery API documentation online for more examples, further explanation, and discussion by other developers in the community. To search a method, simply add its name to the end of the API's URL; for instance, to look up the .slideup() method, navigate to http://api.jquery.com/slideup in your browser.

In the next part of this book, you'll brush up on your PHP skills, including object-oriented programming, before jumping into the back-end development of the events calendar you'll be building from Chapter 4 on.

Getting Into Advanced PHP Programming

At this point, you're going to put your new jQuery knowledge aside for a bit and focus on the backend using PHP. Part 2 teaches you how to plan and implement an object-oriented backend solution for an events calendar that you will later enhance using your new knowledge of jQuery. This book assumes you have a reasonably sound grasp on the basic concepts of PHP (variables, functions, the basic language constructs); to brush up on your PHP basics, check out *Learn PHP 7* (Apress, 2015).

■ ■ ■

CHAPTER 3

Object-Oriented Programming

In this chapter, you'll learn the concepts behind **object-oriented programming** (OOP), a style of coding in which related actions are grouped into classes to aid in creating more-compact, effective code. The back end of the project you'll be building in this book is heavily based on OOP, so the concepts covered in this chapter will be referenced often throughout the rest of the exercises you'll complete.

Understanding Object-Oriented Programming

As stated above, object-oriented programming is a style of coding that allows developers to group similar tasks into classes. This helps keep your code easy to maintain and in line with the tenant of "don't repeat yourself" (DRY).

■ **Note** For further reading on DRY programming, see `http://en.wikipedia.org/wiki/Don't_repeat_yourself`.

One of the major benefits of DRY programming is that, if a piece of information changes in your program, usually only one change is required to update the code. One of the biggest nightmares for developers is maintaining code where data is declared over and over again, meaning any changes to the program become an infinitely more frustrating game of *Where's Waldo?* as they hunt for duplicated data and functionality.

OOP is intimidating to a lot of developers because it introduces new syntax and, at a glance, appears to be far more complex than simple **procedural**, or inline, code. However, upon closer inspection, OOP is actually a very straightforward and ultimately simpler approach to programming.

Understanding Objects and Classes

Before we get too deep into the finer points of OOP, a basic understanding of the components of objects and classes is necessary. This section will go over the building blocks of classes, their different capabilities, and some of their uses.

Recognizing the Differences Between Objects and Classes

Right off the bat, there's confusion in OOP: seasoned developers start talking about objects and classes, and they appear to be interchangeable terms. This is not the case, however, although the difference can be tough to wrap your head around at first.

A **class** is like a blueprint for a house. It defines the shape of the house on paper, with relationships between the different parts of the house clearly defined and planned out, even though the house doesn't exist.

An **object**, then, is like the actual house built according to that blueprint. The data stored in the object is like the wood, wires, and concrete that makes up the house: without being assembled according to the blueprint, it's just a pile of stuff. However, when it all comes together, it becomes an organized, useful house.

Classes form the structure of data and actions, and use that information to build objects. More than one object can be built from the same class at the same time, each one independent of the others. Continuing with our construction analogy, it's similar to the way an entire subdivision can be built from the same blueprint: 150 different houses that all look the same but have different families and decorations inside.

Structuring Classes

The syntax to create a class is pretty straightforward: declare a class using the `class` keyword, followed by the name of the class and a set of curly braces (`{}`):

```php
<?php

declare(strict_types=1);

class MyClass
{
    // Class properties and methods go here
}

?>
```

▓ **Note** The optional declaration **strict_types=1** is new for PHP 7, and forces strict type checking for scalar type declarations in all function calls and return statements within any file where it appears. See the Appendix for more info about this and other PHP 7 features you'll be using.

After creating the class, a new class can be instantiated and stored in a variable using the new keyword:

```php
$obj = new MyClass;
```

To see the contents of the class, use `var_dump()`:

```php
var_dump($obj);
```

Try out this process by putting all the preceding code in a new file called `test.php` in the `testing` folder:

```php
<?php

declare(strict_types=1);

class MyClass
{
        // Class properties and methods go here
}
```

```
$obj = new MyClass;

var_dump($obj);

?>
```

Load the page in your browser at `http://localhost/testing/test.php` and the following should display:

```
object(MyClass)#1 (0) { }
```

In its simplest form, you've just completed your first OOP script.

Defining Class Properties

To add data to a class, **properties**, or class-specific variables, are used. These work exactly like regular variables, except they're bound to the object and therefore can only be accessed using the object.

To add a property to MyClass, add the following bold code to your script:

```
<?php

declare(strict_types=1);

class MyClass
{
    public $prop1 = "I'm a class property!";
}

$obj = new MyClass;

var_dump($obj);

?>
```

The keyword public determines the visibility of the property, which you'll learn about a little later in this chapter. Next, the property is named using standard variable syntax, and a value is assigned (although class properties *do not* need an initial value).

To read this property and output it to the browser, reference the object from which to read and the property to be read:

```
echo $obj->prop1;
```

Because multiple instances of a class can exist, if the individual object is not referenced, the script is unable to determine which object to read from. The use of the arrow (->) is an OOP construct that accesses the contained properties and methods of a given object.

Modify the script in test.php to read out the property rather than dump the whole class, by modifying the line in bold:

```php
<?php

declare(strict_types=1);

class MyClass
{
    public $prop1 = "I'm a class property!";
}

$obj = new MyClass;

echo $obj->prop1;

?>
```

Reloading your browser now outputs the following:

```
I'm a class property!
```

Defining Class Methods

Methods are class-specific functions. Individual actions that an object will be able to perform are defined within the class as methods.

For instance, to create methods that set and get the value of the class property $prop1, add the following bold lines to your code:

```php
<?php

declare(strict_types=1);

class MyClass
{
    public $prop1 = "I'm a class property!";

    public function setProperty(string $newval)
    {
        $this->prop1 = $newval;
    }

    public function getProperty(): string
    {
        return $this->prop1 . "<br />";
    }
}
```

```php
$obj = new MyClass;

echo $obj->prop1;

?>
```

■ **Note**   OOP allows objects to reference themselves using $this. When working within a method, use $this in the same way you use the object name outside the class.

To use these methods, call them just like regular functions, but first, reference the object to which they belong. Read the property from MyClass, change its value, and read it out again by making the modifications shown in bold:

```php
<?php

declare(strict_types=1);

class MyClass
{
    public $prop1 = "I'm a class property!";

    public function setProperty(string $newval)
    {
        $this->prop1 = $newval;
    }

    public function getProperty(): string
    {
        return $this->prop1 . "<br />";
    }
}

$obj = new MyClass;

echo $obj->getProperty(); // Get the property value

$obj->setProperty("I'm a new property value!"); // Set a new one

echo $obj->getProperty(); // Read it out again to show the change

?>
```

Reload your browser, and you'll see the following:

```
I'm a class property!
I'm a new property value!
```

The power of OOP becomes apparent when you're using multiple instances of the same class. Add an additional instance of MyClass into the mix and start setting and getting properties:

```php
<?php

declare(strict_types=1);

class MyClass
{
    public $prop1 = "I'm a class property!";

    public function setProperty(string $newval)
    {
        $this->prop1 = $newval;
    }

    public function getProperty(): string
    {
        return $this->prop1 . "<br />";
    }
}

// Create two objects
$obj = new MyClass;
$obj2 = new MyClass;

// Get the value of $prop1 from both objects
echo $obj->getProperty();
echo $obj2->getProperty();

// Set new values for both objects
$obj->setProperty("I'm a new property value!");
$obj2->setProperty("I belong to the second instance!");

// Output both objects' $prop1 value
echo $obj->getProperty();
echo $obj2->getProperty();

?>
```

When you load the results in your browser, they read as follows:

```
I'm a class property!
I'm a class property!
I'm a new property value!
I belong to the second instance!
```

As you can see, OOP keeps objects as separate entities, which makes for easy separation of different pieces of code into small, related bundles.

To make the use of objects easier, PHP also provides a number of **magic methods**, or special methods that are called when certain common actions occur within objects. This allows developers to perform a number of useful tasks with relative ease.

Using Constructors and Destructors

When an object is instantiated, it's often desirable to set a few things right off the bat. To handle this, PHP provides the magic method __construct(), which is called automatically whenever a new object is created.

For the purpose of illustrating the concept of constructors, add a constructor to MyClass that will output a message whenever a new instance of the class is created:

```php
<?php

declare(strict_types=1);

class MyClass
{
    public $prop1 = "I'm a class property!";

    public function __construct()
    {
        echo 'The class "', __CLASS__, '" was initiated!<br />';
    }

    public function setProperty(string $newval)
    {
        $this->prop1 = $newval;
    }

    public function getProperty(): string
    {
        return $this->prop1 . "<br />";
    }
}

// Create a new object
$obj = new MyClass;

// Get the value of $prop1
echo $obj->getProperty();

// Output a message at the end of the file
echo "End of file.<br />";

?>
```

91

░░ **Note**   __CLASS__ is what's called a **magic constant**, which, in this case, returns the name of the class in which it is called. There are several available magic constants; you can read more about them in the PHP manual at http://us3.php.net/manual/en/language.constants.predefined.php.

Reloading the file in your browser will produce the following result:

```
The class "MyClass" was initiated!
I'm a class property!
End of file.
```

To call a function when the object is destroyed, the __destruct() magic method is available. This is useful for class cleanup (closing a database connection, for instance).

Output a message when the object is destroyed by defining the magic method __destruct() in MyClass:

```php
<?php

declare(strict_types=1);

class MyClass
{
    public $prop1 = "I'm a class property!";

    public function __construct()
    {
        echo 'The class "', __CLASS__, '" was initiated!<br />';
    }

    public function __destruct()
    {
        echo 'The class "', __CLASS__, '" was destroyed.<br />';
    }

    public function setProperty(string $newval)
    {
        $this->prop1 = $newval;
    }

    public function getProperty(): string
    {
        return $this->prop1 . "<br />";
    }
}
```

```php
// Create a new object
$obj = new MyClass;

// Get the value of $prop1
echo $obj->getProperty();

// Output a message at the end of the file
echo "End of file.<br />";

?>
```

With a destructor defined, reloading the test file results in the following output:

```
The class "MyClass" was initiated!
I'm a class property!
End of file.
The class "MyClass" was destroyed.
```

When the end of a file is reached, PHP automatically releases all resources that were used within it to keep memory available. This triggers the destructor for the MyClass object.

To explicitly trigger the destructor, you can destroy the object using the function unset():

```php
<?php

declare(strict_types=1);

class MyClass
{
    public $prop1 = "I'm a class property!";

    public function __construct()
    {
        echo 'The class "', __CLASS__, '" was initiated!<br />';
    }

    public function __destruct()
    {
        echo 'The class "', __CLASS__, '" was destroyed.<br />';
    }

    public function setProperty(string $newval)
    {
        $this->prop1 = $newval;
    }

    public function getProperty(): string
    {
        return $this->prop1 . "<br />";
    }
}
```

```php
// Create a new object
$obj = new MyClass;

// Get the value of $prop1
echo $obj->getProperty();

// Destroy the object
unset($obj);

// Output a message at the end of the file
echo "End of file.<br />";


?>
```

Now the result changes to the following when loaded in your browser:

```
The class "MyClass" was initiated!
I'm a class property!
The class "MyClass" was destroyed.
End of file.
```

Converting to a String

To avoid an error if a script attempts to output MyClass as a string, a magic method called __toString() is used.

Without __toString(), attempting to output the object as a string results in a fatal error. Attempt to use echo to output the object without a magic method in place, like so:

```php
<?php

declare(strict_types=1);

class MyClass
{
    public $prop1 = "I'm a class property!";

    public function __construct()
    {
        echo 'The class "', __CLASS__, '" was initiated!<br />';
    }

    public function __destruct()
    {
        echo 'The class "', __CLASS__, '" was destroyed.<br />';
    }

    public function setProperty(string $newval)
    {
        $this->prop1 = $newval;
```

```php
    }

    public function getProperty(): string
    {
        return $this->prop1 . "<br />";
    }
}

// Create a new object
$obj = new MyClass;

// Output the object as a string
echo $obj;

// Destroy the object
unset($obj);

// Output a message at the end of the file
echo "End of file.<br />";

?>
```

This results in the following:

The class "MyClass" was initiated!

Catchable fatal error: Object of class MyClass could not be converted to string ↵
in **C:\wamp\www\book\testing\tst01.php** on line **34**

To avoid this error, add a __toString() method:

```php
<?php

declare(strict_types=1);

class MyClass
{
    public $prop1 = "I'm a class property!";

    public function __construct()
    {
        echo 'The class "', __CLASS__, '" was initiated!<br />';
    }

    public function __destruct()
    {
        echo 'The class "', __CLASS__, '" was destroyed.<br />';
    }
```

```php
    public function __toString()
    {
        echo "Using the toString method: ";
        return $this->getProperty();
    }

    public function setProperty($newval)
    {
        $this->prop1 = $newval;
    }

    public function getProperty()
    {
        return $this->prop1 . "<br />";
    }
}

// Create a new object
$obj = new MyClass;

// Output the object as a string
echo $obj;

// Destroy the object
unset($obj);

// Output a message at the end of the file
echo "End of file.<br />";

?>
```

In this case, attempting to convert the object to a string results in a call to the getProperty() method. Load the test script in your browser to see the result:

```
The class "MyClass" was initiated!
Using the toString method: I'm a class property!
The class "MyClass" was destroyed.
End of file.
```

▓ **Tip**   In addition to the magic methods discussed in this section, several others are available. For a complete list of magic methods, see the PHP manual page at http://us2.php.net/manual/en/language.oop5.magic.php.

Using Class Inheritance

Classes can inherit the methods and properties of another class using the extends keyword. For instance, to create a second class that extends MyClass and adds a method, you add the following to your test file:

```php
<?php

declare(strict_types=1);

class MyClass
{
    public $prop1 = "I'm a class property!";

    public function __construct()
    {
        echo 'The class "', __CLASS__, '" was initiated!<br />';
    }

    public function __destruct()
    {
        echo 'The class "', __CLASS__, '" was destroyed.<br />';
    }

    public function __toString()
    {
        echo "Using the toString method: ";
        return $this->getProperty();
    }

    public function setProperty(string $newval)
    {
        $this->prop1 = $newval;
    }

    public function getProperty(): string
    {
        return $this->prop1 . "<br />";
    }
}

class MyOtherClass extends MyClass
{
    public function newMethod(): string
    {
        return "From a new method in " . __CLASS__ . ".<br />";
    }
}
```

```php
// Create a new object
$newobj = new MyOtherClass;

// Output the object as a string
echo $newobj->newMethod();

// Use a method from the parent class
echo $newobj->getProperty();

?>
```

Upon reloading the test file in your browser, the following is output:

```
The class "MyClass" was initiated!
From a new method in MyOtherClass.
I'm a class property!
The class "MyClass" was destroyed.
```

Overwriting Inherited Properties and Methods

To change the behavior of an existing property or method in the new class, you can simply overwrite it by declaring it again in the new class:

```php
<?php

declare(strict_types=1);

class MyClass
{
    public $prop1 = "I'm a class property!";

    public function __construct()
    {
        echo 'The class "', __CLASS__, '" was initiated!<br />';
    }

    public function __destruct()
    {
        echo 'The class "', __CLASS__, '" was destroyed.<br />';
    }

    public function __toString()
    {
        echo "Using the toString method: ";
        return $this->getProperty();
    }
```

```php
    public function setProperty(string $newval)
    {
        $this->prop1 = $newval;
    }

    public function getProperty(): string
    {
        return $this->prop1 . "<br />";
    }
}

class MyOtherClass extends MyClass
{
    public function __construct()
    {
        echo "A new constructor in " . __CLASS__ . ".<br />";
    }

    public function newMethod(): string
    {
        return "From a new method in " . __CLASS__ . ".<br />";
    }
}

// Create a new object
$newobj = new MyOtherClass;

// Output the object as a string
echo $newobj->newMethod();

// Use a method from the parent class
echo $newobj->getProperty();

?>
```

This changes the output in the browser to

```
A new constructor in MyOtherClass.
From a new method in MyOtherClass.
I'm a class property!
The class "MyClass" was destroyed.
```

Preserving Original Method Functionality While Overwriting Methods

To add new functionality to an inherited method while keeping the original method intact, use the parent keyword with the **scope resolution operator** (::):

```php
<?php

declare(strict_types=1);

class MyClass
{
    public $prop1 = "I'm a class property!";

    public function __construct()
    {
        echo 'The class "', __CLASS__, '" was initiated!<br />';
    }

    public function __destruct()
    {
        echo 'The class "', __CLASS__, '" was destroyed.<br />';
    }

    public function __toString()
    {
        echo "Using the toString method: ";
        return $this->getProperty();
    }

    public function setProperty(string $newval)
    {
        $this->prop1 = $newval;
    }

    public function getProperty(): string
    {
        return $this->prop1 . "<br />";
    }
}

class MyOtherClass extends MyClass
{
    public function __construct()
    {
        parent::__construct(); // Call the parent class's constructor
        echo "A new constructor in " . __CLASS__ . ".<br />";
    }
```

```php
    public function newMethod(): string
    {
        return "From a new method in " . __CLASS__ . ".<br />";
    }
}

// Create a new object
$newobj = new MyOtherClass;

// Output the object as a string
echo $newobj->newMethod();

// Use a method from the parent class
echo $newobj->getProperty();

?>
```

This outputs the result of both the parent constructor and the constructor for the new class:

```
The class "MyClass" was initiated!
A new constructor in MyOtherClass.
From a new method in MyOtherClass.
I'm a class property!
The class "MyClass" was destroyed.
```

Assigning the Visibility of Properties and Methods

For added control over objects, methods and properties are assigned **visibility**. This controls how and from where properties and methods can be accessed. There are three visibility keywords: public, protected, and private. In addition to its visibility, a method or property can be declared as static, which allows them to be accessed without an instantiation of the class.

Public Properties and Methods

All the methods and properties you've used so far have been public. This means that they can be accessed anywhere, both within the class and externally.

Protected Properties and Methods

When a property or method is declared protected, it can only be accessed within the class itself or in descendant classes (classes that extend the class containing the protected method).

Declare the getProperty() method as protected in MyClass and try to access it directly from outside the class, like so:

```php
<?php

declare(strict_types=1);
```

```php
class MyClass
{
    public $prop1 = "I'm a class property!";

    public function __construct()
    {
        echo 'The class "', __CLASS__, '" was initiated!<br />';
    }

    public function __destruct()
    {
        echo 'The class "', __CLASS__, '" was destroyed.<br />';
    }

    public function __toString()
    {
        echo "Using the toString method: ";
        return $this->getProperty();
    }

    public function setProperty(string $newval)
    {
        $this->prop1 = $newval;
    }

    protected function getProperty(): string
    {
        return $this->prop1 . "<br />";
    }
}

class MyOtherClass extends MyClass
{
    public function __construct()
    {
        parent::__construct();
            echo "A new constructor in " . __CLASS__ . ".<br />";
    }

    public function newMethod(): string
    {
        return "From a new method in " . __CLASS__ . ".<br />";
    }
}

// Create a new object
$newobj = new MyOtherClass;

// Attempt to call a protected method
echo $newobj->getProperty();

?>
```

Upon attempting to run this script, the following error shows up:

```
The class "MyClass" was initiated!
A new constructor in MyOtherClass.
```

Fatal error: Uncaught Error: Call to protected method MyClass::getProperty() from ↵
context '' in C:\wamp\www\book\testing\test.php:54 Stack trace: #0 {main} thrown ↵
in **C:\wamp\www\book\testing\test.php** on line **54**

Now, create a new method in MyOtherClass to call the getProperty() method:

```php
<?php

declare(strict_types=1);

class MyClass
{
    public $prop1 = "I'm a class property!";

    public function __construct()
    {
        echo 'The class "', __CLASS__, '" was initiated!<br />';
    }

    public function __destruct()
    {
        echo 'The class "', __CLASS__, '" was destroyed.<br />';
    }

    public function __toString()
    {
        echo "Using the toString method: ";
        return $this->getProperty();
    }

    public function setProperty(string $newval)
    {
        $this->prop1 = $newval;
    }

    protected function getProperty(): string
    {
        return $this->prop1 . "<br />";
    }
}
```

```php
class MyOtherClass extends MyClass
{
    public function __construct()
    {
        parent::__construct();
            echo "A new constructor in " . __CLASS__ . ".<br />";
    }

    public function newMethod(): string
    {
        return "From a new method in " . __CLASS__ . ".<br />";
    }

    public function callProtected(): string
    {
        return $this->getProperty();
    }
}

// Create a new object
$newobj = new MyOtherClass;

// Call the protected method from within a public method
echo $newobj->callProtected();

?>
```

This generates the desired result:

```
The class "MyClass" was initiated!
A new constructor in MyOtherClass.
I'm a class property!
The class "MyClass" was destroyed.
```

Private Properties and Methods

A property or method declared `private` is accessible only from within the class that defines it. No code outside the class may directly access that property or method.

To demonstrate this, it is simplest to go all the way back to the first example, and simply declare $prop1 as `private` in MyClass, and then attempt to run the modified code, as shown:

```php
<?php

declare(strict_types=1);

class MyClass
{
    private $prop1 = "I'm a class property!";

}
```

```php
$obj = new MyClass;

echo $obj->prop1;

?>
```

Reload your browser, and the following error appears:

Fatal error: Uncaught Error: Cannot access private property MyClass::$prop1 ⏎
in C:\wamp\www\book\testing\test.php:13 Stack trace: #0 {main} thrown ⏎
in **C:\wamp\www\book\testing\test.php** on line **13**

Limiting access to member properties by keeping them private is generally considered to be good OOP practice. The usual way to manage class properties is to provide public methods to set and get their values, as you have indeed seen above.

The difference here is that by keeping the class property private, you are enforcing access through methods only. Such encapsulation of class properties makes your code both more robust and easier to maintain. By providing methods to client code, you gain much more control over the integrity of class properties, as well as the freedom to redesign the class internals without breaking client code.

Here is the example again with the public methods restored to access the property:

```php
<?php

declare(strict_types=1);

class MyClass
{
    private $prop1 = "I'm a class property!";

    public function setProperty(string $newval)
    {
        $this->prop1 = $newval;
    }

    public function getProperty(): string
    {
        return $this->prop1 . "<br />";
    }
}

$obj = new MyClass;

echo $obj->getProperty();
$obj->setProperty("Now I am different!");

echo $obj->getProperty();

?>
```

This generates the following output:

```
I'm a class property!
Now I am different!
```

This code works very much as before, but with the added benefit of fully encapsulating the class property. Class methods too can be declared private, as we will occasionally do for "helper" methods whose access is limited to other methods within the same class. But private visibility is more commonly applied to class properties, as in this example. We will generally follow this pattern going forward.

Static Properties and Methods

A method or property declared static can be accessed without first instantiating the class; you simply supply the class name, scope resolution operator, and the property or method name.

One of the major benefits to using static properties is that they keep their stored values for the duration of the script. This means that if you modify a static property and access it later in the script, the modified value will still be stored.

To demonstrate this, return to the full example, add a private static property called $count, a public accessor called getCount(), and a static method called plusOne() to MyClass. Then set up a do...while loop to output the incremented value of $count as long as the value is less than 10, like so:

```php
<?php

declare(strict_types=1);

class MyClass
{
    private $prop1 = "I'm a class property!";

    private static $count = 0;

    public function __construct()
    {
        echo 'The class "', __CLASS__, '" was initiated!<br />';
    }

    public function __destruct()
    {
        echo 'The class "', __CLASS__, '" was destroyed.<br />';
    }

    public function __toString()
    {
        echo "Using the toString method: ";
        return $this->getProperty();
    }
```

```php
    public function setProperty(string $newval)
    {
        $this->prop1 = $newval;
    }

    protected function getProperty(): string
    {
        return $this->prop1 . "<br />";
    }

    public static function getCount(): int
    {
        return self::$count;
    }

    public static function plusOne()
    {
        echo "The count is " . ++self::$count . ".<br />";
    }
}

class MyOtherClass extends MyClass
{
    public function __construct()
    {
        parent::__construct();
        echo "A new constructor in " . __CLASS__ . ".<br />";
    }

    public function newMethod(): string
    {
        return "From a new method in " . __CLASS__ . ".<br />";
    }

    public function callProtected()
    {
        return $this->getProperty();
    }
}

do
{
    // Call plusOne without instantiating MyClass
    MyClass::plusOne();
} while ( MyClass::getCount() < 10 );

?>
```

▓ **Note**   When accessing static properties, the dollar sign ($) comes *after* the scope resolution operator.

When you load this script in your browser, the following is output:

```
The count is 1.
The count is 2.
The count is 3.
The count is 4.
The count is 5.
The count is 6.
The count is 7.
The count is 8.
The count is 9.
The count is 10.
```

Commenting with DocBlocks

While not an official part of OOP, the DocBlock commenting style is a widely accepted method of documenting classes. Aside from providing a standard for developers to use when writing code, it has also been adopted by many of the most popular SDKs (software development kits), such as Eclipse (available at http://eclipse.org) and NetBeans (available at http://netbeans.org), and will be used to generate code hints.

A DocBlock is defined by using a block comment that starts with an additional asterisk:

```
/**
 * This is a very basic DocBlock
 */
```

The real power of DocBlocks comes with the ability to use tags, which start with an at symbol (@) immediately followed by the tag name and the value of the tag. These allow developers to define authors of a file, the license for a class, the property or method information, and other useful information.

The most common tags are the following:

@author: The author of the current element (which might be a class, file, method, or any bit of code) is listed using this tag. Multiple author tags can be used in the same DocBlock if more than one author is credited. The format for the author name is John Doe <john.doe@email.com>.

@copyright: This signifies the copyright year and name of the copyright holder for the current element. The format is 2010 Copyright Holder.

@license: This links to the license for the current element. The format for the license information is http://www.example.com/path/to/license.txt License Name.

@var: This holds the type and description of a variable or class property. The format is *type* element description.

@param: This tag shows the type and description of a function or method parameter. The format is *type* $element_name element description.

@return: The type and description of the return value of a function or method are provided in this tag. The format is *type* return element description.

A sample class commented with DocBlocks might look like this:

```php
<?php

declare(strict_types=1);

/**
 * A simple class
 *
 * This is the long description for this class,
 * which can span as many lines as needed. It is
 * not required, whereas the short description is
 * necessary.
 *
 * It can also span multiple paragraphs if the
 * description merits that much verbiage.
 *
 * @author Jason Lengstorf <jason.lengstorf@ennuidesign.com>
 * @copyright 2010 Ennui Design
 * @license http://www.php.net/license/3_01.txt PHP License 3.01
 */
class SimpleClass
{
    /**
     * A private variable
     *
     * @var string stores data for the class
     */
    private $foo;

    /**
     * Sets $foo to a new value upon class instantiation
     *
     * @param string $val a value required for the class
     * @return void
     */
    public function __construct(string $val)
    {
        $this->foo = $val;
    }

    /**
     * Multiplies two integers
     *
     * Accepts a pair of integers and returns the
     * product of the two.
     *
     * @param int $bat a number to be multiplied
     * @param int $baz a number to be multiplied
     * @return int the product of the two parameters
     */
```

```php
    public function bar(int $bat, int $baz): int
    {
        return $bat * $baz;
    }
}

?>
```

Once you scan the preceding class, the benefits of DocBlock are apparent: everything is clearly defined so that the next developer can pick up the code and never have to wonder what a snippet of code does or what it should contain.

▓ **Note**　For more information on DocBlocks, see `http://en.wikipedia.org/wiki/PHPDoc`.

Comparing Object-Oriented and Procedural Code

There's not really a right and wrong way to write code. That being said, this section outlines a strong argument for adopting an object-oriented approach in software development, especially in large applications.

Ease of Implementation

While it may be daunting at first, OOP actually provides an easier approach to dealing with data. Because an object can store data internally, variables don't need to be passed from function to function to work properly.

Also, because multiple instantiations of the same class can exist simultaneously, dealing with large data sets is infinitely easier. For instance, imagine you are processing the information for two people in a file. They need names, occupations, and ages.

The Procedural Approach

Here's the procedural approach to this example:

```php
<?php

declare(strict_types=1);

function changeJob(array $person, string $newjob): array
{
    $person['job'] = $newjob; // Change the person's job
    return $person;
}

function happyBirthday(array $person): array
{
    ++$person['age']; // Add 1 to the person's age
    return $person;
}
```

```php
$person1 = array(
    'name' => 'Tom',
    'job' => 'Button-Pusher',
    'age' => 34
);

$person2 = array(
    'name' => 'John',
    'job' => 'Lever-Puller',
    'age' => 41
);

// Output the starting values for the people
echo "<pre>Person 1: ", print_r($person1, TRUE), "</pre>";
echo "<pre>Person 2: ", print_r($person2, TRUE), "</pre>";

// Tom got a promotion and had a birthday
$person1 = changeJob($person1, 'Box-Mover');
$person1 = happyBirthday($person1);

// John just had a birthday
$person2 = happyBirthday($person2);

// Output the new values for the people
echo "<pre>Person 1: ", print_r($person1, TRUE), "</pre>";
echo "<pre>Person 2: ", print_r($person2, TRUE), "</pre>";

?>
```

When executed, the code outputs the following:

```
Person 1: Array
(
    [name] => Tom
    [job] => Button-Pusher
    [age] => 34
)
Person 2: Array
(
    [name] => John
    [job] => Lever-Puller
    [age] => 41
)
Person 1: Array
(
    [name] => Tom
    [job] => Box-Mover
    [age] => 35
)
```

111

```
Person 2: Array
(
    [name] => John
    [job] => Lever-Puller
    [age] => 42
)
```

While this code isn't necessarily bad, there's a lot to keep in mind while coding. The array of the affected person's attributes must be passed and returned from each function call, which leaves margin for error.

To clean up this example, it is desirable to leave as few things up to the developer as possible. Only absolutely essential information for the current operation should need to be passed to the functions.

This is where OOP steps in and helps you clean things up.

The OOP Approach

Here's the OOP approach to this example:

```php
<?php

declare(strict_types=1);

class Person
{
    private $_name;
    private $_job;
    private $_age;

    public function __construct(string $name, string $job, int $age)
    {
        $this->_name = $name;
        $this->_job = $job;
        $this->_age = $age;
    }

    public function changeJob(string $newjob)
    {
        $this->_job = $newjob;
    }

    public function happyBirthday()
    {
        ++$this->_age;
    }
}

// Create two new people
$person1 = new Person("Tom", "Button-Pusher", 34);
$person2 = new Person("John", "Lever Puller", 41);
```

```
// Output their starting point
echo "<pre>Person 1: ", print_r($person1, TRUE), "</pre>";
echo "<pre>Person 2: ", print_r($person2, TRUE), "</pre>";

// Give Tom a promotion and a birthday
$person1->changeJob("Box-Mover");
$person1->happyBirthday();

// John just gets a year older
$person2->happyBirthday();

// Output the ending values
echo "<pre>Person 1: ", print_r($person1, TRUE), "</pre>";
echo "<pre>Person 2: ", print_r($person2, TRUE), "</pre>";

?>
```

This outputs the following in the browser:

```
Person 1: Person Object
(
    [_name:Person:private] => Tom
    [_job:Person:private] => Button-Pusher
    [_age:Person:private] => 34
)

Person 2: Person Object
(
    [_name:Person:private] => John
    [_job:Person:private] => Lever Puller
    [_age:Person:private] => 41
)

Person 1: Person Object
(
    [_name:Person:private] => Tom
    [_job:Person:private] => Box-Mover
    [_age:Person:private] => 35
)

Person 2: Person Object
(
    [_name:Person:private] => John
    [_job:Person:private] => Lever Puller
    [_age:Person:private] => 42
)
```

There's a little bit more setup involved to make the approach object oriented, but after the class is defined, creating and modifying people is a breeze; a person's information does not need to be passed or returned from methods, and only absolutely essential information is passed to each method.

On the small scale, this difference may not seem like much, but as your applications grow in size, OOP will significantly reduce your workload if implemented properly.

░ **Tip**   Not everything needs to be object oriented. A quick function that handles something small in one place inside the application does not necessarily need to be wrapped in a class. Use your best judgment when deciding between object-oriented and procedural approaches.

Better Organization

Another benefit of OOP is how well it lends itself to being easily packaged and cataloged. Each class can generally be kept in its own separate file, and if a uniform naming convention is used, accessing the classes is extremely simple.

Assume you've got an application with 150 classes that are called dynamically through a controller file at the root of your application filesystem. All 150 classes follow the naming convention class.*classname*.inc.php and reside in the inc folder of your application.

The controller can implement PHP's __autoload() function to dynamically pull in only the classes it needs as they are called, rather than including all 150 in the controller file just in case or coming up with some clever way of including the files in your own code:

```php
<?php
    function __autoload($class_name)
    {
        include_once 'inc/class.' . $class_name . '.inc.php';
    }
?>
```

Having each class in a separate file also makes code more portable and easier to reuse in new applications without a bunch of copying and pasting.

Easier Maintenance

Due to the more compact nature of OOP when done correctly, changes in the code are usually much easier to spot and make than in a long, spaghetti-code, procedural implementation.

If a particular array of information gains a new attribute, a procedural piece of software may require (in a worst-case scenario) that the new attribute be added to *each function that uses the array*.

An OOP application could potentially be updated as easily adding the new property and then adding the methods that deal with said property.

A lot of the benefits covered in this section are the product of OOP in combination with DRY programming practices. It is definitely possible to create easy-to-maintain procedural code that doesn't cause nightmares, and it is equally possible to create awful object-oriented code. This book will attempt to demonstrate a combination of good coding habits in conjunction with OOP to generate clean code that's easy to read and maintain.

Summary

At this point, you should feel comfortable with the object-oriented programming style. The whole core of the event calendar's back end will be based on OOP, so any concepts that may currently seem unclear will be more thoroughly examined as the concepts from this chapter are put into a practical, real-world example.

In the next chapter, you'll start building the back end of the events calendar.

CHAPTER 4

Build an Events Calendar

Now that you're up to speed on the concept of object-oriented programming, you can start working on the project that will be the meat and potatoes of this book: the events calendar. It all starts here, and as this book progresses, you'll be adding more and more functionality using both PHP and jQuery.

Planning the Calendar

Because you're starting from absolute scratch, you need to take a minute to plan the application. This application will be database-driven (using MySQL), so the planning will take part in two stages: first the database structure and then a basic map of the application that will access and modify the database.

Defining the Database Structure

To make building the application much easier, the first thing you should plan is how the data will be stored. This shapes everything in the application.

For a basic events calendar, all the information you'll need to store is the following:

- event_id: An automatically incremented integer that uniquely identifies each event

- event_title: The title of the event

- event_desc: A full description of the event

- event_start: The start time of the event (in format YYYY-MM-DD HH:MM:SS)

- event_end: The end time of the event (in format YYYY-MM-DD HH:MM:SS)

Creating the Class Map

The next step is to lay out the main class that will handle all the actions your application will perform related to the calendar events. This class will be called Calendar; the methods and properties will be laid out like so:

- Build the constructor.

- Make sure a database connection exists or create one.

- Set the following basic properties:

  - A database object

  - The date to use

- The month being viewed
- The year to view
- The number of days in the month
- The weekday on which the month starts
- Generate HTML to build the events form.
  - Check if an event is being edited or created.
  - Load event information into the form if editing is needed.
- Save new events in the database and sanitize input.
- Delete events from the database and confirm deletion.
- Load events information.
  - Load events data from the database.
  - Store each event as an array in the proper day for the month.
- Output HTML with calendar information. Using the events array, loop through each day of the month and attach event titles and times where applicable.
- Display event information as HTML. Accept an event ID and load the description and details for the event

Planning the Application's Folder Structure

This application is going to be somewhat elaborate when it's finished, so it's worth taking a few minutes to think about how files are going to be organized.

For the sake of security, everything possible will be kept out of the **web root,** or publicly available folders: this includes database credentials, the core of the application, and the classes that will run it. With nothing in the web root, mischievous users won't be able to poke around in your folder structure without being on the server itself, which is a good practice for security.

To start, you'll have two folders: `public` to contain all files available for direct access by the application's users, such as CSS, the index file, and JavaScript files, and `sys` to contain the nonpublic files, such as database credentials, the application's classes, and the core PHP files.

Public Files

The `public` folder will serve as the web root. When a user accesses your application's URL, this is the folder in which the server will look first. At the root level, it contains the files accessed by users to view and manipulate the data stored in the database:

- `index.php`: This is the main file, which displays the month in calendar format with event titles displayed in the box of the day on which they occur.
- `view.php`: If users click an event title, they're taken to this page where the event's data is displayed in detail.
- `admin.php`: To create or modify new events, the form displayed on this page is used.
- `confirmdelete.php`: To delete an event, the user must first confirm that choice by submitting the confirmation form on this page.

The public folder will also have a subfolder called assets, which will contain additional files for the site. Those files will be grouped by their usage, which in this section falls into four categories: common files, CSS files, JavaScript files, and form-processing files.

Create four folders within assets called common, css, inc, and js. The common folder will store files that will be used on all the publicly accessible pages (namely the header and footer of the app); the css folder will store site style sheets; the inc folder will store files to process form-submitted input; and the js folder will store site JavaScript files.

Nonpublic Application Files

The sys folder will be broken into three subfolders: class, which will store all class files for the application (such as the Calendar class); config, which stores application configuration information such as database credentials; and core, which holds the files that initialize the application.

When everything is organized and all files are created, the file structure will be well organized and easy to scale in the future (see Figure 4-1).

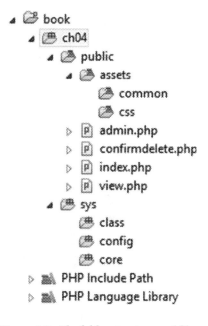

Figure 4-1. *The folder structure and files as they appear in Eclipse 4.5 (Mars) on Windows*

PUBLIC AND NONPUBLIC FOLDERS—WHY BOTHER?

You may be asking yourself right about now, "Why put in the extra effort to create public and nonpublic folders? What's the benefit?"

To answer that question, you need to know a little bit about how web servers work. A server is essentially a computer that stores files and serves selected files to a network (such as the World Wide Web) using a network identifier (an IP address or a URL mapped to an IP address). Hundreds of web sites or other applications can be hosted on one server, each in their own folder.

The server grants access to outside users to these public folders, which means all the files on the folder can be accessed from the network to which the server is connected. In the case of files that contain sensitive information, this isn't always desirable.

Fortunately, files in a public folder can still access files outside of the public folder, even though the users on the network cannot. This allows you to hide your sensitive data from the rest of the world, but keep it accessible to your application.

There are other ways to hide this information, but simply keeping sensitive data nonpublic is the most straightforward, surefire method of doing so.

Modifying the Development Environment

Because you're using public and nonpublic folders for this application, a quick modification to your development environment is necessary: you need to point the server to your public folder, rather that the folder containing both. In this section, you'll learn how to point your server to the public folder.

▓ **Note**　You can skip this section and keep the sys folder inside the public folder without losing any functionality in the application (keep in mind that file paths will differ from those used throughout the exercises in this book). You will, however, open the application to potential security risks. It's highly recommended that you take a minute to follow these steps.

Local Development

To change the document root (public folder) in a local installation, you need to modify the server's configuration file. This book assumes Apache is being used as your server in the XAMPP stack, so you need to locate the httpd.conf file (located at /xamppfiles/etc/httpd.conf on Mac, /opt/lampp/etc/httpd.conf on Linux, and C:\wamp\bin\apache\apache2.4.x\conf\httpd.conf on Windows).

Inside httpd.conf, search for the DocumentRoot directive. This is where you set the path to your public folder. The file should look something like this:

```
#
# DocumentRoot: The directory out of which you will serve your
# documents. By default, all requests are taken from this directory, but
# symbolic links and aliases may be used to point to other locations.
#
DocumentRoot "c:\wamp\www\"
```

Additionally, search for a line in your `httpd.conf` file that references the document root to set permissions. It will look something like this:

```
<Directory "c:/wamp/www/">
```

After locating and altering the paths above, *restart Apache* using the XAMPP control panel. Now, the default folder accessed is the `public` folder of the application. To test this, create the file `index.php` and add the following code snippet:

```
<?php echo "I'm the new document root!"; ?>
```

Navigate to the document root of your development environment in a browser (`localhost` by default) to make sure the reconfiguration worked (see Figure 4-2).

Figure 4-2. *The public folder's index file is displayed after reconfiguring Apache*

Remote Development

Because remote development usually takes place on a hosting company's server, the steps to point your domain to the app's `public` folder will vary from hosting provider to hosting provider, and therefore won't be covered in this book.

However, in many cases, the host will allow you to point a domain to a folder within your hosting account. If this is the case, simply point the domain to the `public` folder, and everything should work properly.

Some hosts do not allow access outside of the document root. If this is the case with your hosting provider, simply place the `sys` folder in the `public` folder and alter the file paths accordingly.

Building the Calendar

With the folder structure ready and your development environment set up, it's time to actually start developing. We'll cover each of the three event views (main view, single event view, and administrative view) in steps, starting with the main calendar view.

Creating the Database

As with the application planning process, the first step in developing the application is to create the database. In your local development environment, pull up phpMyAdmin (`http://localhost/phpmyadmin` in XAMPP), and open the SQL tab (you can also execute these commands in a PHP script if you're not using phpMyAdmin). Create the database, a table to store event data called events, and a few dummy entries using the following SQL:

```
CREATE DATABASE IF NOT EXISTS `php-jquery_example`
  DEFAULT CHARACTER SET utf8
  COLLATE utf8_unicode_ci;

CREATE TABLE IF NOT EXISTS `php-jquery_example`.`events` (
  `event_id` INT(11) NOT NULL AUTO_INCREMENT,
  `event_title` VARCHAR(80) DEFAULT NULL,
  `event_desc` TEXT,
  `event_start` TIMESTAMP NOT NULL DEFAULT '0000-00-00 00:00:00',
  `event_end` TIMESTAMP NOT NULL DEFAULT '0000-00-00 00:00:00',

  PRIMARY KEY (`event_id`),
  INDEX (`event_start`)
) ENGINE=MyISAM CHARACTER SET utf8 COLLATE utf8_unicode_ci;

INSERT INTO `php-jquery_example`.`events`
  (`event_title`, `event_desc`, `event_start`, `event_end`) VALUES
  ('New Year&#039;s Day', 'Happy New Year!',
    '2016-01-01 00:00:00', '2016-01-01 23:59:59'),
  ('Last Day of January', 'Last day of the month! Yay!',
    '2016-01-31 00:00:00', '2016-01-31 23:59:59');
```

░ **Note** All the preceding commands are specific to MySQL. Since this book is focused on jQuery and PHP, we won't go into detail about MySQL here. For more information on MySQL, check out *Beginning PHP and MySQL* by Jason Gilmore (Apress).

After you execute the preceding commands, a new database called php-jquery_example will appear in the left-hand column. Click the database name to display the tables, and then click the events table to view the entries you created (see Figure 4-3).

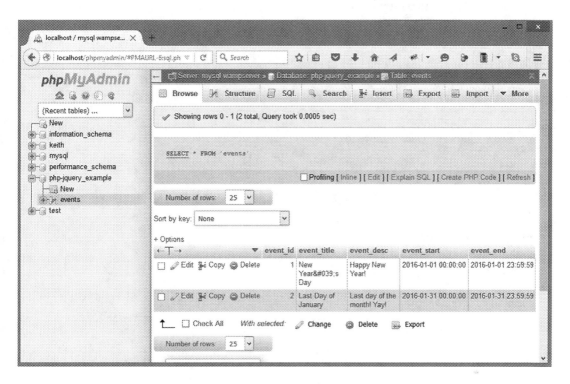

Figure 4-3. *The database, table, and entries after they're created*

Connecting to the Database with a Class

Because you'll be creating multiple classes in this application that need database access, it makes sense to create an object that will open and store that database object. This object will be called DB_Connect, and it will reside in the class folder with the name class.db_connect.inc.php (/sys/class/class.db_connect.inc.php).

This class will have one property and one method, both of which are protected. The property will be called $db and will store a database object. The method will be a constructor; this will accept an optional database object to store in $db, or it will create a new PDO object if no database object is passed.

Insert the following code into class.db_connect.inc.php:

```php
<?php

declare(strict_types=1);

/**
 * Database actions (DB access, validation, etc.)
 *
 * PHP version 7
 *
```

```
 * LICENSE: This source file is subject to the MIT License, available
 * at http://www.opensource.org/licenses/mit-license.html
 *
 * @author     Jason Lengstorf <jason.lengstorf@ennuidesign.com>
 * @copyright  2009 Ennui Design
 * @license    http://www.opensource.org/licenses/mit-license.html
 */
class DB_Connect {

    /**
     * Stores a database object
     *
     * @var object A database object
     */
    protected $db;

    /**
     * Checks for a DB object or creates one if one isn't found
     *
     * @param object $db A database object
     */
    protected function __construct($db=NULL)
    {
        if ( is_object($db) )
        {
            $this->db = $db;
        }
        else
        {
            // Constants are defined in /sys/config/db-cred.inc.php
            $dsn = "mysql:host=" . DB_HOST . ";dbname=" . DB_NAME;
            try
            {
                $this->db = new PDO($dsn, DB_USER, DB_PASS);
            }
            catch ( Exception $e )
            {
                // If the DB connection fails, output the error
                die ( $e->getMessage() );
            }
        }
    }

}

?>
```

▓ **Note** The preceding function uses constants that are not defined just yet. You'll create the files to define
these constants in the next section.

Creating the Class Wrapper

To build the application itself, start by creating the file `class.calendar.inc.php` in the `class` folder that resides within the non-public `sys` folder (`/sys/class/class.calendar.inc.php`). This class will extend the `DB_Connect` class in order to have access to the database object. Open the file in your editor of choice and create the `Calendar` class using the following code:

```php
<?php

declare(strict_types=1);

/**
 * Builds and manipulates an events calendar
 *
 * PHP version 7
 *
 * LICENSE: This source file is subject to the MIT License, available
 * at http://www.opensource.org/licenses/mit-license.html
 *
 * @author      Jason Lengstorf <jason.lengstorf@ennuidesign.com>
 * @copyright   2009 Ennui Design
 * @license     http://www.opensource.org/licenses/mit-license.html
 */
class Calendar extends DB_Connect
{
    // Methods and properties go here
}

?>
```

With the class created, you can start adding the properties and methods to the class.

Adding Class Properties

The `Calendar` class doesn't need any public properties, and you won't be extending it in the examples contained within this book, so all class properties will be private.

As defined in the section on planning, create the properties for the `Calendar` class:

```php
<?php

declare(strict_types=1);

class Calendar extends DB_Connect
{

    /**
     * The date from which the calendar should be built
     *
     * Stored in YYYY-MM-DD HH:MM:SS format
     *
```

```
 * @var string the date to use for the calendar
 */
private $_useDate;

/**
 * The month for which the calendar is being built
 *
 * @var int the month being used
 */
private $_m;

/**
 * The year from which the month's start day is selected
 *
 * @var int the year being used
 */
private $_y;

/**
 * The number of days in the month being used
 *
 * @var int the number of days in the month
 */
private $_daysInMonth;

/**
 * The index of the day of the week the month starts on (0-6)
 *
 * @var int the day of the week the month starts on
 */
private $_startDay;

// Methods go here
}

?>
```

▓ **Note**   For the sake of brevity, DocBlocks will be left out of repeated code snippets.

According to the original planning, the class properties are as follows:

- $_useDate: The date to use when building the calendar in YYYY-MM-DD HH:MM:SS format

- $_m: The month to use when building the calendar

- $_y: The year to use when building the calendar

- $_daysInMonth: How many days are in the current month

- $_startDay: Index from 0-6 representing on what day of the week the month starts

Building the Constructor

Next, you can build the class constructor. Start out by declaring it:

```php
<?php

declare(strict_types=1);

class Calendar extends DB_Connect
{

    private $_useDate;

    private $_m;

    private $_y;

    private $_daysInMonth;

    private $_startDay;

    /**
     * Creates a database object and stores relevant data
     *
     * Upon instantiation, this class accepts a database object
     * that, if not null, is stored in the object's private $_db
     * property. If null, a new PDO object is created and stored
     * instead.
     *
     * Additional info is gathered and stored in this method,
     * including the month from which the calendar is to be built,
     * how many days are in said month, what day the month starts
     * on, and what day it is currently.
     *
     * @param object $dbo a database object
     * @param string $useDate the date to use to build the calendar
     * @return void
     */
    public function __construct($dbo=NULL, $useDate=NULL)
    {

    }

}

?>
```

The constructor will accept two optional parameters: the first is a database object, and the second is the date around which the calendar display should be built.

Checking the Database Connection

To function properly, the class needs a database connection. The constructor will call the parent constructor from DB_Connect to check for an existing database object and use that when available, or it will create a new object if none is supplied.

Set up the call to make this check using the code shown in bold:

```php
<?php

declare(strict_types=1);

class Calendar extends DB_Connect
{

    private $_useDate;

    private $_m;

    private $_y;

    private $_daysInMonth;

    private $_startDay;

    public function __construct($dbo=NULL, $useDate=NULL)
    {
        /*
         * Call the parent constructor to check for
         * a database object
         */
        parent::__construct($dbo);
    }
}

?>
```

■ **Note**   The Calendar class constructor accepts an optional $dbo argument that is passed in turn to the DB_Connect constructor. This allows you to create a database object and pass it for use in the class easily.

Creating a File to Store Database Credentials

To keep the database credentials separate from the rest of the application for easy maintenance, you want to use a configuration file. Create a new file called db-cred.inc.php in the config folder (/sys/config/db-cred.inc.php). Inside, create an array called $C (for constants), and store each piece of data as a new key-value pair:

```php
<?php

declare(strict_types=1);
```

```
/*
 * Create an empty array to store constants
 */
$C = array();

/*
 * The database host URL
 */
$C['DB_HOST'] = 'localhost';

/*
 * The database username
 */
$C['DB_USER'] = 'root';

/*
 * The database password
 */
$C['DB_PASS'] = '';

/*
 * The name of the database to work with
 */
$C['DB_NAME'] = 'php-jquery_example';

?>
```

▓ **Note** Initializing $C as an empty array is a safeguard against any tainted pieces of data being stored in $C and defined as constants. This is a good habit, especially when dealing with sensitive data.

Save this file. If you're not using XAMPP or if you've modified the default database credentials, you'll need to substitute your own host, username, password, and database name in the code.

Creating an Initialization File

At this point, your database credentials still aren't stored as constants. You'll be using an initialization file to handle this.

An **initialization file** collects data, loads files, and organizes information for an application. In this example, it will load and define all necessary constants, create a database object, and set up an automatic loading function for classes. Other functionality will be added later on as it becomes necessary.

Create a file called init.inc.php, and place it in the core folder (/sys/core/init.inc.php). Inside, add the following:

```php
<?php

declare(strict_types=1);
```

```php
/*
 * Include the necessary configuration info
 */
include_once '../sys/config/db-cred.inc.php';

/*
 * Define constants for configuration info
 */
foreach ( $C as $name => $val )
{
    define($name, $val);
}

/*
 * Create a PDO object
 */
$dsn = "mysql:host=" . DB_HOST . ";dbname=" . DB_NAME;
$dbo = new PDO($dsn, DB_USER, DB_PASS);

/*
 * Define the auto-load function for classes
 */
function __autoload($class)
{
    $filename = "../sys/class/class." . $class . ".inc.php";
    if ( file_exists($filename) )
    {
        include_once $filename;
    }
}

?>
```

An automatic loading function is called when a script attempts to instantiate a class that hasn't been loaded yet. It's a convenient way to easily load classes into a script on demand. For more information on automatic loading, visit http://php.net/autoload.

Creating an Index File to Pull It All Together

To see everything in action, modify index.php in the public folder. Inside, simply include the initialization file and instantiate the Calendar class. Next, check if the class loaded properly, and output the object's structure if so:

```php
<?php

declare(strict_types=1);

/*
 * Include necessary files
 */
include_once '../sys/core/init.inc.php';
```

```
/*
 * Load the calendar for January
 */
$cal = new Calendar($dbo, "2016-01-01 12:00:00");

if ( is_object ($cal) )
{
    echo "<pre>", var_dump($cal), "</pre>";
}

?>
```

Once you navigate to http://localhost/, the following message is output:

```
object(Calendar)#2 (6) {
  ["_useDate":"Calendar":private]=>
  NULL
  ["_m":"Calendar":private]=>
  NULL
  ["_y":"Calendar":private]=>
  NULL
  ["_daysInMonth":"Calendar":private]=>
  NULL
  ["_startDay":"Calendar":private]=>
  NULL
  ["db":protected]=>
  object(PDO)#1 (0) {
  }
}
```

Setting Basic Properties

With all that infrastructure taken care of, you can get back to finishing the Calendar class's constructor.

After checking the database object, the constructor needs to store several pieces of data about the month with which it will be building a calendar.

First, it checks if a date was passed to the constructor; if so, that is stored in the $_useDate property; otherwise, the current date is used.

Next, the date is converted to a UNIX timestamp (the number of seconds since the Unix epoch; read more about this at http://en.wikipedia.org/wiki/Unix_time) before the month and year are extracted and stored in $_m and $_y, respectively.

Finally, $_m and $_y are used to determine how many days are in the month being used and which day of the week the month starts on.

The following bold code adds this functionality to the constructor:

```
<?php

declare(strict_types=1);

class Calendar extends DB_Connect
{
```

```php
private $_useDate;

private $_m;

private $_y;

private $_daysInMonth;

private $_startDay;

public function __construct($dbo=NULL, $useDate=NULL)
{
    /*
     * Call the parent constructor to check for
     * a database object
     */
    parent::__construct($dbo);

    /*
     * Gather and store data relevant to the month
     */
    if ( isset($useDate) )
    {
        $this->_useDate = $useDate;
    }
    else
    {
        $this->_useDate = date('Y-m-d H:i:s');
    }

    /*
     * Convert to a timestamp, then determine the month
     * and year to use when building the calendar
     */
    $ts = strtotime($this->_useDate);
    $this->_m = (int)date('m', $ts);
    $this->_y = (int)date('Y', $ts);

    /*
     * Determine how many days are in the month
     */
    $this->_daysInMonth = cal_days_in_month(
            CAL_GREGORIAN,
            $this->_m,
            $this->_y
        );
```

```
    /*
     * Determine what weekday the month starts on
     */
    $ts = mktime(0, 0, 0, $this->_m, 1, $this->_y);
    $this->_startDay = (int)date('w', $ts);
  }

}

?>
```

Now all the properties that were previously NULL will have values when you reload http://localhost/:

```
object(Calendar)#2 (6) {
  ["_useDate":"Calendar":private]=>
  string(19) "2016-01-01 12:00:00"
  ["_m":"Calendar":private]=>
  int(1)
  ["_y":"Calendar":private]=>
  int(2016)
  ["_daysInMonth":"Calendar":private]=>
  int(31)
  ["_startDay":"Calendar":private]=>
  int(5)
  ["db":protected]=>
  object(PDO)#1 (0) {
  }
}
```

Loading Events Data

To load data about events, you need to create a new method to access the database and retrieve them. Because event data will be accessed in two ways (the second of which will be addressed later in this chapter), the act of loading data will be kept generic for easy reuse.

This method will be private and named _loadEventData(). It accepts one optional parameter, the ID of an event, and follows these steps to load events:

- Create a basic SELECT query to load the available fields from the events table.

- Check if an ID was passed, and if so, add a WHERE clause to the query to return only one event.

- Otherwise, do both of the following:

  - Find midnight of the first day of the month and 11:59:59PM on the last day of the month.

  - Add a WHERE...BETWEEN clause to only load dates that fall within the current month.

- Execute the query.

- Return an associative array of the results.

All put together, this method looks like so:

```php
<?php

declare(strict_types=1);

class Calendar extends DB_Connect
{
    private $_useDate;

    private $_m;

    private $_y;

    private $_daysInMonth;

    private $_startDay;

    public function __construct($dbo=NULL, $useDate=NULL) {...}

    /**
     * Loads event(s) info into an array
     *
     * @param int $id an optional event ID to filter results
     * @return array an array of events from the database
     */
    private function _loadEventData($id=NULL)
    {
        $sql = "SELECT
                    `event_id`, `event_title`, `event_desc`,
                    `event_start`, `event_end`
                FROM `events`";

        /*
         * If an event ID is supplied, add a WHERE clause
         * so only that event is returned
         */
        if ( !empty($id) )
        {
            $sql .= "WHERE `event_id`=:id LIMIT 1";
        }

        /*
         * Otherwise, load all events for the month in use
         */
```

```php
        else
        {
            /*
             * Find the first and last days of the month
             */
            $start_ts = mktime(0, 0, 0, $this->_m, 1, $this->_y);
            $end_ts = mktime(23, 59, 59, $this->_m+1, 0, $this->_y);
            $start_date = date('Y-m-d H:i:s', $start_ts);
            $end_date = date('Y-m-d H:i:s', $end_ts);

            /*
             * Filter events to only those happening in the
             * currently selected month
             */
            $sql .= "WHERE `event_start`
                        BETWEEN '$start_date'
                        AND '$end_date'
                    ORDER BY `event_start`";
        }

        try
        {
            $stmt = $this->db->prepare($sql);

            /*
             * Bind the parameter if an ID was passed
             */
            if ( !empty($id) )
            {
                $stmt->bindParam(":id", $id, PDO::PARAM_INT);
            }

            $stmt->execute();
            $results = $stmt->fetchAll(PDO::FETCH_ASSOC);
            $stmt->closeCursor();

            return $results;
        }
        catch ( Exception $e )
        {
            die ( $e->getMessage() );
        }
    }

}

?>
```

■ **Note**   For the sake of brevity, nonreferenced methods are collapsed.

This method returns an array that, when using the test entries you entered into the database previously, looks like this:

```
Array
(
    [0] => Array
        (
            [event_id] => 1
            [event_title] => New Year's Day
            [event_desc] => Happy New Year!
            [event_start] => 2016-01-01 00:00:00
            [event_end] => 2016-01-01 23:59:59
        )

    [1] => Array
        (
            [event_id] => 2
            [event_title] => Last Day of January
            [event_desc] => Last day of the month! Yay!
            [event_start] => 2016-01-31 00:00:00
            [event_end] => 2016-01-31 23:59:59
        )

)
```

Creating an Array of Event Objects for Use in the Calendar

The raw output of _loadEventData() isn't immediately usable in the calendar. Because events need to be displayed on the proper day, the events retrieved from _loadEventData() need to be grouped by the day on which they occur. For easy reference, the event fields will be simplified as well.

The end goal is an array of events that will use the day of the month as its index, containing each event as an object. The two test entries in your database should end up being stored like so when the new method is complete:

```
Array
(
    [1] => Array
        (
            [0] => Event Object
                (
                    [id] => 1
                    [title] => New Year's Day
                    [description] => Happy New Year!
                    [start] => 2016-01-01 00:00:00
                    [end] => 2016-01-01 23:59:59
                )

        )
```

```
    [31] => Array
        (
            [0] => Event Object
                (
                    [id] => 2
                    [title] => Last Day of January
                    [description] => Last day of the month! Yay!
                    [start] => 2016-01-31 00:00:00
                    [end] => 2016-01-31 23:59:59
                )

        )

)

)
```

Creating an Event Class

To accomplish this, you must first create a new class called Event in the class folder (/sys/class/class.
event.inc.php). It will have five public properties ($id, $title, $description, $start, and $end) and a
constructor that will set each of those properties using the associative array returned by the database query.
Create the file, and insert the following code inside it:

```php
<?php

declare(strict_types=1);

/**
 * Stores event information
 *
 * PHP version 7
 *
 * LICENSE: This source file is subject to the MIT License, available
 * at http://www.opensource.org/licenses/mit-license.html
 *
 * @author      Jason Lengstorf <jason.lengstorf@ennuidesign.com>
 * @copyright   2010 Ennui Design
 * @license     http://www.opensource.org/licenses/mit-license.html
 */
class Event
{

    /**
     * The event ID
     *
     * @var int
     */
    public $id;

    /**
     * The event title
     *
```

```php
     * @var string
     */
    public $title;

    /**
     * The event description
     *
     * @var string
     */
    public $description;

    /**
     * The event start time
     *
     * @var string
     */
    public $start;

    /**
     * The event end time
     *
     * @var string
     */
    public $end;

    /**
     * Accepts an array of event data and stores it
     *
     * @param array $event Associative array of event data
     * @return void
     */
    public function __construct($event)
    {
        if ( is_array($event) )
        {
            $this->id = $event['event_id'];
            $this->title = $event['event_title'];
            $this->description = $event['event_desc'];
            $this->start = $event['event_start'];
            $this->end = $event['event_end'];
        }
        else
        {
            throw new Exception("No event data was supplied.");
        }
    }

}

?>
```

Creating the Method to Store Event Objects in an Array

Now that each event can be stored as an object, you can create the method that will loop through the available events and store them in an array corresponding to the dates on which they occur. First, load the event data from the database using _loadEventData(). Next, extract the day of the month from each event's start date and add a new value to the array at that day's index. In the Calendar class, create a new method called _createEventObj() and set it to private. Load the events from the database, and create the new array using the following bold code:

```php
<?php

declare(strict_types=1);

class Calendar extends DB_Connect
{

    private $_useDate;

    private $_m;

    private $_y;

    private $_daysInMonth;

    private $_startDay;

    public function __construct($dbo=NULL, $useDate=NULL) {...}

    private function _loadEventData($id=NULL) {...}

    /**
     * Loads all events for the month into an array
     *
     * @return array events info
     */
    private function _createEventObj()
    {
        /*
         * Load the events array
         */
        $arr = $this->_loadEventData();

        /*
         * Create a new array, then organize the events
         * by the day of the month on which they occur
         */
        $events = array();
        foreach ( $arr as $event )
        {
            $day = date('j', strtotime($event['event_start']));
```

```php
            try
            {
                $events[$day][] = new Event($event);
            }
            catch ( Exception $e )
            {
                die ( $e->getMessage() );
            }
        }
        return $events;
    }

}

?>
```

Now the events can be loaded and organized in such a way that the method to output the actual calendar, HTML, can easily put dates in the proper place.

Outputting HTML to Display the Calendar and Events

At this point, you have the database set up, test events stored, and methods in place to load and organize the event data into an easy-to-use array. You're ready to put the pieces together and build a calendar!

The calendar will be built by a public method called buildCalendar(). This will generate a calendar with the following attributes:

- A heading that will show the month and year being displayed

- Weekday abbreviations to make the calendar look like a calendar

- Numbered boxes that contain events if they exist for the given date

To start, declare the buildCalendar() method in the Calendar class, and create the heading in an H2 element. Also, create an array of weekday abbreviations and loop through them to generate an unordered list. Add the following bold code to do so:

```php
<?php

declare(strict_types=1);

class Calendar extends DB_Connect
{

    private $_useDate;

    private $_m;

    private $_y;

    private $_daysInMonth;

    private $_startDay;
```

```php
public function __construct($dbo=NULL, $useDate=NULL) {...}

private function _loadEventData($id=NULL) {...}

private function _createEventObj() {...}

/**
 * Returns HTML markup to display the calendar and events
 *
 * Using the information stored in class properties, the
 * events for the given month are loaded, the calendar is
 * generated, and the whole thing is returned as valid markup.
 *
 * @return string the calendar HTML markup
 */
public function buildCalendar()
{
    /*
     * Determine the calendar month and create an array of
     * weekday abbreviations to label the calendar columns
     */
    $cal_month = date('F Y', strtotime($this->_useDate));
    define('WEEKDAYS', array('Sun', 'Mon', 'Tue',
            'Wed', 'Thu', 'Fri', 'Sat'));

    /*
     * Add a header to the calendar markup
     */
    $html = "\n\t<h2>$cal_month</h2>";
    for ( $d=0, $labels=NULL; $d<7; ++$d )
    {
        $labels .= "\n\t\t<li>" . WEEKDAYS[$d] . "</li>";
    }
    $html .= "\n\t<ul class=\"weekdays\">"
        . $labels . "\n\t</ul>";

    /*
     * Return the markup for output
     */
    return $html;
}

}

?>
```

Modifying the Index File

To see the output of the buildCalendar() method, you need to modify index.php in the public folder to call the method. Update the file with the code shown in bold:

```php
<?php

declare(strict_types=1);

/*
 * Include necessary files
 */
include_once '../sys/core/init.inc.php';

/*
 * Load the calendar for January
 */
$cal = new Calendar($dbo, "2016-01-01 12:00:00");

/*
 * Display the calendar HTML
 */
echo $cal->buildCalendar();

?>
```

Pull up the file in your browser to see the results so far (Figure 4-4).

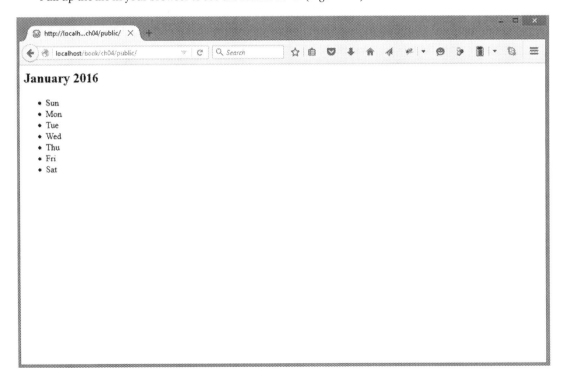

Figure 4-4. *The heading and weekday abbreviations*

Building the Calendar

The next step is to build the actual calendar days. Several steps need to be completed for this to work out.

1. Create a new unordered list.

2. Set up a loop (with an iteration counter, a calendar date counter, today's date, and the month and year stored as variables) that runs as long as the calendar date counter is less than the number of days in the month.

3. Add a `fill` class to the days of the week that occur before the first.

4. Add a `today` class if the current date is contained within the same month and year and matches the date being generated.

5. Create an opening and closing list item tag for each day.

6. Check if the current calendar box falls within the current month, and add the date if so.

7. Check if the current calendar box is a Saturday, and close the list and open a new one if so.

8. Assemble the pieces of the list item and append them to the markup.

9. After the loop, run another loop to add filler days until the calendar week is completed.

10. Close the final unordered list and return the markup.

To start, complete Steps 1 and 2 by adding the following bold code to the `buildCalendar()` method:

```php
public function buildCalendar()
{
    /*
     * Determine the calendar month and create an array of
     * weekday abbreviations to label the calendar columns
     */
    $cal_month = date('F Y', strtotime($this->_useDate));
    define('WEEKDAYS', array('Sun', 'Mon', 'Tue',
            'Wed', 'Thu', 'Fri', 'Sat'));

    /*
     * Add a header to the calendar markup
     */
    $html = "\n\t<h2>$cal_month</h2>";
    for ( $d=0, $labels=NULL; $d<7; ++$d )
    {
        $labels .= "\n\t\t<li>" . WEEKDAYS[$d] . "</li>";
    }
    $html .= "\n\t<ul class=\"weekdays\">"
        . $labels . "\n\t</ul>";
```

```
    /*
     * Create the calendar markup
     */
    $html .= "\n\t<ul>"; // Start a new unordered list
    for ( $i=1, $c=1, $t=date('j'), $m=date('m'), $y=date('Y');
            $c<=$this->_daysInMonth; ++$i )
    {
        // More steps go here
    }

    /*
     * Return the markup for output
     */
    return $html;
}
```

Next, add the bold code below to complete Steps 3–5:

```
public function buildCalendar()
{
    /*
     * Determine the calendar month and create an array of
     * weekday abbreviations to label the calendar columns
     */
    $cal_month = date('F Y', strtotime($this->_useDate));
    define('WEEKDAYS', array('Sun', 'Mon', 'Tue',
            'Wed', 'Thu', 'Fri', 'Sat'));

    /*
     * Add a header to the calendar markup
     */
    $html = "\n\t<h2>$cal_month</h2>";
    for ( $d=0, $labels=NULL; $d<7; ++$d )
    {
        $labels .= "\n\t\t<li>" . WEEKDAYS[$d] . "</li>";
    }
    $html .= "\n\t<ul class=\"weekdays\">"
        . $labels . "\n\t</ul>";

    /*
     * Create the calendar markup
     */
    $html .= "\n\t<ul>"; // Start a new unordered list
    for ( $i=1, $c=1, $t=date('j'), $m=date('m'), $y=date('Y');
            $c<=$this->_daysInMonth; ++$i )
    {
        /*
         * Apply a "fill" class to the boxes occurring before
         * the first of the month
         */
        $class = $i<=$this->_startDay ? "fill" : NULL;
```

```
    /*
     * Add a "today" class if the current date matches
     * the current date
     */
    if ( $c==$t && $m==$this->_m && $y==$this->_y )
    {
        $class = "today";
    }

    /*
     * Build the opening and closing list item tags
     */
    $ls = sprintf("\n\t\t<li class=\"%s\">", $class);
    $le = "\n\t\t</li>";

    // More steps go here
    }

    /*
     * Return the markup for output
     */
    return $html;
}
```

To complete Steps 6-10 (actually build the dates, check if the week needs to wrap, assemble the date markup, finish the last week out with filler, and return the markup), add the following bold code:

```
public function buildCalendar()
{
    /*
     * Determine the calendar month and create an array of
     * weekday abbreviations to label the calendar columns
     */
    $cal_month = date('F Y', strtotime($this->_useDate));
    define('WEEKDAYS', array('Sun', 'Mon', 'Tue',
            'Wed', 'Thu', 'Fri', 'Sat'));

    /*
     * Add a header to the calendar markup
     */
    $html = "\n\t<h2>$cal_month</h2>";
    for ( $d=0, $labels=NULL; $d<7; ++$d )
    {
        $labels .= "\n\t\t<li>" . WEEKDAYS[$d] . "</li>";
    }
    $html .= "\n\t<ul class=\"weekdays\">"
        . $labels . "\n\t</ul>";

    /*
     * Create the calendar markup
     */
```

```php
$html .= "\n\t<ul>"; // Start a new unordered list
for ( $i=1, $c=1, $t=date('j'), $m=date('m'), $y=date('Y');
        $c<=$this->_daysInMonth; ++$i )
{
    /*
     * Apply a "fill" class to the boxes occurring before
     * the first of the month
     */
    $class = $i<=$this->_startDay ? "fill" : NULL;

    /*
     * Add a "today" class if the current date matches
     * the current date
     */
    if ( $c+1==$t && $m==$this->_m && $y==$this->_y )
    {
        $class = "today";
    }

    /*
     * Build the opening and closing list item tags
     */
    $ls = sprintf("\n\t\t<li class=\"%s\">", $class);
    $le = "\n\t\t</li>";

    /*
     * Add the day of the month to identify the calendar box
     */
    if ( $this->_startDay<$i && $this->_daysInMonth>=$c )
    {
        $date = sprintf("\n\t\t\t<strong>%02d</strong>",$c++);
    }
    else { $date=" "; }

    /*
     * If the current day is a Saturday, wrap to the next row
     */
    $wrap = $i!=0 && $i%7==0 ? "\n\t</ul>\n\t<ul>" : NULL;

    /*
     * Assemble the pieces into a finished item
     */
    $html .= $ls . $date . $le . $wrap;
}
```

```
/*
 * Add filler to finish out the last week
 */
while ( $i%7!=1 )
{
    $html .= "\n\t\t<li class=\"fill\"> </li>";
    ++$i;
}

/*
 * Close the final unordered list
 */
$html .= "\n\t</ul>\n\n";

/*
 * Return the markup for output
 */
return $html;
}
```

Test the function as it stands now. Figure 4-5 shows the unordered lists in a browser.

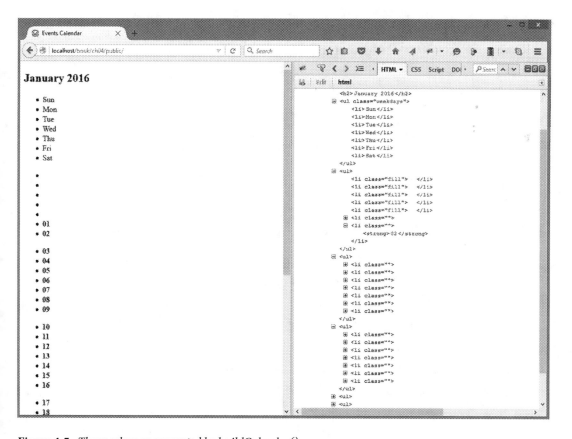

Figure 4-5. *The markup as generated by buildCalendar()*

Displaying Events in the Calendar

Adding the events to the calendar display is as easy as loading the events array from _createEventObj()
and looping through the events stored in the index that matches the current day if any exist. Add event data
to the calendar markup using the following bold code:

```php
public function buildCalendar()
{
    /*
     * Determine the calendar month and create an array of
     * weekday abbreviations to label the calendar columns
     */
    $cal_month = date('F Y', strtotime($this->_useDate));
    define('WEEKDAYS', array('Sun', 'Mon', 'Tue',
            'Wed', 'Thu', 'Fri', 'Sat'));

    /*
     * Add a header to the calendar markup
     */
    $html = "\n\t<h2>$cal_month</h2>";
    for ( $d=0, $labels=NULL; $d<7; ++$d )
    {
        $labels .= "\n\t\t<li>" . WEEKDAYS[$d] . "</li>";
    }
    $html .= "\n\t<ul class=\"weekdays\">"
        . $labels . "\n\t</ul>";

    /*
     * Load events data
     */
    $events = $this->_createEventObj();

    /*
     * Create the calendar markup
     */
    $html .= "\n\t<ul>"; // Start a new unordered list
    for ( $i=1, $c=1, $t=date('j'), $m=date('m'), $y=date('Y');
            $c<=$this->_daysInMonth; ++$i )
    {
        /*
         * Apply a "fill" class to the boxes occurring before
         * the first of the month
         */
        $class = $i<=$this->_startDay ? "fill" : NULL;

        /*
         * Add a "today" class if the current date matches
         * the current date
         */
```

```php
if ( $c+1==$t && $m==$this->_m && $y==$this->_y )
{
    $class = "today";
}

/*
 * Build the opening and closing list item tags
 */
$ls = sprintf("\n\t\t<li class=\"%s\">", $class);
$le = "\n\t\t</li>";

/*
 * Add the day of the month to identify the calendar box
 */
if ( $this->_startDay<$i && $this->_daysInMonth>=$c )
{
    /*
     * Format events data
     */
    $event_info = NULL; // clear the variable
    if ( isset($events[$c]) )
    {
        foreach ( $events[$c] as $event )
        {
            $link = '<a href="view.php?event_id='
                    . $event->id . '">' . $event->title
                    . '</a>';
            $event_info .= "\n\t\t\t$link";
        }
    }

    $date = sprintf("\n\t\t\t<strong>%02d</strong>",$c++);
}
else { $date=" "; }

/*
 * If the current day is a Saturday, wrap to the next row
 */
$wrap = $i!=0 && $i%7==0 ? "\n\t</ul>\n\t<ul>" : NULL;

/*
 * Assemble the pieces into a finished item
 */
$html .= $ls . $date . $event_info . $le . $wrap;
}
```

```
    /*
     * Add filler to finish out the last week
     */
    while ( $i%7!=1 )
    {
        $html .= "\n\t\t<li class=\"fill\"> </li>";
        ++$i;
    }

    /*
     * Close the final unordered list
     */
    $html .= "\n\t</ul>\n\n";

    /*
     * Return the markup for output
     */
    return $html;
}
```

▓ **Caution**   Don't forget to add the new $event_info variable into the markup at the bottom of the loop!

When the database events are loaded into the calendar display, the titles show up next to the appropriate date (see Figure 4-6).

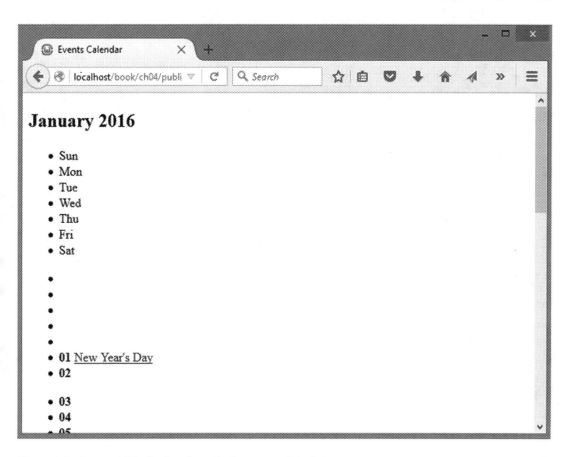

Figure 4-6. *An event title displayed next to the appropriate date*

■ **Note** The linked event titles point to a file called `view.php` that doesn't exist yet. This file will be built and explained in the "Outputting HTML to Display Full Event Descriptions" section later in this chapter.

Making the Calendar Look Like a Calendar

At this point, your markup is proper and your events are there, but the generated code doesn't look much like a calendar at all.

To rectify this, take a moment to complete the HTML markup and style the page using CSS.

■ **Note** Because this book is not about CSS, the rules used won't be explained in detail. For more information on CSS, check out *Beginning CSS3* by David Powers (Apress).

In a nutshell, the CSS file will do the following:

- Float each list item to the left.

- Adjust margins and borders to make the dates look like a traditional calendar.

- Add a hover effect so the day over which the mouse is hovering will be highlighted.

- Style event titles.

- Add hover effects for event titles as well.

- Add some CSS3 flair, including rounded corners and drop shadows, for fun.

■ **Tip**   For more information on CSS3, visit `http://css3.info/`.

Create a new file called `style.css` in the `css` folder (`/public/assets/css/style.css`) and add the following rules:

```css
body {
    background-color: #789;
    font-family: georgia, serif;
    font-size: 13px;
}

#content {
    display: block;
    width: 812px;
    margin: 40px auto 10px;
    padding: 10px;
    background-color: #FFF;
    -moz-border-radius: 6px;
    -webkit-border-radius: 6px;
    border-radius: 6px;
    border:2px solid black;
    -moz-box-shadow: 0 0 14px #123;
    -webkit-box-shadow: 0 0 14px #123;
    box-shadow: 0 0 14px #123;
}

h2,p {
    margin: 0 auto 14px;
    text-align: center;
}

ul {
    display: block;
    clear: left;
    height: 82px;
    width: 812px;
    margin: 0 auto;
    padding: 0;
```

```
    list-style: none;
    background-color: #FFF;
    text-align: center;
    border: 1px solid black;
    border-top: 0;
    border-bottom: 2px solid black;
}

li {
    position: relative;
    float: left;
    margin: 0;
    padding: 20px 2px 2px;
    border-left: 1px solid black;
    border-right: 1px solid black;
    width: 110px;
    height: 60px;
    overflow: hidden;
    background-color: white;
}

li:hover {
    background-color: #FCB;
    z-index: 1;
    -moz-box-shadow: 0 0 10px #789;
    -webkit-box-shadow: 0 0 10px #789;
    box-shadow: 0 0 10px #789;
}

.weekdays {
    height: 20px;
    border-top: 2px solid black;
}

.weekdays li {
    height: 16px;
    padding: 2px 2px;
    background-color: #BCF;
}

.fill {
    background-color: #BCD;
}

.weekdays li:hover,li.fill:hover {
    background-color: #BCD;
    -moz-box-shadow: none;
    -webkit-box-shadow: none;
    box-shadow: none;
}
```

```css
.weekdays li:hover,.today {
    background-color: #BCF;
}

li strong {
    position: absolute;
    top: 2px;
    right: 2px;
}

li a {
    position: relative;
    display: block;
    border: 1px dotted black;
    margin: 2px;
    padding: 2px;
    font-size: 11px;
    background-color: #DEF;
    text-align: left;
    -moz-border-radius: 6px;
    -webkit-border-radius: 6px;
    border-radius: 6px;
    z-index: 1;
    text-decoration: none;
    color: black;
    font-weight: bold;
    font-style: italic;
}

li a:hover {
    background-color: #BCF;
    z-index: 2;
    -moz-box-shadow: 0 0 6px #789;
    -webkit-box-shadow: 0 0 6px #789;
    box-shadow: 0 0 6px #789;
}
```

Save the style sheet, and close it; you won't need to modify it again in this chapter. In the next section, you'll create common files that will, among other things, include these styles into the page.

Creating the Common Files—Header and Footer

This application will have multiple pages viewed by your users, and they all need a common set of HTML elements, style sheets, and more. To simplify maintenance as much as possible, you'll be using two files, header.inc.php and footer.inc.php, to contain these common elements.

First, create a file called header.inc.php in the common folder (/public/assets/common/header.inc.php). This file will hold the DOCTYPE declaration for the HTML and create a head section that contains a Content-Type meta tag, the document title, and links to any CSS files required for the document.

Because the document title will vary from page to page, you'll be setting a variable, $page_title, to store each page's title.

Also, because more than one CSS file may be needed for a page, an array of CSS file names will be passed in a variable called $css_files and looped through to generate the proper markup.

Inside this file, place the following code:

```
<!DOCTYPE html
  PUBLIC "-//W3C//DTD XHTML 1.0 Strict//EN"
  "http://www.w3.org/TR/xhtml1/DTD/xhtml1-strict.dtd">

<html xmlns="http://www.w3.org/1999/xhtml" xml:lang="en" lang="en">

<head>
    <meta http-equiv="Content-Type"
          content="text/html;charset=utf-8" />
    <title><?php echo $page_title; ?></title>
<?php foreach ( $css_files as $css ): ?>
    <link rel="stylesheet" type="text/css" media="screen,projection"
          href="assets/css/<?php echo $css; ?>" />
<?php endforeach; ?>
</head>

<body>
```

Next, create a file called footer.inc.php in the common folder (/public/assets/common/footer.inc.php) to contain the closing parts of the markup.

For now, this file doesn't need to do much: it simply closes the body and html tags opened in header.inc.php. As you continue developing this application, more will be added here.

Insert the following into footer.inc.php:

```
</body>

</html>
```

Adding the Files to the Index

To bring the new pieces together, you need to modify the index file. First, add values to the $page_title and $css_files variables, and then include the header file.

Also, to wrap the page content, add in a new div with the ID content that wraps around the call to buildCalendar().

Finally, add a call to the footer file to finish the page. When it's completed, the index file will be modified with the code shown in bold:

```
<?php

declare(strict_types=1);

/*
 * Include necessary files
 */
include_once '../sys/core/init.inc.php';
```

```php
/*
 * Load the calendar
 */
$cal = new Calendar($dbo, "2016-01-01 12:00:00");

/*
 * Set up the page title and CSS files
 */
$page_title = "Events Calendar";
$css_files = array('style.css');

/*
 * Include the header
 */
include_once 'assets/common/header.inc.php';

?>

<div id="content">
<?php

/*
 * Display the calendar HTML
 */
echo $cal->buildCalendar();

?>

</div><!-- end #content -->
<?php

/*
 * Include the footer
 */
include_once 'assets/common/footer.inc.php';

?>
```

After saving the changes, reload your browser to see the results, shown in Figure 4-7.

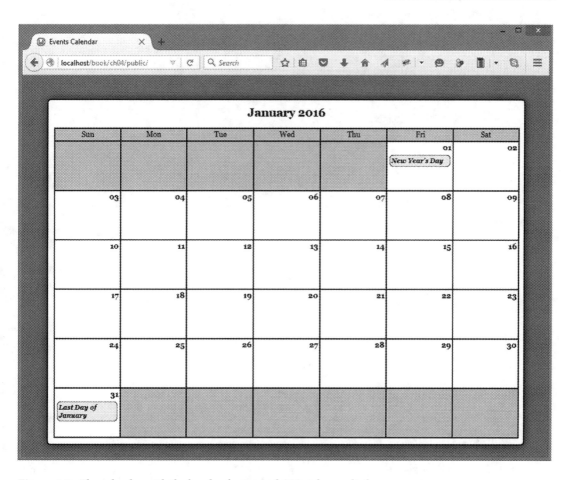

Figure 4-7. *The calendar with the header, footer, and CSS styles applied*

Outputting HTML to Display Full Event Descriptions

Next, you need to allow the user to view the details of an event. This will be done in three steps.

1. Create a method to format an array of a single event's data when loaded by ID.

2. Create a method to generate markup containing the data as loaded by the first method.

3. Create a new file to display the markup generated by the second method.

Creating a Method to Format Single Event Data

Similar to _createEventObj(), the purpose of this method, which you'll call _loadEventById(), is to generate an Event object from the result set returned by _loadEventData().

Because the markup generation is fairly simple when only using one event, all this method will do is load the desired event by its ID using _loadEventData() and then return the first (and only, due to the LIMIT 1 clause) result from the method.

Add the following method to the Calendar class:

```php
<?php

declare(strict_types=1);

class Calendar extends DB_Connect
{
    private $_useDate;

    private $_m;

    private $_y;

    private $_daysInMonth;

    private $_startDay;

    public function __construct($dbo=NULL, $useDate=NULL) {...}

    public function buildCalendar() {...}

    private function _loadEventData($id=NULL) {...}

    private function _createEventObj() {...}

    /**
     * Returns a single event object
     *
     * @param int $id an event ID
     * @return object the event object
     */
    private function _loadEventById($id)
    {
        /*
         * If no ID is passed, return NULL
         */
        if ( empty($id) )
        {
            return NULL;
        }

        /*
         * Load the events info array
         */
        $event = $this->_loadEventData($id);

        /*
         * Return an event object
         */
```

```php
        if ( isset($event[0]) )
        {
            return new Event($event[0]);
        }
        else
        {
            return NULL;
        }
    }

}

?>
```

When called, this method will return an object (for the ID of 1) that looks like this:

```
Event Object
(
    [id] => 1
    [title] => New Year's Day
    [description] => Happy New Year!
    [start] => 2016-01-01 00:00:00
    [end] => 2016-01-01 23:59:59
)
```

Creating a Method to Generate Markup

Now that an array of a single event's data is available, you can build a new public method to format the event data into HTML markup. This method will be called displayEvent(); it will accept an event's ID and generate HTML markup using the following steps.

1. Load the event data using _loadEventById().

2. Use the start and end dates to generate strings to describe the event.

3. Return the HTML markup to display the event.

Create the displayEvent() method by adding the bold code to the Calendar class:

```php
<?php

declare(strict_types=1);

class Calendar extends DB_Connect
{

    private $_useDate;

    private $_m;

    private $_y;

    private $_daysInMonth;
```

```php
    private $_startDay;

    public function __construct($dbo=NULL, $useDate=NULL) {...}

    public function buildCalendar() {...}

    /**
     * Displays a given event's information
     *
     * @param int $id the event ID
     * @return string basic markup to display the event info
     */
    public function displayEvent($id)
    {
        /*
         * Make sure an ID was passed
         */
        if ( empty($id) ) { return NULL; }

        /*
         * Make sure the ID is an integer
         */
        $id = preg_replace('/[^0-9]/', '', $id);

        /*
         * Load the event data from the DB
         */
        $event = $this->_loadEventById($id);

        /*
         * Generate strings for the date, start, and end time
         */
        $ts = strtotime($event->start);
        $date = date('F d, Y', $ts);
        $start = date('g:ia', $ts);
        $end = date('g:ia', strtotime($event->end));

        /*
         * Generate and return the markup
         */
        return "<h2>$event->title</h2>"
            . "\n\t<p class=\"dates\">$date, $start&mdash;$end</p>"
            . "\n\t<p>$event->description</p>";
    }

    private function _loadEventData($id=NULL) {...}

    private function _createEventObj() {...}

    private function _loadEventById($id) {...}
}
?>
```

Creating a New File to Display Full Events

To display the output of displayEvent(), you'll create a new file. This file will be called view.php, and it will reside in the public folder (/public/view.php).

This file will be called with a query string containing the ID of the event to be displayed. If no ID is supplied, the user will be sent back out to the main view of the calendar.

At the top of view.php, check for an event ID, and then load the initialization file; the page title and CSS file are set up in variables, and the header file is called. After that, a new instance of the Calendar class is created.

Next, set up a new div with the ID of content and call the displayEvent() method. Add a link to go back to the main calendar page, close the div, and include the footer.

All things considered, the file should end up looking like this:

```php
<?php

declare(strict_types=1);

/*
 * Make sure the event ID was passed
 */
if ( isset($_GET['event_id']) )
{
    /*
     * Make sure the ID is an integer
     */
    $id = preg_replace('/[^0-9]/', '', $_GET['event_id']);

    /*
     * If the ID isn't valid, send the user to the main page
     */
    if ( empty($id) )
    {
        header("Location: ./");
        exit;
    }
}
else
{
    /*
     * Send the user to the main page if no ID is supplied
     */
    header("Location: ./");
    exit;
}

/*
 * Include necessary files
 */
include_once '../sys/core/init.inc.php';

/*
 * Output the header
 */
```

```php
$page_title = "View Event";
$css_files = array("style.css");
include_once 'assets/common/header.inc.php';

/*
 * Load the calendar
 */
$cal = new Calendar($dbo);

?>

<div id="content">
<?php echo $cal->displayEvent($id) ?>

    <a href="./">&laquo; Back to the calendar</a>
</div><!-- end #content -->

<?php

/*
 * Output the footer
 */
include_once 'assets/common/footer.inc.php';

?>
```

Test this file by going back to the main calendar and clicking an event title. The view.php file loads and displays the event information in a format that matches the calendar (see Figure 4-8).

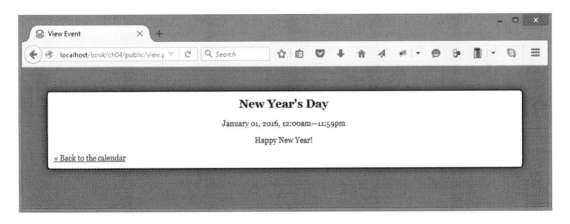

Figure 4-8. *The event information displayed after clicking an event title*

Summary

You now have a fully functional events calendar, which you created using object-oriented PHP and MySQL. Along the way, you learned how to handle dates, how to organize entries into objects for easy access, and how to output markup and stylesheets to resemble a traditional calendar. In the next chapter, you'll build controls to add, edit, and create events.

CHAPTER 5

Add Controls to Create, Edit, and Delete Events

Now that the calendar can be viewed, you need to add controls that will allow administrators to create, edit, and delete events.

Generating a Form to Create or Edit Events

To edit an event or add new events to the calendar, you need to use a form. You do this by adding a method called displayForm() that generates a form for editing and creating events to the Calendar class.

This simple method accomplishes the following tasks:

- Checks for an integer passed as the event ID.

- Instantiates empty variables for the different fields used to describe events.

- Loads event data if an event ID was passed.

- Stores event data in the variables instantiated earlier if it exists.

- Outputs a form.

Note By explicitly sanitizing the event ID passed in the $_POST superglobal, you ensure that the ID is safe to use since any non-integer values will be converted to 0.

You build the displayForm() method by adding the following bold code to the Calendar class:

```php
<?php

declare(strict_types=1);

class Calendar extends DB_Connect
{

    private $_useDate;

    private $_m;
```

```php
    private $_y;

    private $_daysInMonth;

    private $_startDay;

    public function __construct($db=NULL, $useDate=NULL) {...}

    public function buildCalendar() {...}

    public function displayEvent($id) {...}

    /**
     * Generates a form to edit or create events
     *
     * @return string the HTML markup for the editing form
     */
    public function displayForm()
    {
        /*
         * Check if an ID was passed
         */
        if ( isset($_POST['event_id']) )
        {
            $id = (int) $_POST['event_id'];
                // Force integer type to sanitize data
        }
        else
        {
            $id = NULL;
        }

        /*
         * Instantiate the headline/submit button text
         */
        $submit = "Create a New Event";

        /*
         * If no ID is passed, start with an empty event object.
         */
        $event = new Event();

        /*
         * Otherwise load the associated event
         */
        if ( !empty($id) )
        {
            $event = $this->_loadEventById($id);
```

```php
        /*
         * If no object is returned, return NULL
         */
        if ( !is_object($event) ) { return NULL; }

        $submit = "Edit This Event";
    }

    /*
     * Build the markup
     */
    return <<<FORM_MARKUP

<form action="assets/inc/process.inc.php" method="post">
    <fieldset>
        <legend>$submit</legend>
        <label for="event_title">Event Title</label>
        <input type="text" name="event_title"
            id="event_title" value="$event->title" />
        <label for="event_start">Start Time</label>
        <input type="text" name="event_start"
            id="event_start" value="$event->start" />
        <label for="event_end">End Time</label>
        <input type="text" name="event_end"
            id="event_end" value="$event->end" />
        <label for="event_description">Event Description</label>
        <textarea name="event_description"
            id="event_description">$event->description</textarea>
        <input type="hidden" name="event_id" value="$event->id" />
        <input type="hidden" name="token" value="$_SESSION[token]" />
        <input type="hidden" name="action" value="event_edit" />
        <input type="submit" name="event_submit" value="$submit" />
        or <a href="./">cancel</a>
    </fieldset>
</form>
FORM_MARKUP;
    }

    private function _loadEventData($id=NULL) {...}

    private function _createEventObj() {...}

    private function _loadEventById($id) {...}

}

?>
```

Adding a Token to the Form

If you look at the preceding form, there's a hidden input named token that holds a session value, also called token. This is a security measure to prevent *cross-site request forgeries* (CSRF), which are form submissions that are faked by submitting a form to your app's processing file from somewhere other than the form itself. This is a common tactic used by spammers to send multiple forged entry submissions, which is annoying, potentially harmful, and definitely undesirable.

This token is created by generating a random hash and storing it in the session, and then posting the token along with the form data. If the token in the $_POST superglobal matches the one in the $_SESSION superglobal, then it's a reasonably sure bet that the submission is legitimate.

You add an anti-CSRF token into your application by modifying the initialization file with the code shown in bold:

```php
<?php

declare(strict_types=1);

/*
 * Enable sessions if needed.
 * Avoid pesky warning if session already active.
 */
$status = session_status();
if ($status == PHP_SESSION_NONE){
    //There is no active session
    session_start();
}

/*
 * Generate an anti-CSRF token if one doesn't exist
 */
if ( !isset($_SESSION['token']) )
{
    $_SESSION['token'] = sha1(uniqid((string)mt_rand(), TRUE));
}

/*
 * Include the necessary configuration info
 */
include_once '../sys/config/db-cred.inc.php'; // DB info

/*
 * Define constants for configuration info
 */
foreach ( $C as $name => $val )
{
    define($name, $val);
}

/*
 * Create a PDO object
 */
```

```php
$dsn = "mysql:host=" . DB_HOST . ";dbname=" . DB_NAME;
$dbo = new PDO($dsn, DB_USER, DB_PASS);

/*
 * Define the auto-load function for classes
 */
function __autoload($class)
{
    $filename = "../sys/class/class." . $class . ".inc.php";
    if ( file_exists($filename) )
    {
        include_once $filename;
    }
}

?>
```

▓ **Caution**   You may want to include a time limit for tokens to increase security further. Making sure a token is no older than 20 minutes, for instance, helps prevent a user from leaving a computer unattended and having a mischievous user start poking around later. For more information on tokens and preventing CSRF, visit Chris Shiflett's blog and read his article on the topic at `http://shiflett.org/csrf`.

Creating a File to Display the Form

Now that the method exists to display the form, you need to create a file that will call that method. This file will be called `admin.php`, and it will reside in the root level of the `public` folder (`/public/admin.php`).

Similar to `view.php`, this file accomplishes the following:

- Loads the initialization file.
- Sets up a page title and CSS file array.
- Includes the header.
- Creates a new instance of the `Calendar` class.
- Calls the `displayForm()` method.
- Includes the footer.

Next, add the following inside the new `admin.php` file:

```php
<?php

declare(strict_types=1);

/*
 * Include necessary files
 */
include_once '../sys/core/init.inc.php';
```

```php
/*
 * Output the header
 */
$page_title = "Add/Edit Event";
$css_files = array("style.css");
include_once 'assets/common/header.inc.php';

/*
 * Load the calendar
 */
$cal = new Calendar($dbo);

?>

<div id="content">
<?php echo $cal->displayForm(); ?>

</div><!-- end #content -->

<?php

/*
 * Output the footer
 */
include_once 'assets/common/footer.inc.php';

?>
```

After saving this code, navigate to `http://localhost/admin.php` to see the resulting form, shown in Figure 5-1.

Figure 5-1. *The form before adding any CSS styles*

Adding a New Stylesheet for Administrative Features

Obviously, the preceding form needs some visual enhancement to make it more usable. However, this form will ultimately be accessible only to administrators (because you don't want just anyone making changes to your calendar), so the CSS rules will be separated out to a separate stylesheet called admin.css. You can find this file in the css folder (/public/assets/css/).

Again, since this book is not about CSS, the rules won't be explained. Essentially, the following CSS makes the form elements look more like what your user expects a form to look like; it also adds a couple rules for elements that will be created shortly.

Now add the following code into admin.css:

```css
fieldset {
    border: 0;
}

legend {
    font-size: 24px;
    font-weight: bold;
}

input[type=text],input[type=password],label {
    display: block;
    width: 70%;
    font-weight: bold;
}

textarea {
    width: 99%;
    height: 200px;
}

input[type=text],input[type=password],textarea {
    border: 1px solid #123;
    -moz-border-radius: 6px;
    -webkit-border-radius: 6px;
    border-radius: 6px;
    -moz-box-shadow: inset 1px 2px 4px #789;
    -webkit-box-shadow: inset 1px 2px 4px #789;
    box-shadow: inset 1px 2px 4px #789;
    padding: 4px;
    margin: 0 0 4px;
    font-size: 16px;
    font-family: georgia, serif;
}

input[type=submit] {
    margin: 4px 0;
    padding: 4px;
    border: 1px solid #123;
    -moz-border-radius: 6px;
    -webkit-border-radius: 6px;
```

167

```
    border-radius: 6px;
    -moz-box-shadow: inset -2px -1px 3px #345,
        inset 1px 1px 3px #BCF,
        1px 2px 6px #789;
    -webkit-box-shadow: inset -2px -1px 3px #345,
        inset 1px 1px 3px #BCF,
        1px 2px 6px #789;
    box-shadow: inset -2px -1px 3px #345,
        inset 1px 1px 3px #BCF,
        1px 2px 6px #789;
    background-color: #789;
    font-family: georgia, serif;
    text-transform: uppercase;
    font-weight: bold;
    font-size: 14px;
    text-shadow: 0px 0px 1px #fff;
}

.admin-options {
    text-align: center;
}

.admin-options form,.admin-options p {
    display: inline;
}

a.admin {
    display: inline-block;
    margin: 4px 0;
    padding: 4px;
    border: 1px solid #123;
    -moz-border-radius: 6px;
    -webkit-border-radius: 6px;
    border-radius: 6px;
    -moz-box-shadow: inset -2px -1px 3px #345,
        inset 1px 1px 3px #BCF,
        1px 2px 6px #789;
    -webkit-box-shadow: inset -2px -1px 3px #345,
        inset 1px 1px 3px #BCF,
        1px 2px 6px #789;
    box-shadow: inset -2px -1px 3px #345,
        inset 1px 1px 3px #BCF,
        1px 2px 6px #789;
    background-color: #789;
    color: black;
    text-decoration: none;
    font-family: georgia, serif;
    text-transform: uppercase;
    font-weight: bold;
    font-size: 14px;
    text-shadow: 0px 0px 1px #fff;
}
```

Save this file, then add admin.css to the $css_files array in admin.php by making the changes shown in bold:

```php
<?php

declare(strict_types=1);

/*
 * Include necessary files
 */
include_once '../sys/core/init.inc.php';

/*
 * Output the header
 */
$page_title = "Add/Edit Event";
$css_files = array("style.css", "admin.css");
include_once 'assets/common/header.inc.php';

/*
 * Load the calendar
 */
$cal = new Calendar($dbo);

?>

<div id="content">
<?php echo $cal->displayForm(); ?>

</div><!-- end #content -->

<?php

/*
 * Output the footer
 */
include_once 'assets/common/footer.inc.php';

?>
```

After saving the preceding code, reload `http://localhost/admin.php` to see the styled form (see Figure 5-2).

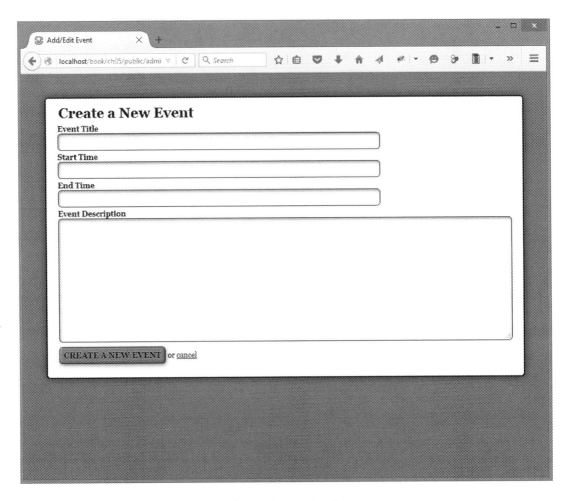

Figure 5-2. *The form to add or edit events after applying CSS styles*

Saving New Events in the Database

To save events entered in the form, you create a new method in the `Calendar` class called `processForm()` that accomplishes the following:

- Sanitizes the data passed from the form via `POST`.
- Determines whether an event is being edited or created.
- Generates an `INSERT` statement if no event is being edited, or generates an `UPDATE` statement if an event ID was posted.
- Creates a prepared statement and binds the parameters.
- Executes the query and returns `TRUE` or the error message on failure.

The following code creates the processForm() method in the Calendar class:

```php
<?php

declare(strict_types=1);

class Calendar extends DB_Connect
{

    private $_useDate;

    private $_m;

    private $_y;

    private $_daysInMonth;

    private $_startDay;

    public function __construct($dbo=NULL, $useDate=NULL) {...}

    public function buildCalendar() {...}

    public function displayEvent($id) {...}

    public function displayForm() {...}

    /**
     * Validates the form and saves/edits the event
     *
     * @return mixed TRUE on success, an error message on failure
     */
    public function processForm()
    {
        /*
         * Exit if the action isn't set properly
         */
        if ( $_POST['action']!='event_edit' )
        {
            return "The method processForm was accessed incorrectly";
        }

        /*
         * Escape data from the form
         */
        $title = htmlentities($_POST['event_title'], ENT_QUOTES);
        $desc = htmlentities($_POST['event_description'], ENT_QUOTES);
        $start = htmlentities($_POST['event_start'], ENT_QUOTES);
        $end = htmlentities($_POST['event_end'], ENT_QUOTES);
```

```php
    /*
     * If no event ID passed, create a new event
     */
    if ( empty($_POST['event_id']) )
    {
        $sql = "INSERT INTO `events`
                    (`event_title`, `event_desc`, `event_start`,
                        `event_end`)
                VALUES
                    (:title, :description, :start, :end)";
    }

    /*
     * Update the event if it's being edited
     */
    else
    {
        /*
         * Cast the event ID as an integer for security
         */
        $id = (int) $_POST['event_id'];
        $sql = "UPDATE `events`
                SET
                    `event_title`=:title,
                    `event_desc`=:description,
                    `event_start`=:start,
                    `event_end`=:end
                WHERE `event_id`=$id";
    }

    /*
     * Execute the create or edit query after binding the data
     */
    try
    {
        $stmt = $this->db->prepare($sql);
        $stmt->bindParam(":title", $title, PDO::PARAM_STR);
        $stmt->bindParam(":description", $desc, PDO::PARAM_STR);
        $stmt->bindParam(":start", $start, PDO::PARAM_STR);
        $stmt->bindParam(":end", $end, PDO::PARAM_STR);
        $stmt->execute();
        $stmt->closeCursor();
        return TRUE;
    }
    catch ( Exception $e )
    {
        return $e->getMessage();
    }
}
```

```php
    private function _loadEventData($id=NULL) {...}

    private function _createEventObj() {...}

    private function _loadEventById($id) {...}

}

?>
```

Adding a Processing File to Call the Processing Method

The form to add and edit events is submitted to a file called process.inc.php, which is located in the inc folder (/public/assets/inc/process.inc.php). This file checks the submitted form data and saves or updates entries by performing the following steps:

1. Enables the session.

2. Includes the database credentials and the Calendar class.

3. Defines constants (as occurs in the initialization file).

4. Creates an array that stores information about each action.

5. Verifies that the token was submitted and is correct, and that the submitted action exists in the lookup array. If so, go to Step 6. If not, go to Step 7.

6. Creates a new instance of the Calendar class.

   • Calls the processForm() method.

   • Sends the user back to the main view or outputs an error on failure.

7. Sends the user back out to the main view with no action if the token doesn't match.

The array created in Step 4 allows you to avoid a long, repetitive string of if...elseif blocks to test for each individual action. Using the action as the array key and storing the object, method name, and page to which the user should be redirected as array values means that you can write a single block of logic using the variables from the array.

Insert the following code into process.inc.php to complete the steps just described:

```php
<?php

declare(strict_types=1);

/*
 * Enable sessions if needed.
 * Avoid pesky warning if session already active.
 */
$status = session_status();
if ($status == PHP_SESSION_NONE){
    //There is no active session
    session_start();
}
```

```php
/*
 * Include necessary files
 */
include_once '../../../sys/config/db-cred.inc.php';

/*
 * Define constants for config info
 */
foreach ( $C as $name => $val )
{
    define($name, $val);
}

/*
 * Create a lookup array for form actions
 */
define('ACTIONS', array(
        'event_edit' => array(
                'object' => 'Calendar',
                'method' => 'processForm',
                'header' => 'Location: ../../'
            )
        )
    );

/*
 * Need a PDO object.
 */
$dsn = "mysql:host=" . DB_HOST . ";dbname=" . DB_NAME;
$dbo = new PDO($dsn, DB_USER, DB_PASS);

/*
 * Make sure the anti-CSRF token was passed and that the
 * requested action exists in the lookup array
 */
if ( $_POST['token']==$_SESSION['token']
        && isset(ACTIONS[$_POST['action']]) )
{
    $use_array = ACTIONS[$_POST['action']];
    $obj = new $use_array['object']($dbo);
    $method = $use_array['method'];
    if ( TRUE === $msg=$obj->$method() )
    {
        header($use_array['header']);
        exit;
    }
    else
    {
        // If an error occured, output it and end execution
        die ( $msg );
    }
}
```

```
else
{
    // Redirect to the main index if the token/action is invalid
    header("Location: ../../");
    exit;
}

function __autoload($class_name)
{
    $filename = '../../../sys/class/class.'
        . strtolower($class_name) . '.inc.php';
    if ( file_exists($filename) )
    {
        include_once $filename;
    }
}

?>
```

Save this file, and then navigate to http://localhost/admin.php and create a new event with the following information:

- **Event Title:** Dinner Party

- **Start Time:** 2016-01-22 17:00:00

- **End Time:** 2016-01-22 19:00:00

- **Description:** Five-course meal with wine pairings at John's house

After clicking the "Create new event" button, the calendar is updated with the new event, as shown in Figure 5-3.

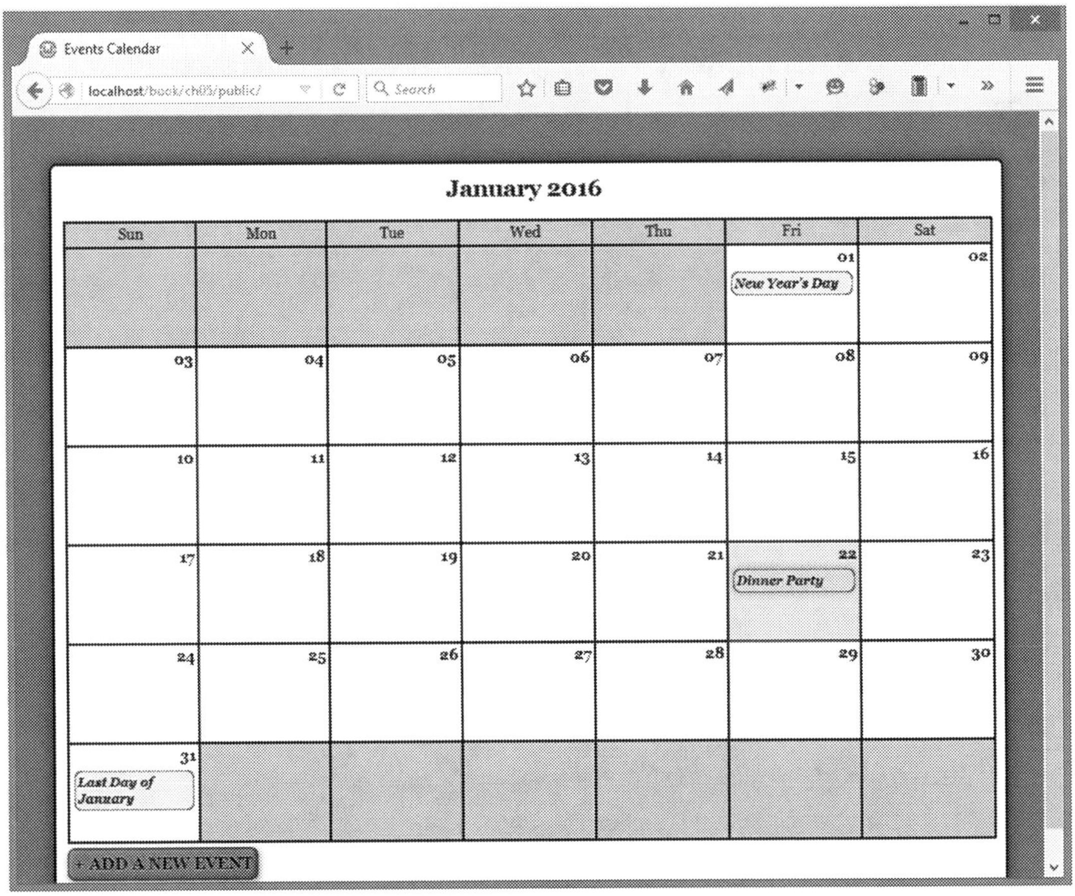

Figure 5-3. *The new event as it appears when hovered over*

Adding a Button to the Main View to Create New Events

To make it easier for your authorized users to create new events, add a button to the calendar that takes the user to the form in `admin.php`. Do this by creating a new private method called `_adminGeneralOptions()` in the `Calendar` class:

```php
<?php

declare(strict_types=1);

class Calendar extends DB_Connect
{
    private $_useDate;

    private $_m;
```

```php
    private $_y;

    private $_daysInMonth;

    private $_startDay;

    public function __construct($dbo=NULL, $useDate=NULL) {...}

    public function buildCalendar() {...}

    public function displayEvent($id) {...}

    public function displayForm() {...}

    public function processForm() {...}

    private function _loadEventData($id=NULL) {...}

    private function _createEventObj() {...}

    private function _loadEventById($id) {...}

    /**
     * Generates markup to display administrative links
     *
     * @return string markup to display the administrative links
     */
    private function _adminGeneralOptions()
    {
        /*
         * Display admin controls
         */
        return <<<ADMIN_OPTIONS

    <a href="admin.php" class="admin">+ Add a New Event</a>
ADMIN_OPTIONS;
    }

}

?>
```

▓ **Note**   Checks to ensure that this button is only displayed to authorized users will be added Chapter 6.

Next, modify the buildCalendar() method to call your new _adminGeneralOptions() method by inserting the following bold code:

```
public function buildCalendar()
{
    // To save space, the bulk of this method has been omitted

    /*
     * Close the final unordered list
     */
    $html .= "\n\t</ul>\n\n";

    /*
     * If logged in, display the admin options
     */
    $admin = $this->_adminGeneralOptions();

    /*
     * Return the markup for output
     */
    return $html . $admin;
}
```

Finally, add the admin stylesheet (admin.css) to index.php using the following code in bold to make sure the link displays correctly:

```
<?php

declare(strict_types=1);

/*
 * Include necessary files
 */
include_once '../sys/core/init.inc.php';

/*
 * Load the calendar
 */
$cal = new Calendar($dbo, "2016-01-01 12:00:00");

/*
 * Set up the page title and CSS files
 */
$page_title = "Events Calendar";
$css_files = array('style.css', 'admin.css');

/*
 * Include the header
 */
include_once 'assets/common/header.inc.php';
```

```php
?>

<div id="content">
<?php

/*
 * Display the calendar HTML
 */
echo $cal->buildCalendar();

?>

</div><!-- end #content -->
<?php

/*
 * Include the footer
 */
include_once 'assets/common/footer.inc.php';

?>
```

Save the file and reload http://localhost/ to see the button (see Figure 5-4).

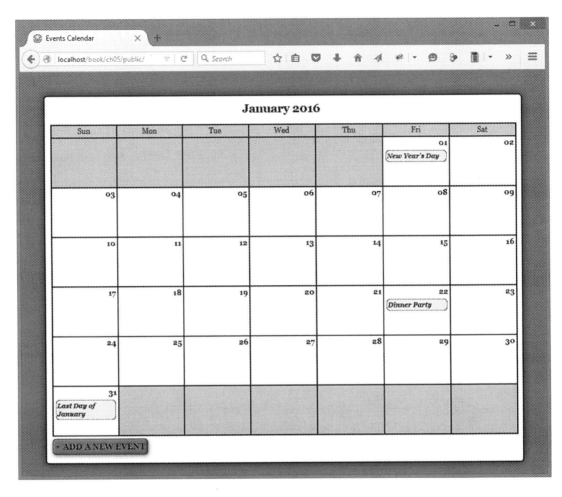

Figure 5-4. *The Admin button appears in the bottom left of the calendar*

Adding Edit Controls to the Full Event View

Next, you need to make it possible for authorized users to edit events. You will do this by adding a button to the full view of an event in `view.php`.

However, unlike the simple link used to create a new option, an Edit button will require an actual form submission. To keep this code manageable, you'll create a new private method called `_adminEntryOptions()` in the `Calendar` class that will generate the markup for the form.

For now, this form will simply return the form markup to display the Edit button. More will be added to the form as you continue on through the exercises in this book.

You create this method by adding the following bold code to the Calendar class:

```php
<?php

declare(strict_types=1);

class Calendar extends DB_Connect
{

    private $_useDate;

    private $_m;

    private $_y;

    private $_daysInMonth;

    private $_startDay;

    public function __construct($dbo=NULL, $useDate=NULL) {...}

    public function buildCalendar() {...}

    public function displayEvent($id) {...}

    public function displayForm() {...}

    public function processForm() {...}

    private function _loadEventData($id=NULL) {...}

    private function _createEventObj() {...}

    private function _loadEventById($id) {...}

    private function _adminGeneralOptions() {...}

    /**
     * Generates edit and delete options for a given event ID
     *
     * @param int $id the event ID to generate options for
     * @return string the markup for the edit/delete options
     */
    private function _adminEntryOptions($id)
    {
        return <<<ADMIN_OPTIONS

<div class="admin-options">
<form action="admin.php" method="post">
    <p>
        <input type="submit" name="edit_event"
            value="Edit This Event" />
```

```
            <input type="hidden" name="event_id"
                  value="$id" />
        </p>
    </form>
    </div><!-- end .admin-options -->
ADMIN_OPTIONS;
    }


}

?>
```

Modifying the Full Event Display Method to Show Admin Controls

Before the Edit button will be displayed, the _adminEntryOptions() method needs to be called from within the displayEvent() method. This is as simple as storing the return value of _adminEntryOptions() in a variable, $admin, and outputting that variable along with the rest of the entry markup.

Add the following bold modifications to displayEvent() in the Calendar class:

```
/**
 * Displays a given event's information
 *
 * @param int $id the event ID
 * @return string basic markup to display the event info
 */
public function displayEvent($id)
{
    /*
     * Make sure an ID was passed
     */
    if ( empty($id) ) { return NULL; }

    /*
     * Make sure the ID is an integer
     */
    $id = preg_replace('/[^0-9]/', '', $id);

    /*
     * Load the event data from the DB
     */
    $event = $this->_loadEventById($id);
    /*
     * Generate strings for the date, start, and end time
     */
    $ts = strtotime($event->start);
    $date = date('F d, Y', $ts);
    $start = date('g:ia', $ts);
    $end = date('g:ia', strtotime($event->end));

    /*
     * Load admin options if the user is logged in
     */
```

```
$admin = $this->_adminEntryOptions($id);
/*
 * Generate and return the markup
 */
return "<h2>$event->title</h2>"
    . "\n\t<p class=\"dates\">$date, $start&mdash;$end</p>"
```

. `"\n\t<p>$event->description</p>$admin";`
```
    }
```

▒ **Note**   Make sure that you include the $admin variable at the end of the `return` string.

As with the "Create a new entry" button, checks will be added later to ensure that only authorized users see the editing controls.

Adding the Admin Stylesheet to the Full Event View Page

The last step before the Edit button is ready for use is to include the admin.css stylesheet in the $css_files variable of view.php:

```php
<?php

declare(strict_types=1);

/*
 * Make sure the event ID was passed
 */
if ( isset($_GET['event_id']) )
{
    /*
     * Collect the event ID from the URL string
     */
    $id = htmlentities($_GET['event_id'], ENT_QUOTES);
}
else
{
    /*
     * Send the user to the main page if no ID is supplied
     */
    header("Location: ./");
    exit;
}

/*
 * Include necessary files
 */
include_once '../sys/core/init.inc.php';
```

```php
/*
 * Output the header
 */
$page_title = "View Event";
$css_files = array("style.css", "admin.css");
include_once 'assets/common/header.inc.php';

/*
 * Load the calendar
 */
$cal = new Calendar($dbo);

?>

<div id="content">
<?php echo $cal->displayEvent($id) ?>

    <a href="./">&laquo; Back to the calendar</a>
</div><!-- end #content -->

<?php

/*
 * Output the footer
 */
include_once 'assets/common/footer.inc.php';

?>
```

Save this file, and then click an event to see the Edit button (see Figure 5-5).

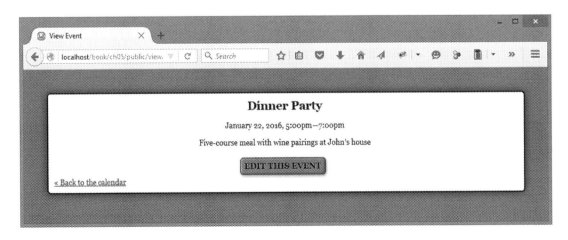

Figure 5-5. *The Edit button as it appears when viewing a full event description*

Clicking the Edit button will bring up the form on admin.php with all the event's data loaded in the form (see Figure 5-6).

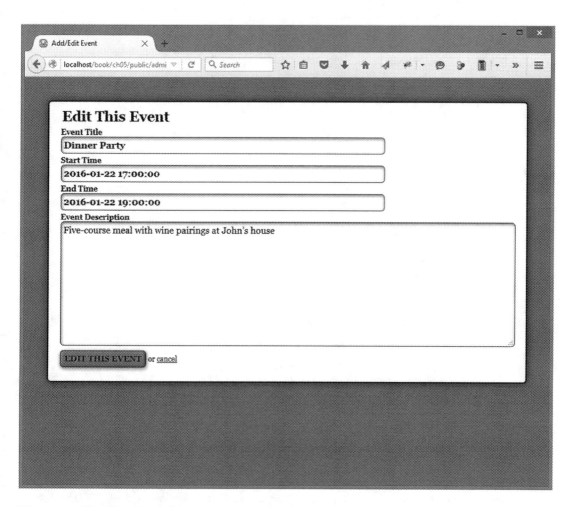

Figure 5-6. *The admin form when an event is being edited*

Deleting Events

The last step in creating the Calendar class is to allow authorized users to delete events. Event deletion is different from creating or editing events in that you want to confirm a user's intentions before deleting the event. Otherwise an accidental click could result in frustration and inconvenience for the user.

This means that you must implement the Delete button in two stages.

1. The Delete button is clicked, and the user is taken to a confirmation page.

2. The confirmation button is clicked, and the event is removed from the database.

Generating a Delete Button

To start, add a Delete button to the full view edit controls by modifying _adminEntryOptions() in the Calendar class with the code shown in bold:

```
/**
 * Generates edit and delete options for a given event ID
 *
 * @param int $id the event ID to generate options for
 * @return string the markup for the edit/delete options
 */
private function _adminEntryOptions($id)
{
    return <<<ADMIN_OPTIONS

<div class="admin-options">
<form action="admin.php" method="post">
    <p>
        <input type="submit" name="edit_event"
            value="Edit This Event" />
        <input type="hidden" name="event_id"
            value="$id" />
    </p>
</form>
<form action="confirmdelete.php" method="post">
    <p>
        <input type="submit" name="delete_event"
            value="Delete This Event" />
        <input type="hidden" name="event_id"
            value="$id" />
    </p>
</form>
</div><!-- end .admin-options -->
ADMIN_OPTIONS;
    }
```

This adds a button that sends the user to a yet-to-be-created confirmation page called confirmdelete. php, which you'll build later in this section. After saving the preceding changes, you will see both edit and delete options when viewing a full event description (see Figure 5-7).

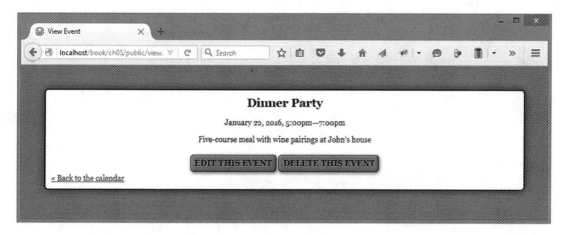

Figure 5-7. *The Delete button as it appears on the full event view*

Creating a Method to Require Confirmation

When a user clicks the Delete button, she is sent to a confirmation page that contains a form to make sure she really wants to delete the event. That form will be generated by a new public method in the Calendar class called confirmDelete().

This method confirms that an event should be deleted by performing the following actions:

1. Checks if the confirmation form was submitted and a valid token was passed. If so, go to Step 2. If not, go to Step 3.

2. Checks whether the button clicked was the Confirmation button.

    - If so, it deletes the event.

    - If not, it sends the user back out to the main calendar view.

3. It loads the event data and displays the confirmation form.

You accomplish the preceding steps by adding the new method, shown in bold, to the Calendar class:

```php
<?php

declare(strict_types=1);

class Calendar extends DB_Connect
{

    private $_useDate;

    private $_m;

    private $_y;

    private $_daysInMonth;

    private $_startDay;
```

```php
    public function __construct($dbo=NULL, $useDate=NULL) {...}

    public function buildCalendar() {...}

    public function displayEvent($id) {...}

    public function displayForm() {...}

    public function processForm() {...}

    /**
     * Confirms that an event should be deleted and does so
     *
     * Upon clicking the button to delete an event, this
     * generates a confirmation box. If the user confirms,
     * this deletes the event from the database and sends the
     * user back out to the main calendar view. If the user
     * decides not to delete the event, they're sent back to
     * the main calendar view without deleting anything.
     *
     * @param int $id the event ID
     * @return mixed the form if confirming, void or error if deleting
     */
    public function confirmDelete($id)
    {
        /*
         * Make sure an ID was passed
         */
        if ( empty($id) ) { return NULL; }

        /*
         * Make sure the ID is an integer
         */
        $id = preg_replace('/[^0-9]/', '', $id);

        /*
         * If the confirmation form was submitted and the form
         * has a valid token, check the form submission
         */
        if ( isset($_POST['confirm_delete'])
                && $_POST['token']==$_SESSION['token'] )
        {
            /*
             * If the deletion is confirmed, remove the event
             * from the database
             */
            if ( $_POST['confirm_delete']=="Yes, Delete It" )
            {
                $sql = "DELETE FROM `events`
                        WHERE `event_id`=:id
                        LIMIT 1";
```

```php
        try
        {
            $stmt = $this->db->prepare($sql);
            $stmt->bindParam(
                    ":id",
                    $id,
                    PDO::PARAM_INT
                );
            $stmt->execute();
            $stmt->closeCursor();
            header("Location: ./");
            return;
        }
        catch ( Exception $e )
        {
            return $e->getMessage();
        }
    }

    /*
     * If not confirmed, sends the user to the main view
     */
    else
    {
        header("Location: ./");
        return;
    }
}

/*
 * If the confirmation form hasn't been submitted, display it
 */
$event = $this->_loadEventById($id);

/*
 * If no object is returned, return to the main view
 */
if ( !is_object($event) ) { header("Location: ./"); }

return <<<CONFIRM_DELETE

<form action="confirmdelete.php" method="post">
    <h2>
        Are you sure you want to delete "$event->title"?
    </h2>
    <p>There is <strong>no undo</strong> if you continue.</p>
    <p>
        <input type="submit" name="confirm_delete"
            value="Yes, Delete It" />
        <input type="submit" name="confirm_delete"
            value="Nope! Just Kidding!" />
```

```
            <input type="hidden" name="event_id"
                value="$event->id" />
            <input type="hidden" name="token"
                value="$_SESSION[token]" />
        </p>
    </form>
CONFIRM_DELETE;
    }

    private function _loadEventData($id=NULL) {...}

    private function _createEventObj() {...}

    private function _loadEventById($id) {...}

    private function _adminGeneralOptions() {...}

    private function _adminEntryOptions($id) {...}

}

?>
```

Creating a File to Display the Confirmation Form

In order to call the confirmDelete() method, the file confirmdelete.php needs to be created. This file will reside in the root level of the public folder (/public/confirmdelete.php), and it will be very similar to index.php. This file accomplishes the following tasks:

- Ensures an event ID was passed and stored in the $id variable; sends the user to the main view otherwise.

- Loads the initialization file.

- Creates a new instance of the Calendar object.

- Loads the return value of confirmDelete() into a variable, $markup.

- Defines the $page_title and $css_files variables and includes the header.

- Outputs the data stored in $markup.

- Outputs the footer.

⬛ **Note** The reason you load the output of confirmDelete() into a variable before including the header is because the method sometimes uses header() to send the user elsewhere in the app; if the header file was included before calling confirmDelete(), the script would fail in certain cases because no data can be output to the browser before header() is called or a fatal error occurs. For more information on the header() function, visit http://php.net/header.

Now add the following code inside confirmdelete.php:

```php
<?php

declare(strict_types=1);

/*
 * Make sure the event ID was passed
 */
if ( isset($_POST['event_id']) )
{
    /*
     * Collect the event ID from the URL string
     */
    $id = (int) $_POST['event_id'];
}
else
{
    /*
     * Send the user to the main page if no ID is supplied
     */
    header("Location: ./");
    exit;
}

/*
 * Include necessary files
 */
include_once '../sys/core/init.inc.php';

/*
 * Load the calendar
 */
$cal = new Calendar($dbo);
$markup = $cal->confirmDelete($id);

/*
 * Output the header
 */
$page_title = "View Event";
$css_files = array("style.css", "admin.css");
include_once 'assets/common/header.inc.php';

?>

<div id="content">
<?php echo $markup; ?>

</div><!-- end #content -->

<?php
```

```
/*
 * Output the footer
 */
include_once 'assets/common/footer.inc.php';

?>
```

Save this file, and then test the system by deleting the "Dinner Party" entry. After showing you the full event description, the calendar takes you to the confirmation form (see Figure 5-8).

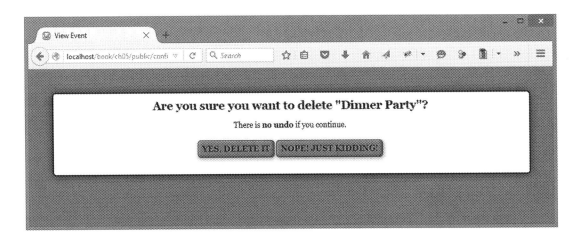

Figure 5-8. *The confirmation form a user sees after clicking the Delete button*

After clicking the "Yes, Delete It" button, the event is removed from the calendar (see Figure 5-9).

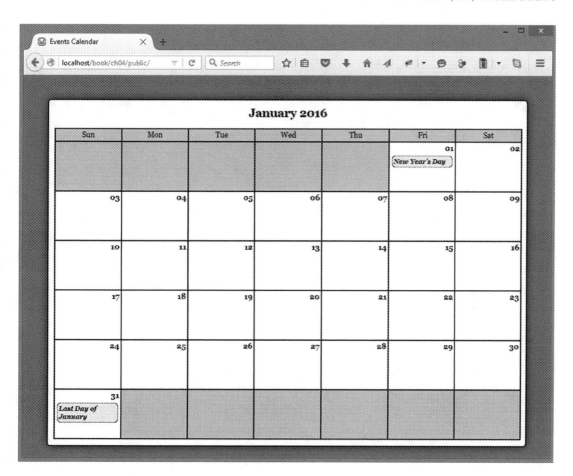

Figure 5-9. *After the user confirms the deletion, the event is removed from the calendar*

Summary

At this point, you have a fully functional events calendar. You've learned how to create a form to create, edit, save, and delete events, including how to confirm event deletion. However, the administrative controls are currently available to anyone who visits the site.

In the next chapter, you'll build a class to grant authorized users access to your site's administrative controls.

■ ■ ■

CHAPTER 6

Password Protecting Sensitive Actions and Areas

Now that your app can add, edit, and remove events, you need to protect those actions by requiring users to log in before they can make any changes. You'll need to create a new table in the database and a new class in the app to make this happen; you'll also need to make a few modifications to existing files.

Building the Admin Table in the Database

To store information about users authorized to modify events, you'll need to create a new database table. This table will be called users, and it will store four pieces of information about each user: an ID, name, password hash, and email address.

To create this table, navigate to http://localhost/phpmyadmin and select the SQL tab to execute the following command:

```
CREATE TABLE IF NOT EXISTS `php-jquery_example`.`users` (
  `user_id` INT(11) NOT NULL AUTO_INCREMENT,
  `user_name` VARCHAR(80) DEFAULT NULL,
  `user_pass` VARCHAR(47) DEFAULT NULL,
  `user_email` VARCHAR(80) DEFAULT NULL,
  PRIMARY KEY (`user_id`),
  UNIQUE (`user_name`)
) ENGINE=MyISAM CHARACTER SET utf8 COLLATE utf8_unicode_ci;
```

After this code executes, select the php-jquery_example database from the left-hand column and click the users table to view the new table (see Figure 6-1).

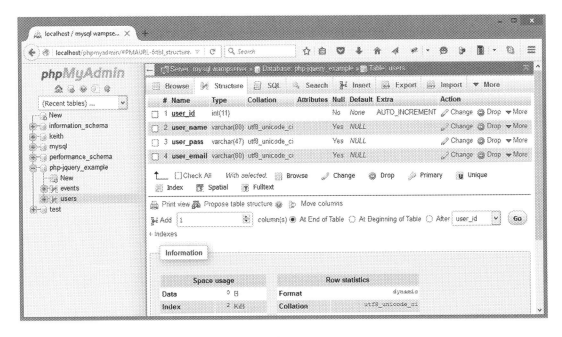

Figure 6-1. *The users table as it appears in phpMyAdmin*

Building a File to Display a Login Form

In order to log in, users will need access to a login form. This will be displayed on a page called `login.php`, which is stored in the public folder (`/public/login.php`). This file will be similar to `admin.php`, except it will simply output the form since none of its information is variable.

The form will accept a username and a password, and it will pass the session token and an action of `user_login` as well. Insert the following code into `login.php` to create this form:

```php
<?php

declare(strict_types=1);

/*
 * Include necessary files
 */
include_once '../sys/core/init.inc.php';

/*
 * Output the header
 */
$page_title = "Please Log In";
$css_files = array("style.css", "admin.css");
include_once 'assets/common/header.inc.php';

?>
```

```
<div id="content">

    <form action="assets/inc/process.inc.php" method="post">
        <fieldset>
            <legend>Please Log In</legend>
            <label for="uname">Username</label>
            <input type="text" name="uname"
                   id="uname" value="" />
            <label for="pword">Password</label>
            <input type="password" name="pword"
                   id="pword" value="" />
            <input type="hidden" name="token"
                value="<?php echo $_SESSION['token']; ?>" />
            <input type="hidden" name="action"
                value="user_login" />
            <input type="submit" name="login_submit"
                value="Log In" />
            or <a href="./">cancel</a>
        </fieldset>
    </form>

</div><!-- end #content -->

<?php

/*
 * Output the footer
 */
include_once 'assets/common/footer.inc.php';

?>
```

Save this code and navigate to `http://localhost/login.php` in your browser to see the resulting login form (see Figure 6-2).

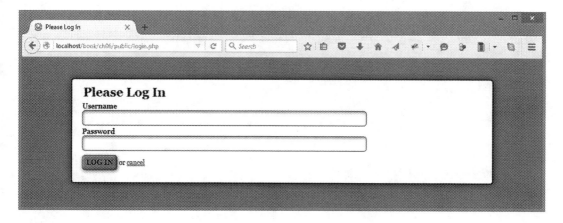

Figure 6-2. The login form

Creating the Admin Class

With your table in place, you can now start structuring the class that will interact with it. In the class folder, create a new file called class.admin.inc.php (/sys/class/class.admin.inc.php). This class will contain methods to allow users to log in and log out.

Defining the Class

First, you define the class, which will extend DB_Connect in order to have database access. This class will have one private property, $_saltLength, which you'll learn about a little later in this section.

The constructor will call the parent constructor to ensure a database object exists, and then it will check whether an integer was passed as the constructor's second argument. If so, the integer is used as the value of $_saltLength.

Now insert the following code into class.admin.inc.php to define the class, the property, and the constructor:

```php
<?php

declare(strict_types=1);

/**
 * Manages administrative actions
 *
 * PHP version 7
 *
 * LICENSE: This source file is subject to the MIT License, available
 * at http://www.opensource.org/licenses/mit-license.html
 *
 * @author     Jason Lengstorf <jason.lengstorf@ennuidesign.com>
 * @copyright  2010 Ennui Design
 * @license    http://www.opensource.org/licenses/mit-license.html
 */
class Admin extends DB_Connect
{

    /**
     * Determines the length of the salt to use in hashed passwords
     *
     * @var int the length of the password salt to use
     */
    private $_saltLength = 7;

    /**
     * Stores or creates a DB object and sets the salt length
     *
     * @param object $db a database object
     * @param int $saltLength length for the password hash
     */
```

```php
    public function __construct($db=NULL, $saltLength=NULL)
    {
        parent::__construct($db);

        /*
         * If an int was passed, set the length of the salt
         */
        if ( is_int($saltLength) )
        {
            $this->_saltLength = $saltLength;
        }
    }

}

?>
```

Building a Method to Check the Login Credentials

The data from login.php needs to be validated in order to verify that a user is authorized to make changes to the events table. You can follow these steps to accomplish this.

1. Verify that the form was submitted using the proper action.

2. Sanitize the user input with htmlentities().

3. Retrieve user data that has a matching username from the database.

4. Store the user information in a variable, $user, and make sure it isn't empty.

5. Generate a salted hash from the user-supplied password and the password stored in the database.

6. Make sure the hashes match.

7. Store user data in the current session using an array and return TRUE.

■ **Note**   Salted hashes will be covered in the next section, "Building a Method to Create Salted Hashes."

Start by defining the method in the Admin class and completing the preceding Steps 1 and 2 using the following bold code:

```php
<?php

declare(strict_types=1);

class Admin extends DB_Connect
{

    private $_saltLength = 7;

    public function __construct($db=NULL, $saltLength=NULL) {...}
```

```
/**
 * Checks login credentials for a valid user
 *
 * @return mixed TRUE on success, message on error
 */
public function processLoginForm()
{
    /*
     * Fails if the proper action was not submitted
     */
    if ( $_POST['action']!='user_login' )
    {
        return "Invalid action supplied for processLoginForm.";
    }

    /*
     * Escapes the user input for security
     */
    $uname = htmlentities($_POST['uname'], ENT_QUOTES);
    $pword = htmlentities($_POST['pword'], ENT_QUOTES);

    // finish processing...
}

}

?>
```

Next, complete Steps 3 and 4 by adding the following code shown in bold:

```
public function processLoginForm()
{
    /*
     * Fails if the proper action was not submitted
     */
    if ( $_POST['action']!='user_login' )
    {
        return "Invalid action supplied for processLoginForm.";
    }

    /*
     * Escapes the user input for security
     */
    $uname = htmlentities($_POST['uname'], ENT_QUOTES);
    $pword = htmlentities($_POST['pword'], ENT_QUOTES);

    /*
     * Retrieves the matching info from the DB if it exists
     */
```

```
$sql = "SELECT
            `user_id`, `user_name`, `user_email`, `user_pass`
        FROM `users`
        WHERE
            `user_name` = :uname
        LIMIT 1";
try
{
    $stmt = $this->db->prepare($sql);
    $stmt->bindParam(':uname', $uname, PDO::PARAM_STR);
    $stmt->execute();
    $user = array_shift($stmt->fetchAll());
    $stmt->closeCursor();
}
catch ( Exception $e )
{
    die ( $e->getMessage() );
}

/*
 * Fails if username doesn't match a DB entry
 */
if ( !isset($user) )
{
    return "Your username or password is invalid.";
}

// finish processing...
}
```

Now the user's data is stored in the variable $user (or the method failed because no match was found for the supplied username in the users table).

Finishing Steps 5-7 completes the method; do this by adding the following bold code:

```
public function processLoginForm()
{
    /*
     * Fails if the proper action was not submitted
     */
    if ( $_POST['action']!='user_login' )
    {
        return "Invalid action supplied for processLoginForm.";
    }

    /*
     * Escapes the user input for security
     */
    $uname = htmlentities($_POST['uname'], ENT_QUOTES);
    $pword = htmlentities($_POST['pword'], ENT_QUOTES);
```

```php
/*
 * Retrieves the matching info from the DB if it exists
 */
$sql = "SELECT
            `user_id`, `user_name`, `user_email`, `user_pass`
        FROM `users`
        WHERE
            `user_name` = :uname..
        LIMIT 1";
try
{
    $stmt = $this->db->prepare($sql);
    $stmt->bindParam(':uname', $uname, PDO::PARAM_STR);
    $stmt->execute();
    $user = array_shift($stmt->fetchAll());
    $stmt->closeCursor();
}
catch ( Exception $e )
{
    die ( $e->getMessage() );
}

/*
 * Fails if username doesn't match a DB entry
 */
if ( !isset($user) )
{
    return "No user found with that ID.";
}

/*
 * Get the hash of the user-supplied password
 */
$hash = $this->_getSaltedHash($pword, $user['user_pass']);

/*
 * Checks if the hashed password matches the stored hash
 */
if ( $user['user_pass']==$hash )..
{
    /*
     * Stores user info in the session as an array
     */
    $_SESSION['user'] = array(
            'id' => $user['user_id'],
            'name' => $user['user_name'],
            'email' => $user['user_email']
        );

    return TRUE;
}
```

```
    /*
     * Fails if the passwords don't match
     */
    else
    {
        return "Your username or password is invalid.";
    }
}
```

This method will now validate a login form submission. However, it doesn't work just quite yet; first, you need to build the _getSaltedHash() method.

Building a Method to Create Salted Hashes

In order to validate a user's password hash stored in the database, you need a function to generate a salted hash from the user's supplied password (a *hash* is an encrypted string generated by a security algorithm such as MD5 or SHA1).

■ **Note**   For more information on password hashing and security algorithms, visit http://en.wikipedia.org/wiki/Cryptographic_hash_function.

INCREASING SECURITY WITH SALTED PASSWORDS

Even though PHP provides functions to *hash*, or encrypt, strings, you should use additional security measures to ensure that your information is entirely secure. One of the simplest and most effective ways to heighten security is through the use of *salts*, which are additional strings used when hashing passwords.

Using Rainbow Tables and Common Encryption Algorithms

Common encryptions algorithms, such as SHA1 and MD5, have been fully mapped using *rainbow tables*,[1] which are reverse lookup tables for password hashes. In a nutshell, a rainbow table allows an attacker to search for the hash produced by a given encryption algorithm in a large table that contains every possible hash and a value that will produce that hash.

Rainbow tables have been generated for MD5 and SHA1, so it's possible for an attacker to crack your users' passwords with relative ease if no extra security measures are taken.

---

[1] http://en.wikipedia.org/wiki/Rainbow_table

Improving Security with Salted Hashes

While not bulletproof, adding a salt to your hashing algorithm will make cracking your users' passwords much more cumbersome for attackers. A salt is a string, either predefined or random, that is used in addition to the user input when hashing.

Without using a salt, a password may be hashed like this:

```
$hash = sha1($password);
```

To add a random salt to the preceding hash, you could apply the following code to it:

```
$salt = substr(md5(time()), 0, 7); // create a random salt
$hash = $salt . sha1($salt . $password);
```

The preceding code generates a random seven-digit salt. The salt is prepended to the password string before hashing; this means that even if two users have the same password, their individual password hashes will be different.

However, in order to reproduce that hash, the salt needs to be available. For this reason, the salt is also prepended, unencrypted, to the hash. This way, when a user signs in, you're able to extract the salt from the hash when it's retrieved from the database and use it to recreate the salted hash of the user's password:

```
$salt = substr($dbhash, 0, 7); // extract salt from stored hash
$hash = $salt . sha1($salt . $_POST['password']);

if ( $dbhash==$hash )
{
    echo "Match!";
}
else
{
    echo "No match.";
}
```

Incorporating Salted Hashes and Rainbow Tables

By adding a salt, rainbow tables are rendered useless. A new table will need to be generated, taking the salt into account in order to crack user passwords; while this isn't impossible, it's time-consuming for the attacker and adds an extra layer of security to your app.

In most applications (especially those that don't store much in the way of sensitive personal information such as credit card information), a salted password is deterrent enough to ward off potential attackers.

As an additional countermeasure, it is also advisable to add a check for repeated failed attempts to log in. This way, an attacker has a finite number of attempts to crack a password before being locked out of the system. This can also prevent **denial of service attacks** (attacks in which a huge volume of requests are sent in an attempt to overload a site and take it offline).

Creating this function is relatively straightforward, requiring only a few steps.

1. Check whether a salt was supplied; if not, generate a new salt by hashing the current UNIX timestamp, and then take a substring of the returned value at the length specified in $_saltLength and store it as $salt.

2. Otherwise, take a substring of the supplied salted hash from the database at the length specified in $_saltLength and store it as $salt.

3. Prepend the salt to the hash of the salt and the password, and return the new string.

Complete all three steps by inserting the following method into the Admin class:

```php
<?php

declare(strict_types=1);

class Admin extends DB_Connect
{

    private $_saltLength = 7;

    public function __construct($db=NULL, $saltLength=NULL) {...}

    public function processLoginForm() {...}

    /**
     * Generates a salted hash of a supplied string
     *
     * @param string $string to be hashed
     * @param string $salt extract the hash from here
     * @return string the salted hash
     */
    private function _getSaltedHash($string, $salt=NULL)
    {
        /*
         * Generate a salt if no salt is passed
         */
        if ( $salt==NULL )
        {
            $salt = substr(md5((string)time()), 0, $this->_saltLength);
        }

        /*
         * Extract the salt from the string if one is passed
         */
        else
        {
            $salt = substr($salt, 0, $this->_saltLength);
        }
```

```
        /*
         * Add the salt to the hash and return it
         */
        return $salt . sha1($salt . $string);
    }

}

?>
```

Creating a Test Method for Salted Hashes

To see how salted hashes work, create a quick test method for _getSaltedHash() called testSaltedHash().
This will be a public function that calls and outputs the values, enabling you to see how the script functions.

In the Admin class, define the testSaltedHash() method:

```
<?php

declare(strict_types=1);

class Admin extends DB_Connect
{

    private $_saltLength = 7;

    public function __construct($db=NULL, $saltLength=NULL) {...}

    public function processLoginForm() {...}

    private function _getSaltedHash($string, $salt=NULL) {...}

    public function testSaltedHash($string, $salt=NULL)
    {
        return $this->_getSaltedHash($string, $salt);
    }

}

?>
```

Next, add a new file called test.php to use this function and place it in the public folder
(/public/test.php). Inside this function, call the initialization file, create a new Admin class, and output
three hashes of this word: *test*. Create the first hash with no salt, and then sleep for one second to get a new
timestamp. Create the second hash with no salt, and then sleep for another second. Finally, create the third
hash using the salt from the second hash. Insert the following code to accomplish this test:

```
<?php

declare(strict_types=1);

// Include necessary files
include_once '../sys/core/init.inc.php';
```

```php
// Load the admin object
$obj = new Admin($dbo);

// Load a hash of the word test and output it
$hash1 = $obj->testSaltedHash("test");
echo "Hash 1 without a salt:<br />", $hash1, "<br /><br />";

// Pause execution for a second to get a different timestamp
sleep(1);

// Load a second hash of the word test
$hash2 = $obj->testSaltedHash("test");
echo "Hash 2 without a salt:<br />", $hash2, "<br /><br />";

// Pause execution for a second to get a different timestamp
sleep(1);

// Rehash the word test with the existing salt
$hash3 = $obj->testSaltedHash("test", $hash2);
echo "Hash 3 with the salt from hash 2:<br />", $hash3;

?>
```

▓ **Note**   The sleep() function delays execution of a script by a given number of seconds, passed as its sole argument. You can learn more about this function at http://php.net/sleep.

Your results will not be identical because the timestamp hashes used for the salt will differ; however, your results should look something like this:

```
Hash 1 without a salt:
fa260349138b9541c4b2895aeb0f0effe490194f4ef6c30

Hash 2 without a salt:
8d130612280d9e54c5fa4558cf80fac18a0514456dc11dc

Hash 3 with the salt from hash 2:
8d130612280d9e54c5fa4558cf80fac18a0514456dc11dc
```

As you can see, hashes of the word *test* don't match up when passed separately; however, if you supply an existing salted hash of *test*, the same hash is produced. This way, even if two users have the same password, their stored hashes will be different, making it much more difficult for potential attackers to crack passwords.

▓ **Note**   Bear in mind that no algorithm is 100% effective. However, using techniques like salted hashes makes it possible to reduce the possibility of an attack significantly.

Creating a User to Test Administrative Access

In order to test the administrative functions, you'll need a username/password pair to exist in your users table. For simplicity, the username will be testuser, the password will be admin, and the email address will be admin@example.com. Keep in mind that *this is not a secure password*; it is being used for illustration purposes only, and it should be changed before you use it with any production scripts.

Begin by generating a hash of the password, admin, which is easy using the test method testSaltedHash() and test.php. Add the following bold code to test.php to generate a salted hash of your test user's password:

```php
<?php

declare(strict_types=1);

// Include necessary files
include_once '../sys/core/init.inc.php';

// Load the admin object
$obj = new Admin($dbo);

// Generate a salted hash of "admin"
$pass = $obj->testSaltedHash("admin");
echo 'Hash of "admin":<br />', $pass, "<br /><br />";

?>
```

Navigate to http://localhost/test.php, and you'll see output similar to the following:

```
Hash of "admin":
0c6c835a48f6c5577e322f49c96ce0c719a8c272d4d8609
```

Copy the hash, navigate to http://localhost/phpmyadmin, and then click the SQL tab. Execute the following query to insert a test user into the table:

```sql
INSERT INTO `php-jquery_example`.`users`
  (`user_name`, `user_pass`, `user_email`)
VALUES
  (
    'testuser',
    'a1645e41f29c45c46539192fe29627751e1838f7311eeb4',
    'admin@example.com'
  );
```

After executing the preceding code, click the php-jquery_example database, and then the users table. Select the Browse tab to view the user info in the table (see Figure 6-3).

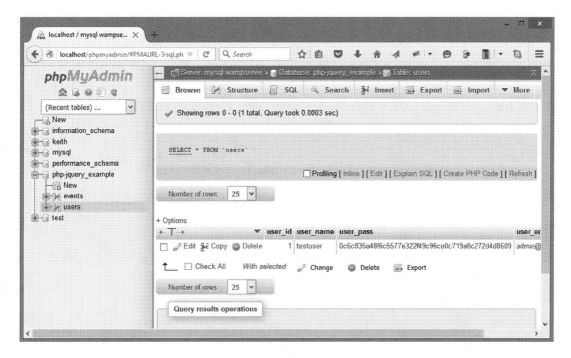

Figure 6-3. *The test user data after inserting it into the database*

Now that a user exists in the user database with a salted hash stored, you can delete both the testSaltedHash() method from the Admin class and the entire test.php file.

Modifying the App to Handle the Login Form Submission

At this point, you're almost ready to test a user login. Before it will work, however, you need to modify process.inc.php to handle form submissions from the login form.

Due to the way the file is set up, this change is as simple as adding a new element to the ACTIONS array. Open process.inc.php and insert the following bold code:

```php
<?php

declare(strict_types=1);

/*
 * Enable sessions if needed.
 * Avoid pesky warning if session already active.
 */
$status = session_status();
if ($status == PHP_SESSION_NONE){
    //There is no active session
    session_start();
}
```

```php
/*
 * Include necessary files
 */
include_once '../../../sys/config/db-cred.inc.php';

/*
 * Define constants for config info
 */
foreach ( $C as $name => $val )
{
    define($name, $val);
}

/*
 * Create a lookup array for form actions
 */
define(ACTIONS, array(
        'event_edit' => array(
                'object' => 'Calendar',
                'method' => 'processForm',
                'header' => 'Location: ../../'
            ),
        'user_login' => array(
                'object' => 'Admin',
                'method' => 'processLoginForm',
                'header' => 'Location: ../../'
            )
        )
    );

/*
 * Need a PDO object.
 */
$dsn = "mysql:host=" . DB_HOST . ";dbname=" . DB_NAME;
$dbo = new PDO($dsn, DB_USER, DB_PASS);

/*
 * Make sure the anti-CSRF token was passed and that the
 * requested action exists in the lookup array
 */
if ( $_POST['token']==$_SESSION['token']
        && isset(ACTIONS[$_POST['action']]) )
{
    $use_array = ACTIONS[$_POST['action']];
    $obj = new $use_array['object']($dbo);
    $method = $use_array['method'];
    if ( TRUE === $msg=$obj->$method() )
    {
        header($use_array['header']);
        exit;
    }
```

```
    else
    {
        // If an error occured, output it and end execution
        die ( $msg );
    }
}
else
{
    // Redirect to the main index if the token/action is invalid
    header("Location: ../../");
    exit;
}

function __autoload($class_name)
{
    $filename = '../../../sys/class/class.'
        . strtolower($class_name) . '.inc.php';
    if ( file_exists($filename) )
    {
        include_once $filename;
    }
}

?>
```

Now you can officially test a login. Because no checks for a login are in place yet, simply add a conditional comment in index.php to show login or logout status by inserting the following bold line into the file:

```
<?php

declare(strict_types=1);

/*
 * Include necessary files
 */
include_once '../sys/core/init.inc.php';

/*
 * Load the calendar
 */
$cal = new Calendar($dbo, "2016-01-01 12:00:00");

/*
 * Set up the page title and CSS files
 */
$page_title = "Events Calendar";
$css_files = array('style.css', 'admin.css');
```

```php
/*
 * Include the header
 */
include_once 'assets/common/header.inc.php';

?>

<div id="content">
<?php

/*
 * Display the calendar HTML
 */
echo $cal->buildCalendar();

?>

</div><!-- end #content -->
<p>
<?php

    echo isset($_SESSION['user']) ? "Logged In!" : "Logged Out!";

?>
</p>

<?php

/*
 * Include the footer
 */
include_once 'assets/common/footer.inc.php';

?>
```

Now save this file and navigate to http://localhost/ to see the "Logged Out!" message below the calendar (see Figure 6-4).

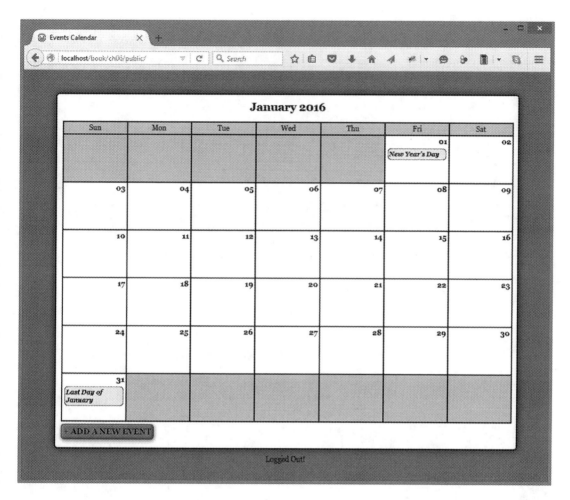

Figure 6-4. *Before the user logs in, the "Logged Out!" message appears below the calendar*

Next, navigate to http://localhost/login.php and enter the username testuser with the password of admin (see Figure 6-5).

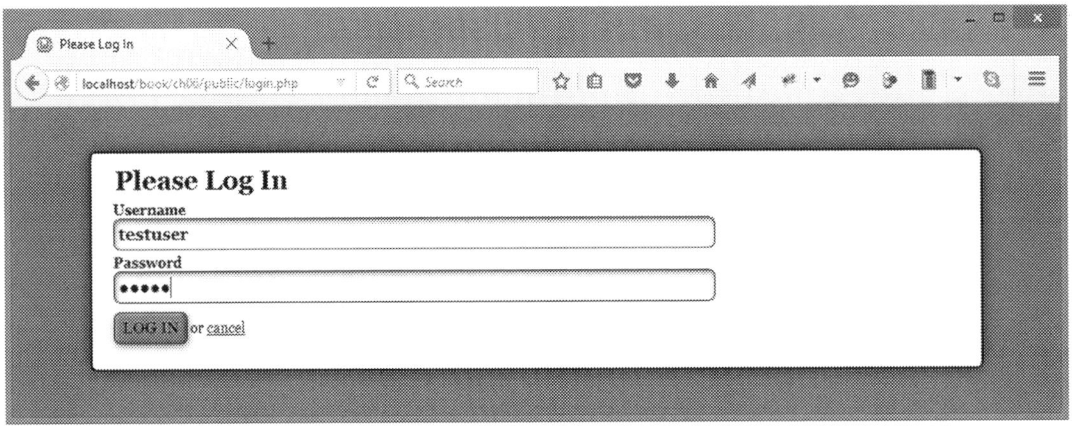

Figure 6-5. The login form with the username and password information entered

After clicking the Log In button, you'll be redirected back to the calendar; however, now the message below the calendar will read "Logged In!" (see Figure 6-6).

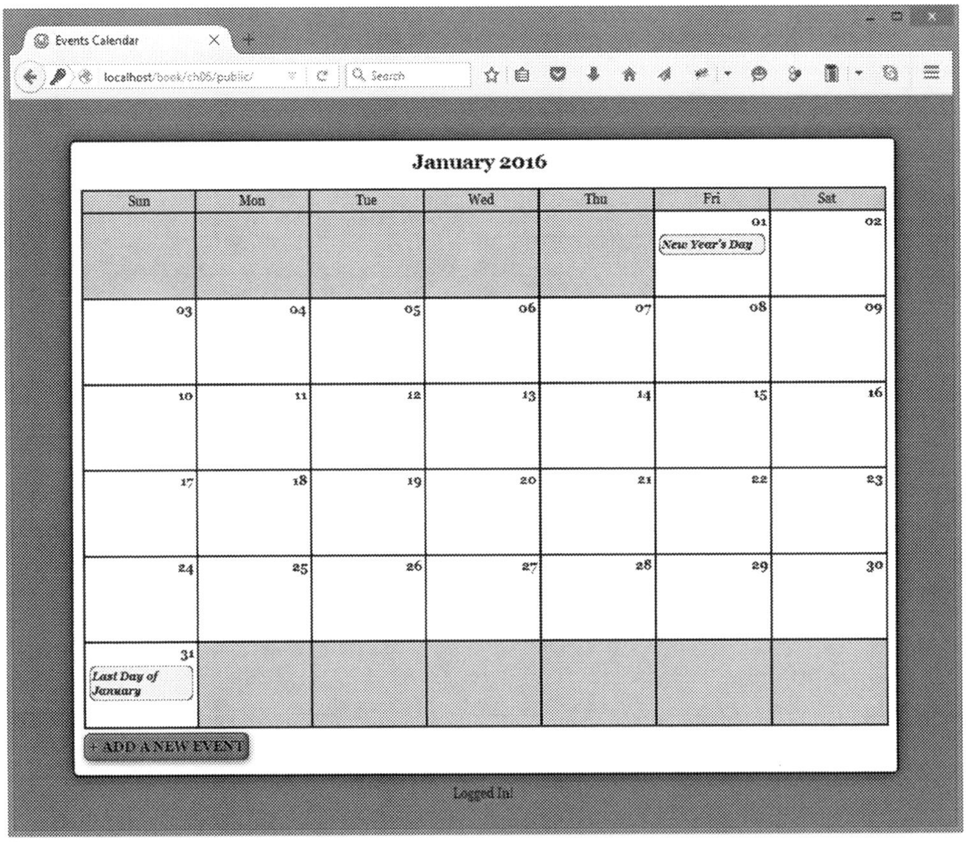

Figure 6-6. After the user logs in, the "Logged In!" message appears below the calendar

Allowing the User to Log Out

Next, you need to add a method that allows the user to log out. You will do this using a form that submits information to process.inc.php. The method _adminGeneralOptions() in the Calendar class generates the form.

Adding a Log Out Button to the Calendar

To add a button that allows users to log out, modify _adminGeneralOptions() in the Calendar class. In addition to providing a button for adding new events, this method will now also output a form that submits the site token and an action value of user_logout to process.inc.php. Open the Calendar class and modify _adminGeneralOptions() with the following bold code:

```
    private function _adminGeneralOptions()
    {
        /*
         * Display admin controls
         */
        return <<<ADMIN_OPTIONS

<a href="admin.php" class="admin">+ Add a New Event</a>
<form action="assets/inc/process.inc.php" method="post">
    <div>
        <input type="submit" value="Log Out" class="logout" />
        <input type="hidden" name="token"
            value="$_SESSION[token]" />
        <input type="hidden" name="action"
            value="user_logout" />
    </div>
</form>
ADMIN_OPTIONS;
    }
```

Now save the changes and refresh http://localhost/ in your browser to see the new button (see Figure 6-7).

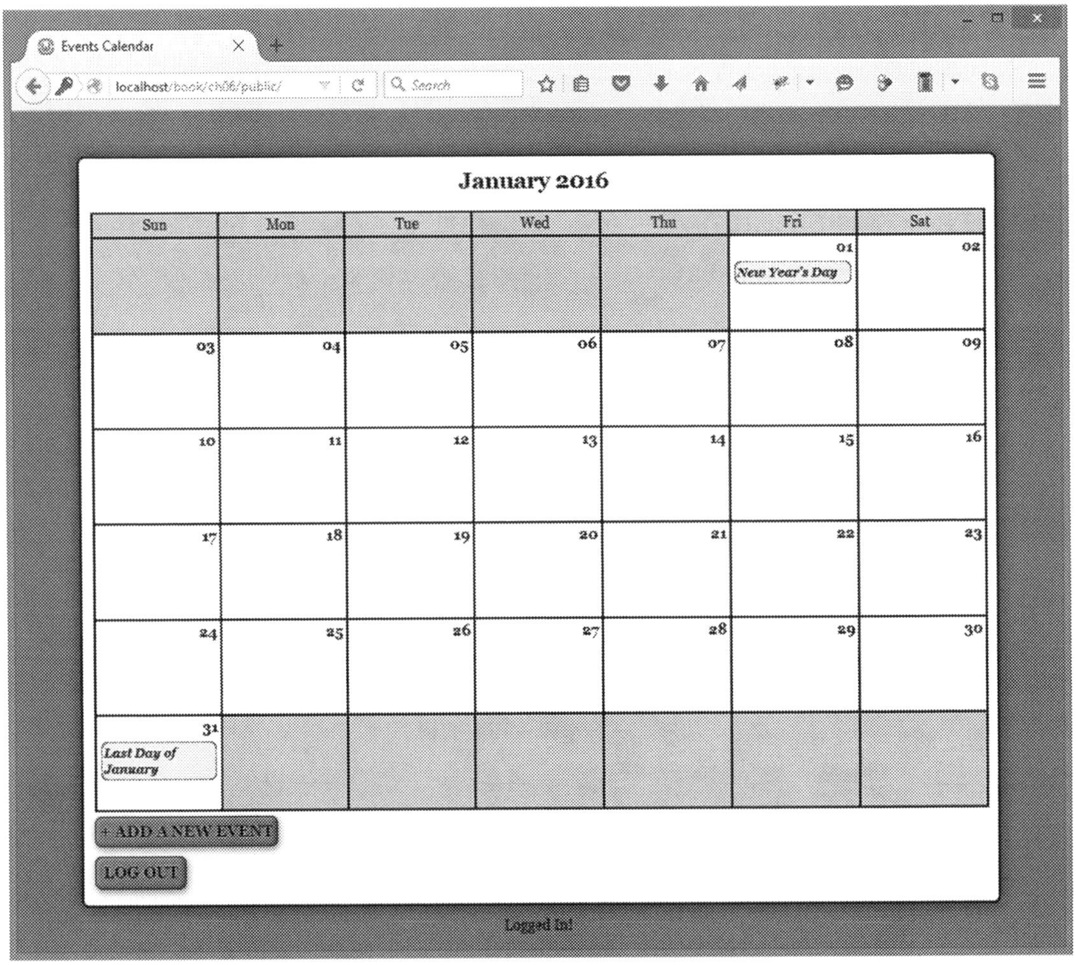

Figure 6-7. *The Log Out button as it appears after you modify the Calendar class*

Creating a Method to Process the Logout

To process the logout, a new public method called processLogout() needs to be added to the Admin class. This method does a quick check to make sure the proper action, user_logout, was supplied, and then uses session_destroy() to remove the user data array by destroying the current session entirely.

You add this method to the Admin class by inserting the following bold code:

```
<?php

declare(strict_types=1);

class Admin extends DB_Connect
{

    private $_saltLength = 7;
```

```php
    public function __construct($db=NULL, $saltLength=NULL) {...}

    public function processLoginForm() {...}

    /**
     * Logs out the user
     *
     * @return mixed TRUE on success or messsage on failure
     */
    public function processLogout()
    {
        /*
         * Fails if the proper action was not submitted
         */
        if ( $_POST['action']!='user_logout' )
        {
            return "Invalid action supplied for processLogout.";
        }

        /*
         * Removes the user array from the current session
         */
        session_destroy();
        return TRUE;
    }

    private function _getSaltedHash($string, $salt=NULL) {...}

}

?>
```

Modifying the App to Handle the User Logout

The last step you need to take before users can successfully log out is to add another array element to the ACTIONS array in process.inc.php. Insert the following bold code into process.inc.php to complete the logout process:

```php
<?php

declare(strict_types=1);

/*
 * Enable sessions if needed.
 * Avoid pesky warning if session already active.
 */
$status = session_status();
if ($status == PHP_SESSION_NONE){
    //There is no active session
    session_start();
}
```

217

```php
/*
 * Include necessary files
 */
include_once '../../../sys/config/db-cred.inc.php';

/*
 * Define constants for config info
 */
foreach ( $C as $name => $val )
{
    define($name, $val);
}

/*
 * Create a lookup array for form actions
 */
define(ACTIONS, array(
        'event_edit' => array(
                'object' => 'Calendar',
                'method' => 'processForm',
                'header' => 'Location: ../../'
            ),
        'user_login' => array(
                'object' => 'Admin',
                'method' => 'processLoginForm',
                'header' => 'Location: ../../'
            ),
        'user_logout' => array(
                'object' => 'Admin',
                'method' => 'processLogout',
                'header' => 'Location: ../../'
            )
        )
    );

/*
 * Make sure the anti-CSRF token was passed and that the
 * requested action exists in the lookup array
 */
if ( $_POST['token']==$_SESSION['token']
        && isset(ACTIONS[$_POST['action']]) )
{
    $use_array = ACTIONS[$_POST['action']];
    $obj = new $use_array['object']($dbo);
    $method = $use_array['method'];
    if ( TRUE === $msg=$obj->$method() )
    {
        header($use_array['header']);
        exit;
    }
```

```php
    else
    {
        // If an error occured, output it and end execution
        die ( $msg );
    }
}
else
{
    // Redirect to the main index if the token/action is invalid
    header("Location: ../../");
    exit;
}

function __autoload($class_name)
{
    $filename = '../../../sys/class/class.'
        . strtolower($class_name) . '.inc.php';
    if ( file_exists($filename) )
    {
        include_once $filename;
    }
}

?>
```

Save this file, then navigate to http://localhost/, and click the Log Out button at the bottom of the calendar. Clicking this button causes the message below the calendar to now read "Logged Out!" (see Figure 6-8).

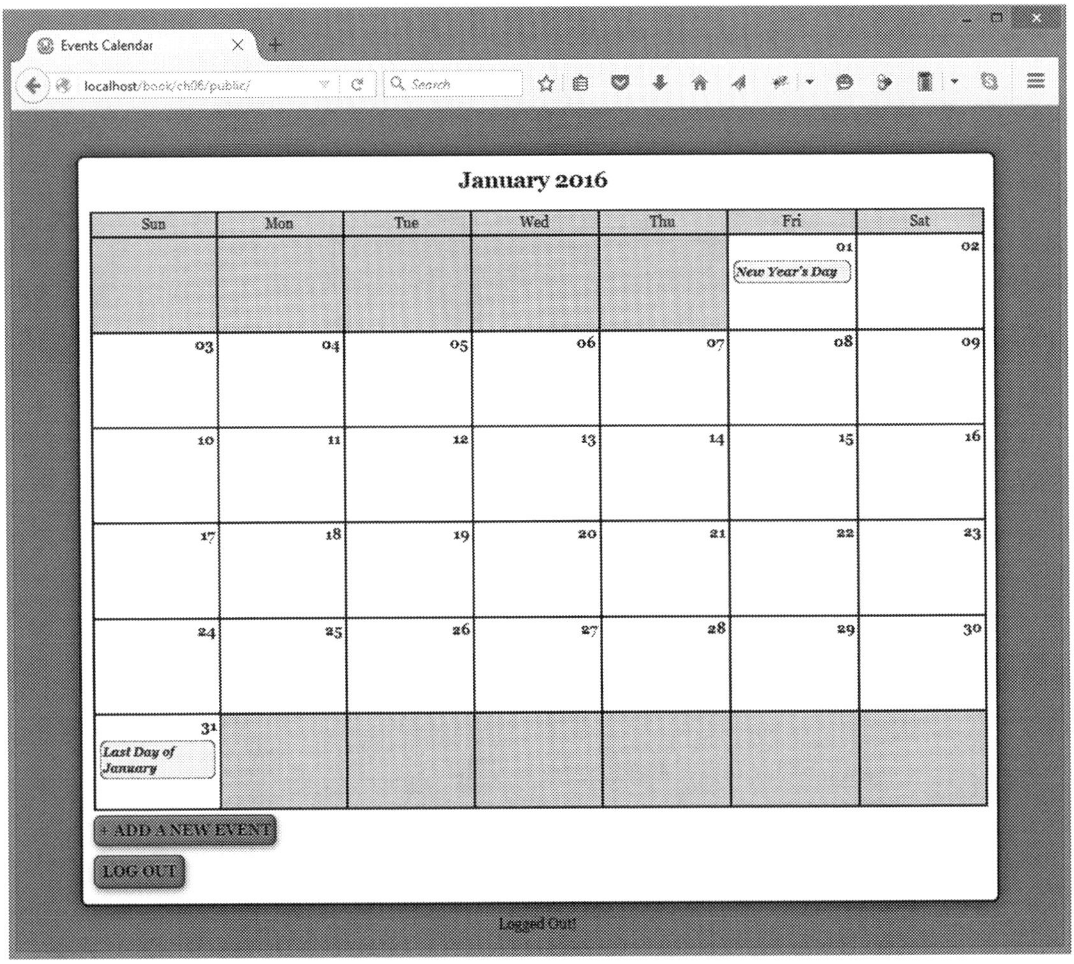

Figure 6-8. *Clicking the Log Out button removes the user data from the session*

▥ **Note** Even though we have established that the login is functioning, we'll still continue showing the Logged In!/Logged Out! messages during the course of our work. But if you wish, you may remove the message logic and the paragraph tags that enclose it from `index.php`.

Displaying Admin Tools Only to Administrators

Your users can log in and log out; the last steps you need to take are to make sure that all actions and options that require administrative access are only shown to users who are logged in.

Showing Admin Options to Administrators

The buttons for adding and editing events should not be displayed unless a user is logged in. To perform this check, you need to modify both the _adminGeneralOptions() and _adminEntryOptions() methods in the Calendar class.

Modifying the General Admin Options Method

Now let's take a look at the calendar's general options. If the user is logged in, you want to show her the options to create a new entry and to log out.

However, if the user is logged out, she should see a link to log in. Perform this check by making the modifications shown in bold to the _adminGeneralOptions() method in the Calendar class:

```php
<?php

declare(strict_types=1);

class Calendar extends DB_Connect
{

    private $_useDate;

    private $_m;

    private $_y;

    private $_daysInMonth;

    private $_startDay;

    public function __construct($db=NULL, $useDate=NULL) {...}

    public function buildCalendar() {...}

    public function displayForm() {...}

    public function processForm() {...}

    public function confirmDelete($id) {...}

    private function _loadEventData($id=NULL) {...}

    private function _createEventObj() {...}

    private function _loadEventById($id) {...}
```

```php
    private function _adminGeneralOptions()
    {
        /*
         * If the user is logged in, display admin controls
         */
        if ( isset($_SESSION['user']) )
        {
            return <<<ADMIN_OPTIONS

    <a href="admin.php" class="admin">+ Add a New Event</a>
    <form action="assets/inc/process.inc.php" method="post">
        <div>
            <input type="submit" value="Log Out" class="logout" />
            <input type="hidden" name="token"
                value="$_SESSION[token]" />
            <input type="hidden" name="action"
                value="user_logout" />
        </div>
    </form>
ADMIN_OPTIONS;
        }
        else
        {
            return <<<ADMIN_OPTIONS

    <a href="login.php">Log In</a>
ADMIN_OPTIONS;
        }
    }

    private function _adminEntryOptions($id) {...}

}

?>
```

After saving the changes, reload `http://localhost/` while logged out to see the administrative options replaced with a simple Log In link (see Figure 6-9).

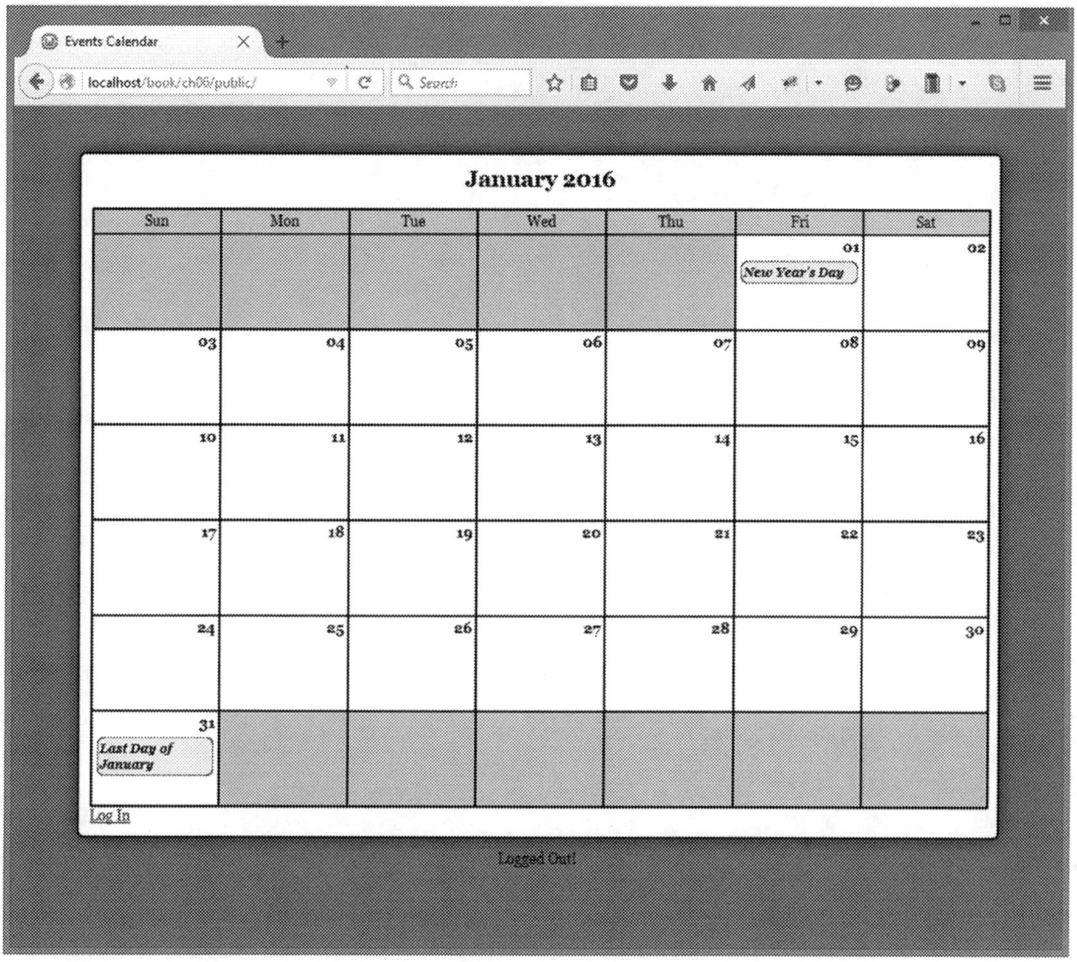

Figure 6-9. *While a user is logged out, a Log In link is displayed in the lower left corner*

Modifying the Event Options Method

Next, you want add code to prevent the editing and deletion of events by unauthorized users; you do this by modifying _adminEventOptions() in the Calendar class with the following bold code:

```php
<?php

declare(strict_types=1);

class Calendar extends DB_Connect
{

    private $_useDate;

    private $_m;
```

```php
    private $_y;

    private $_daysInMonth;

    private $_startDay;

    public function __construct($db=NULL, $useDate=NULL) {...}

    public function buildCalendar() {...}

    public function displayForm() {...}

    public function processForm() {...}

    public function confirmDelete($id) {...}

    private function _loadEventData($id=NULL) {...}

    private function _createEventObj() {...}

    private function _loadEventById($id) {...}

    private function _adminGeneralOptions() {...}

    private function _adminEntryOptions($id)
    {
        if ( isset($_SESSION['user']) )
        {
            return <<<ADMIN_OPTIONS

<div class="admin-options">
<form action="admin.php" method="post">
    <p>
        <input type="submit" name="edit_event"
            value="Edit This Event" />
        <input type="hidden" name="event_id"
            value="$id" />
    </p>
</form>
<form action="confirmdelete.php" method="post">
    <p>
        <input type="submit" name="delete_event"
            value="Delete This Event" />
        <input type="hidden" name="event_id"
            value="$id" />
    </p>
</form>
</div><!-- end .admin-options -->
```

```
ADMIN_OPTIONS;
            }
            else
            {
                return NULL;
            }
      }

}

?>
```

After inserting these changes, navigate to `http://localhost/` while logged out and click an event to bring up its full view; the administrative options will not be displayed (see Figure 6-10).

Figure 6-10. *The full event view while logged out*

Limiting Access to Administrative Pages

As an additional security precaution, you should ensure that any pages that only authorized users should have access to, such as the event creation/editing form, check for proper authorization before executing.

Disallowing Access to the Event Creation Form Without Login

You can prevent a mischievous user from finding the event creation form while logged out by performing a simple check that you add to the file. If the user is not logged in, he'll be sent to the main calendar view before the script has the chance to execute.

To implement this change, open `admin.php` and insert the code shown in bold:

```php
<?php

declare(strict_types=1);

/*
 * Include necessary files
 */
include_once '../sys/core/init.inc.php';
```

```php
/*
 * If the user is not logged in, send them to the main file
 */
if ( !isset($_SESSION['user']) )
{
    header("Location: ./");
    exit;
}

/*
 * Output the header
 */
$page_title = "Add/Edit Event";
$css_files = array("style.css", "admin.css");
include_once 'assets/common/header.inc.php';

/*
 * Load the calendar
 */
$cal = new Calendar($dbo);

?>

<div id="content">
<?php echo $cal->displayForm(); ?>

</div><!-- end #content -->

<?php

/*
 * Output the footer
 */
include_once 'assets/common/footer.inc.php';

?>
```

After saving this file, attempt to navigate to http://localhost/admin.php while logged out. You'll automatically be sent to http://localhost/.

Ensuring Only Logged In Users Can Delete Events

Also, to keep unauthorized users from deleting events, insert a check for a valid user session in the confirmdelete.php file:

```php
<?php

declare(strict_types=1);

/*
 * Enable sessions if needed.
 * Avoid pesky warning if session already active.
 */
$status = session_status();
if ($status == PHP_SESSION_NONE){
    //There is no active session
    session_start();
}

/*
 * Make sure an event ID was passed and the user is logged in
 */
if ( isset($_POST['event_id']) && isset($_SESSION['user']) )
{
    /*
     * Collect the event ID from the URL string
     */
    $id = (int) $_POST['event_id'];
}
else
{
    /*
     * Send the user to the main page if no ID is supplied
     * or the user is not logged in
     */
    header("Location: ./");
    exit;
}

/*
 * Include necessary files
 */
include_once '../sys/core/init.inc.php';

/*
 * Load the calendar
 */
$cal = new Calendar($dbo);
$markup = $cal->confirmDelete($id);
```

```
/*
 * Output the header
 */
$page_title = "View Event";
$css_files = array("style.css", "admin.css");
include_once 'assets/common/header.inc.php';

?>

<div id="content">
<?php echo $markup; ?>

</div><!-- end #content -->

<?php

/*
 * Output the footer
 */
include_once 'assets/common/footer.inc.php';

?>
```

Now save this code and try to directly access http://localhost/confirmdelete.php while logged out. As expected, you'll be redirected to http://localhost/ instead.

Summary

In this chapter, you learned how to add user authorization to your calendar app, which means only authorized users can now make modifications to the calendar. You learned how to create the Admin class, check login credentials, display admin tools to admins only, and limit access to admin pages.

In the next chapter, you'll start integrating jQuery into the application to progressively enhance the user experience.

PART 3

Combining jQuery with PHP Applications

With the calendar running properly, you can now enhance the application with jQuery to improve the user experience. In the following chapters, you'll create a layer of JavaScript that will sit on top of your app to add AJAX functionality.

▩ ▩ ▩

CHAPTER 7

Enhancing the User Interface with jQuery

The application as it stands now is fully functional. Events can be viewed, and users with administrative clearance can log in to create, edit, or delete events.

The next step is to add a layer of polish to the app that creates that finished look and feel, which you'll accomplish using a technique called progressive enhancement to add AJAX functionality to the app.

Adding Progressive Enhancements with jQuery

Progressive enhancement is a term originally coined by Steven Champeon[1] in 2003 to describe a web-development technique in which applications are designed to be accessible to any Internet connection and browser using semantic HTML and other technologies that are applied in layers (such as CSS files and JavaScript code).

For an application to follow the principles of progressive enhancement, it must adhere to the following guidelines:

- Basic content is accessible to all browsers using the simplest, most semantic HTML markup possible.

- All of the basic functionality of the app works in all browsers.

- The user's preferences are respected; this means that the web app doesn't override browser settings (such as window size).

- Externally linked CSS handles the styling and presentation of the document.

- Externally linked JavaScript enhances the user experience, but it remains *unobtrusive*, or non-essential to the application's operation.

Your application already meets the first four guidelines (it's not pretty, but the application will work with styles disabled). So as long as your JavaScript doesn't create any new functionality that can't be accessed with JavaScript disabled, you will have successfully created a progressively enhanced web application.

---

[1] www.hesketh.com/about-us/leadership-team/

Setting Progressive Enhancement Goals

Using the principles of progressive enhancement, you'll add the ability to view event information without a page refresh in a *modal window*, a content area that sits on top of existing markup to display additional information. Such windows are usually triggered by JavaScript, and they are used on many of today's most popular web sites.

In your calendar application, you'll use a modal window to display event details after a user clicks the event title. This will be done without a page refresh using AJAX.

Including jQuery in the Calendar App

As you learned in the introduction to jQuery earlier in this book, using jQuery syntax requires that you first include the jQuery library. It is good practice to place your `<script>` tags near the bottom of your HTML markup, if possible, just before the close body tag (`</body>`). This way, the HTML can load first, sparing the user from having to wait for the (generally slower) script files to load before seeing any of the page. Additionally, it prevents JavaScript errors that can result from code interacting with incompletely loaded page elements.

To make it easy to consistently follow this practice, you'll include the jQuery library and all subsequent files in `footer.inc.php` (`/public/assets/common/footer.inc.php`). Begin by including the latest version of jQuery in your app; you accomplish this by adding the following bold lines to `footer.inc.php`:

```
<script src="https://ajax.googleapis.com/ajax/libs/jquery/2.1.4/jquery.min.js">
</script>
</body>

</html>
```

Save this code, then load `http://localhost/` in your browser. Open the Firebug console and execute the following command to ensure that jQuery is loaded in your app:

```
$("h2").text();
```

After running this command, the console will display the following output:

```
>>> $("h2").text();
"January 2016
```

▓ **Note** Because you're using the Google-hosted jQuery library, you need to have an Internet connection available, in addition to your Apache server. If you do not have access to an Internet connection or prefer not to use one, download the latest version of jQuery from `http://jquery.com/` and include it instead.

Creating a JavaScript Initialization File

Your app is following progressive enhancement guidelines, so all scripts will be housed in an external file called `init.js`. It will reside in the public js folder (`/public/assets/js/init.js`), and it will contain all of the custom jQuery code for your app.

Including the Initialization File in the Application

Before any of your scripts will be available to your app, you will need to include the initialization file in the application. Your app will use jQuery syntax, so the initialization file needs to be included after the script that loads the jQuery library in footer.inc.php.

You include the file in your app by inserting the following bold code into footer.inc.php:

```
<script src="https://ajax.googleapis.com/ajax/libs/jquery/2.1.4/jquery.min.js">
</script>
<script src="assets/js/init.js"></script>
</body>

</html>
```

Ensuring the Document Is Ready Before Script Execution

After creating init.js, use the document.ready shortcut from jQuery to ensure that no scripts execute before the document is actually ready to be manipulated. Insert the following code into init.js:

```
"use strict";  // enforce variable declarations - safer coding

// Makes sure the document is ready before executing scripts
jQuery(function($){

  // A quick check to make sure the script loaded properly
  console.log("init.js was loaded successfully.");

});
```

Save this file and load http://localhost/ in your browser with the Firebug console open. After the file is loaded, you should see the following result appear in the console:

```
init.js was loaded successfully.
```

Creating a New Stylesheet for Elements Created by jQuery

To ensure the elements created with jQuery look right when you start building them, you're going to jump a bit ahead here and create a new CSS file to store styling information for the elements you'll create with the jQuery scripts you're about to write.

This file will be called ajax.css, and it will reside in the css folder (/public/assets/css/ajax.css). After creating it, place the following style rules inside it:

```
.modal-overlay {
    position: fixed;
    top: 0;
    left: 0;
    bottom: 0;
    width: 100%;
```

```css
        height: 100%;
        background-color: rgba(0,0,0,.5);
        z-index: 4;
}

.modal-window {
        position: absolute;
        top: 140px;
        left: 50%;
        width: 300px;
        height: auto;
        margin-left: -150px;
        padding: 20px;
        border: 2px solid #000;
        background-color: #FFF;
        -moz-border-radius: 6px;
        -webkit-border-radius: 6px;
        border-radius: 6px;
        -moz-box-shadow: 0 0 14px #123;
        -webkit-box-shadow: 0 0 14px #123;
        box-shadow: 0 0 14px #123;
        z-index: 5;
}

.modal-close-btn {
        position: absolute;
        top: 0;
        right: 4px;
        margin: 0;
        padding: 0;
        text-decoration: none;
        color: black;
        font-size: 16px;
}

.modal-close-btn:before {
        position: relative;
        top: -1px;
        content: "Close";
        text-transform: uppercase;
        font-size: 10px;
}
```

Including the Stylesheet in the Index File

Next, open index.php and include the new stylesheet in the $css_files array by adding the line in bold:

```php
<?php

declare(strict_types=1);

/*
 * Include necessary files
 */
include_once '../sys/core/init.inc.php';

/*
 * Load the calendar
 */
$cal = new Calendar($dbo, "2016-01-01 12:00:00");

/*
 * Set up the page title and CSS files
 */
$page_title = "Events Calendar";
$css_files = array('style.css', 'admin.css', 'ajax.css');

/*
 * Include the header
 */
include_once 'assets/common/header.inc.php';

?>

<div id="content">
<?php

/*
 * Display the calendar HTML
 */
echo $cal->buildCalendar();

?>

</div><!-- end #content -->

<?php

/*
 * Include the footer
 */
include_once 'assets/common/footer.inc.php';

?>
```

Creating a Modal Window for Event Data

The modal window you'll create for this app will be fairly simple; the script to create it will follow these steps.

1. Prevent the default action (opening the detailed event view in `view.php`).

2. Add an `active` class to the event link in the calendar.

3. Extract the query string from the event link's `href` attribute.

4. Create a button that will close the modal window when clicked.

5. Create the modal window itself and put the Close button inside it.

6. Use AJAX to retrieve the information from the database and display it in the modal window.

All of the preceding steps will be carried out when the click event is fired for an event title link.

Binding a Function to the Click Event of Title Links

Begin by adding a new selector to `init.js` that selects all anchor elements that are direct descendants of list items (`li>a`) and use the `.on()` method to bind a handler to the click event (jQuery versions 1.x would have used the `.live()` method, but that has been deprecated).

Because you'll need to bind to many dynamically created elements, you will consistently use the three-argument form of `.on()`: `$(selector).on(event, childSelector, function)` where *selector* is a parent container (not dynamic), and *childSelector* represents the (often) dynamically created element. For maximum flexibility, you'll use "body" as the parent container.

Insert the following bold code into `init.js`:

```
"use strict";  // enforce variable declarations - safer coding

// Makes sure the document is ready before executing scripts
jQuery(function($){

// Pulls up events in a modal window
$("body").on("click", " li>a", function(event){

        // Event handler scripts go here

    });

});
```

Preventing the Default Action and Adding an Active Class

Next, you need to prevent the default action by using `.preventDefault()`, then add an `active` class to the clicked element using `.addClass()`.

This is accomplished by adding the following bold code:

```
"use strict";  // enforce variable declarations - safer coding

// Makes sure the document is ready before executing scripts
jQuery(function($){
```

```
// Pulls up events in a modal window
$("body").on("click", "li>a", function(event){

        // Stops the link from loading view.php
        event.preventDefault();

        // Adds an "active" class to the link
        $(this).addClass("active");

        // Proves the event handler worked by logging the link text
        console.log( $(this).text() );

    });

});
```

After saving this code, reload `http://localhost/` in your browser and click any of the event titles. Instead of going to the event details on `view.php`, the title of the event is output in the console. For instance, if you click the New Year's Day event, you will see the following output in the console:

```
New Year's Day
```

Extracting the Query String with Regular Expressions

The modal window is being created to display event information, so you'll need some way of knowing which event should be displayed. Without adding any extra markup, you can actually pull the event ID right out of the `href` attribute using regular expressions.

To do this, you need to extract the query string from the link. (If the `href` attribute value is `http://localhost/view.php?event_id=1`, the query string is `event_id=1`.)

You will extract the query string using two items: `.replace()`, a native JavaScript function that accepts a string or regular expression pattern to match, and a string or pattern that matches should be replaced with.

Using the Lazy Approach: String-Based Replacement

At a glance, the obvious solution might seem to be the following:

```
var data = string.replace("http://localhost/view.php?", "");
```

And, yes, this does work, producing the output `"event_id=1"` (if you assume the original value of `$string` was `http://localhost/view.php?event_id=1`). Unfortunately, this approach is not flexible enough; for example, what if the application is moved to another domain name? Or, what if the file name is changed to `event.php`? Either change breaks the preceding logic and requires an update to the script.

Adopting a Better Solution: Regular Expressions

However, there is a better solution: *regular expressions*. Regular expressions are a powerful pattern-matching tool available in most modern programming languages.

To extract the query string, you'll use a pattern that looks for the first question mark (?) in a string, and then returns everything after it. The pattern will look like this:

```
/.*?\?(.*)$/
```

Regular expressions in JavaScript are delimited by forward slashes (/) at each end of the expression. Inside this expression, the pattern looks for zero or more of any character (from left to right) until the first time it reaches a question mark; it then stores all characters after the question mark until the end of the string as a named group for use in the replacement.

▓ **Note**   You'll learn much more about regular expressions and how they work in Chapter 9.

Incorporating a Regular Expression into a Script

You want to extract the href value of the link that was clicked, so you'll use the this keyword. In order to use jQuery methods, you have to pass this as the selector to the jQuery function first. Now access the href value with the .attr() method, call .replace(), and extract the query string.

When using regular expressions in .replace(), no quotes are used to enclose the pattern. Using the regular expression just described, modify init.js to store the query string from the clicked link in a variable called data; do this by adding the code shown in bold:

```
"use strict";   // enforce variable declarations - safer coding

// Makes sure the document is ready before executing scripts
jQuery(function($){

// Pulls up events in a modal window
$("body").on("click", "li>a", function(event){

        // Stops the link from loading view.php
        event.preventDefault();

        // Adds an "active" class to the link
        $(this).addClass("active");

        // Gets the query string from the link href
        var data = $(this)
                        .attr("href")
                        .replace(/.+?\?(.*)$/, "$1");

        // Logs the query string
        console.log( data );
    });

});
```

Save this code, reload `http://localhost/`, and click a link. You should see something similar to the following appear in the console:

```
event_id=1
```

Creating a Modal Window

The next step is to generate the HTML markup that will actually create the modal window and overlay. This markup is extremely simple: it will basically consist of a div element wrapped around other content. For example, the New Year's Day event modal window markup will look like this:

```
<div class="modal-window">
    <h2>New Year's Day</h2>
    <p class="dates">January 01, 2016, 12:00am–11:59pm</p>
    <p>Happy New Year!</p>
</div>
```

You are going to use this same modal window for other features as well (such as for displaying the editing form for events), so the actual creation of the modal window is going to be abstracted in a separate function for easy reuse. Because you will reuse more than one function, you'll organize your script by placing all utility functions in an *object literal*, which is a comma-separated list of name-value pairs (for more information, see the sidebar called "Using an Object Literal for Utility Functions").

Creating the Utility Function to Check for a Modal Window

At the top of init.js, declare a new object literal called fx to store your utility functions:

```
"use strict";  // enforce variable declarations - safer coding

// Makes sure the document is ready before executing scripts
jQuery(function($){

// Functions to manipulate the modal window
var fx = {};

// Pulls up events in a modal window
$("body").on("click", "li>a", function(event){

        // Stops the link from loading view.php
        event.preventDefault();

        // Adds an "active" class to the link
        $(this).addClass("active");

        // Gets the query string from the link href
        var data = $(this)
                        .attr("href")
                        .replace(/.+?\?(.*)$/, "$1");
```

```
        // Logs the query string
        console.log( data );

    });

});
```

The first function to be stored in fx will be called initModal, and it will check whether a modal window already exists. If it does, the function will select it; otherwise, it will create a new one and append it to the body tag.

To see if an element already exists, use the length property after executing the jQuery function with a selector for that element. If the length property returns 0, the element does not currently exist in the Document Object Model (DOM).

Perform the check and return a modal window by inserting the following bold code into fx inside init.js:

```
// Functions to manipulate the modal window
var fx = {

        // Checks for a modal window and returns it, or
        // else creates a new one and returns that
        "initModal" : function() {
                // If no elements are matched, the length
                // property will return 0
                if ( $(".modal-window").length==0 )
                {
                    // Creates a div, adds a class, and
                    // appends it to the body tag
                    return $("<div>")
                            .addClass("modal-window")
                            .appendTo("body");
                }
                else
                {
                    // Returns the modal window if one
                    // already exists in the DOM
                    return $(".modal-window");
                }
        }

    };
```

Calling the Utility Function from the Event Handler

Next, modify the click event handler to load the result of fx.initModal into a variable for use in the script by adding the following bold code in init.js:

```
// Pulls up events in a modal window
$("body").on("click", "li>a", function(event){

        // Stops the link from loading view.php
        event.preventDefault();

        // Adds an "active" class to the link
        $(this).addClass("active");

        // Gets the query string from the link href
        var data = $(this)
                        .attr("href")
                        .replace(/.+?\?(.*)$/, "$1"),

        // Checks if the modal window exists and
        // selects it, or creates a new one
        modal = fx.initModal();

    });
```

▓ **Note**   The semicolon after the data variable has been replaced with a comma in this example.

Save and reload http://localhost/ and then click one of the event titles to cause a modal window to appear on the screen (see Figure 7-1).

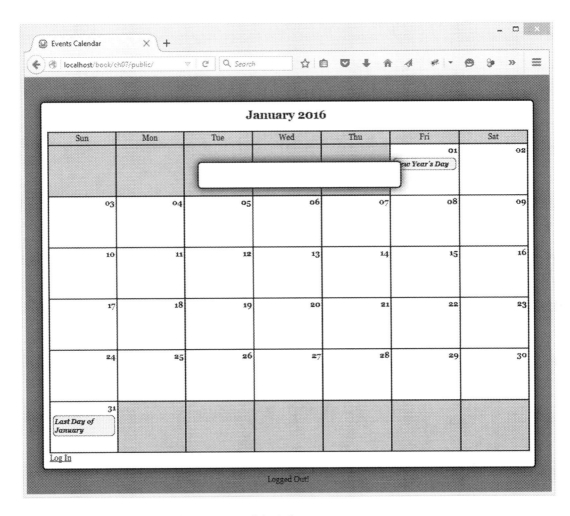

Figure 7-1. *Clicking an event title causes a modal window to appear*

USING AN OBJECT LITERAL FOR UTILITY FUNCTIONS

Utility functions often come into play when writing applications. The more complex the app, the more likely it is that a large number of utility functions will exist for it, and the harder it is to keep those functions organized.

One option for keeping utility functions organized is to use object literals. This allows developers to put the functions in one place or even to group functions according to their usage.

Understanding Object Literals

At its simplest, an object literal is a variable in JavaScript that is an empty set of curly braces, signifying an empty object literal:

```
var obj = {};
```

You can add any number of values to the object literal using comma-separated name-value pairs:

```
var obj = {
    "name" : "Jason Lengstorf",
    "age" : "25"
};
```

To access a value, simply append a dot (.) and the name of the property you wish to access:

```
alert(obj.name); // alerts "Jason Lengstorf"
```

What makes object literals so useful is that you can also store functions in them:

```
var obj = {
    "func" : function() { alert("Object literals rule!"); }
};
```

To call a function stored in an object literal, use the same syntax that you would to access a value; however, you must also include the parentheses at the end. Otherwise, JavaScript assumes you're trying to store that function in another variable and simply returns it:

```
obj.func(); // alerts "Object literals rule!"
```

Functions in object literals can accept parameters as well:

```
var obj = {
    "func" : function(text){ alert(text); }
};
obj.func("I'm a parameter!"); // alerts "I'm a parameter!"
```

Object Literals vs. Procedural Programming

Keeping functions organized in an object literal makes code more legible and—if the developer makes an effort to keep the functions abstract enough—can cut down on the time spent maintaining the code in the future because everything is compartmentalized and easy to find.

That said, object literals are not always the best solution. In instances where you may be dealing with multiple objects, it can be better to use a full-on object-oriented approach. If hardly any scripting is required, an object literal may be overkill.

At the end of the day, it's up to you as a developer to decide what the best approach is for your project. Ultimately, it's a matter of taste and comfort; you need to decide what makes your development process easiest.

Retrieving and Displaying Event Information with AJAX

Now that the modal window loads, it's time to load the event information and display it. To do this, you'll be using the $.ajax() method.

Using the $.ajax() method, you will send data to a processing file (which you'll build in the next section) using the POST method, and then insert the response into the modal window.

Creating a File to Handle AJAX Requests

Before you put together the call to $.ajax(), it helps to know where and how the data should be sent. In the inc folder, create a new file called ajax.inc.php (/public/assets/inc/ajax.inc.php). This file will work very similarly to process.inc.php, except it will deal exclusively with AJAX calls. Because a value returned from a PHP function can't be read by JavaScript unless the value is actually output (using echo or its ilk), process.inc.php will not function properly for this aspect of the application.

Essentially, ajax.inc.php will use a lookup array to determine which objects and methods need to be used, and then output the returned values using echo for use with AJAX.

Start by enabling sessions, loading the necessary configuration information, defining a constant, and putting together an auto-load function. Now add the following to ajax.inc.php:

```php
<?php

declare(strict_types=1);

/*
 * Enable sessions if needed.
 * Avoid pesky warning if session already active.
 */
$status = session_status();
if ($status == PHP_SESSION_NONE){
    //There is no active session
    session_start();
}

/*
 * Include necessary files
 */
include_once '../../../sys/config/db-cred.inc.php';

/*
 * Define constants for config info
 */
foreach ( $C as $name => $val )
{
    define($name, $val);
}

function __autoload($class_name)
{
    $filename = '../../../sys/class/class.'
        . strtolower($class_name) . '.inc.php';
    if ( file_exists($filename) )
```

```
    {
        include_once $filename;
    }
}

?>
```

Next, define the lookup array with information for loading event data, and then put together the code that will instantiate an object, call the method, and output the returned value using the bold code that follows:

```
<?php

declare(strict_types=1);

/*
 * Enable sessions if needed.
 * Avoid pesky warning if session already active.
 */
$status = session_status();
if ($status == PHP_SESSION_NONE){
    //There is no active session
    session_start();
}

/*
 * Include necessary files
 */
include_once '../../../sys/config/db-cred.inc.php';

/*
 * Define constants for config info
 */
foreach ( $C as $name => $val )
{
    define($name, $val);
}

/*
 * Create a lookup array for form actions
 */
define(ACTIONS, array(
        'event_view' => array(
                'object' => 'Calendar',
                'method' => 'displayEvent'
            )
        )
    );
```

```php
/*
 * Make sure the anti-CSRF token was passed and that the
 * requested action exists in the lookup array
 */
if ( isset(ACTIONS[$_POST['action']]) )
{
    $use_array = ACTIONS[$_POST['action']];
    $obj = new $use_array['object']($dbo);
    $method = $use_array['method'];

    /*
     * Check for an ID and sanitize it if found
     */
    if ( isset($_POST['event_id']) )
    {
        $id = (int) $_POST['event_id'];
    }
    else { $id = NULL; }

    echo $obj->$method($id);
}

function __autoload($class_name)
{
    $filename = '../../../sys/class/class.'
        . strtolower($class_name) . '.inc.php';
    if ( file_exists($filename) )
    {
        include_once $filename;
    }
}

?>
```

The only real differences from `process.inc.php` in the preceding code are the lack of a *header* key in the lookup array and the use of echo to output the return value of called methods.

Loading Event Data Using AJAX

Moving back to `init.js`, you can now add the call to `$.ajax()`. There will eventually be several calls to `$.ajax()` in your application, so store the location of the processing file in a variable for easy maintenance if the file location or name could ever change. Add this variable to the top of `init.js` by inserting the code shown in bold:

```js
"use strict";  // enforce variable declarations - safer coding

// Makes sure the document is ready before executing scripts
jQuery(function($){

// File to which AJAX requests should be sent
var processFile = "assets/inc/ajax.inc.php",
```

```
// Functions to manipulate the modal window
    fx = {

        // Checks for a modal window and returns it, or
        // else creates a new one and returns that
        "initModal" : function() {
                // If no elements are matched, the length
                // property will be 0
                if ( $(".modal-window").length==0 )
                {
                    // Creates a div, adds a class, and
                    // appends it to the body tag
                    return $("<div>")
                            .addClass("modal-window")
                            .appendTo("body");
                }
                else
                {
                    // Returns the modal window if one
                    // already exists in the DOM
                    return $(".modal-window");
                }
            }

    };

// Pulls up events in a modal window
$("body").on("click", "li>a", function(event){

        // Stops the link from loading view.php
        event.preventDefault();

        // Adds an "active" class to the link
        $(this).addClass("active");

        // Gets the query string from the link href
        var data = $(this)
                        .attr("href")
                        .replace(/.+?\?(.*)$/, "$1"),

        // Checks if the modal window exists and
        // selects it, or creates a new one
            modal = fx.initModal();

    });

});
```

Next, set up the call to $.ajax() in the event handler. It will use the POST method, point to the processFile, and send the appropriate data. Because the query string extracted from the link does not include an action field, insert one manually here. Finally, use .append() to insert the returned markup into the modal window if the call succeeds or to display an error message if it fails.

Do this by inserting the following bold lines into init.js:

```
// Pulls up events in a modal window
$("body").on("click", "li>a", function(event){

        // Stops the link from loading view.php
        event.preventDefault();

        // Adds an "active" class to the link
        $(this).addClass("active");

        // Gets the query string from the link href
        var data = $(this)
                        .attr("href")
                        .replace(/.+?\?(.*)$/, "$1"),

        // Checks if the modal window exists and
        // selects it, or creates a new one
            modal = fx.initModal();

        // Loads the event data from the DB
        $.ajax({
                type: "POST",
                url: processFile,
                data: "action=event_view&" + data,
                success: function(data){
                        // Alert event data for now
                        modal.append(data);
                    },
                error: function(msg) {
                        modal.append(msg);
                    }
        });

});
```

Save your changes, reload http://localhost/, and click an event title to see the event information loaded into the modal window (see Figure 7-2).

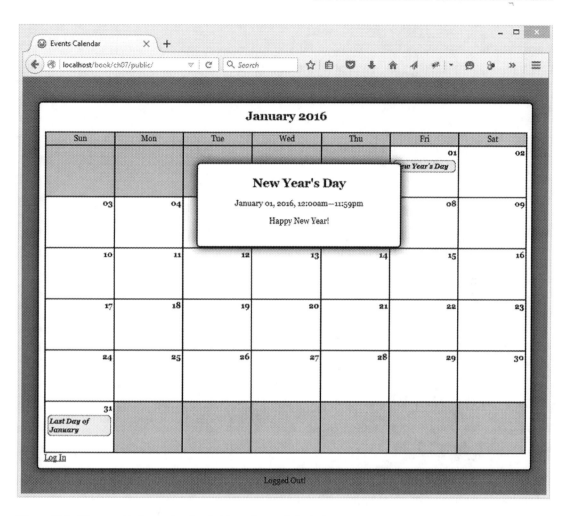

Figure 7-2. *The event information loaded into the modal window*

Adding a Close Button

As it stands right now, the only way to get rid of the modal window after clicking an event title is to reload the page. Of course, this isn't good enough, so you need to add a Close button.

To accomplish this, you need to create a new link and bind a click event handler to it that removes the modal window from the DOM. To give it a traditional Close button feel, use the multiplication symbol as its content (and the CSS in ajax.css adds the word "close" in front of it). Also, add an href attribute to make sure hovering over the link causes the mouse to behave as though the button is clickable.

Next, add a Close button by inserting the following bold code into init.js:

```
// Pulls up events in a modal window
$("body").on("click", "li>a", function(event){

        // Stops the link from loading view.php
        event.preventDefault();
```

```
        // Adds an "active" class to the link
        $(this).addClass("active");

        // Gets the query string from the link href
        var data = $(this)
                        .attr("href")
                        .replace(/.+?\?(.*)$/, "$1"),

        // Checks if the modal window exists and
        // selects it, or creates a new one
            modal = fx.initModal();

        // Creates a button to close the window
        $("<a>")
            .attr("href", "#")
            .addClass("modal-close-btn")
            .html("&times;")
            .click(function(event){
                        // Prevent the default action
                        event.preventDefault();

                        // Removes modal window
                        $(".modal-window")
                            .remove();
                })
            .appendTo(modal);

        // Loads the event data from the DB
        $.ajax({
            type: "POST",
            url: processFile,
            data: "action=event_view&" + data,
            success: function(data){
                    // Alert event data for now
                    modal.append(data);
            },
            error: function(msg) {
                    modal.append(msg);
            }
        });

    });
```

After saving the preceding code, load http://localhost/ and click an event title to see the new Close button (see Figure 7-3). Click the Close button to remove the modal window.

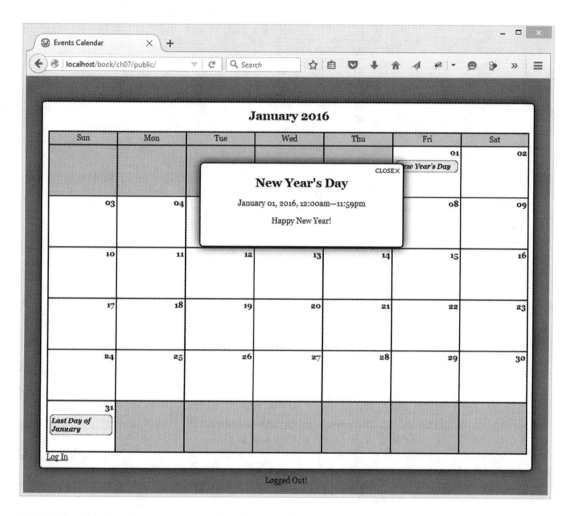

Figure 7-3. *The Close button is now visible in the modal window*

Adding Effects to the Creation and Destruction of the Modal Window

To give the modal window a little more style and polish, you'll add effects to make the box fade in when it's created and fade out when it's removed. Also, to help draw focus to the modal window when it's active, you'll add an overlay to the site that will darken everything but the modal window.

Fading Out the Modal Window

First, you need to add effects to fade out the modal window. This function will be triggered in several ways, some of which also trigger events; to handle this, you create a conditional statement that checks whether an event was triggered, and then prevents the default action if that's the case.

Next, remove the class active from all links, since none of them are in use when the modal window isn't visible.

Finally, you select and fade out the modal window using .fadeOut(). In the callback function of .fadeOut(), the modal window will be removed from the DOM entirely.

You add this function by inserting the following bold code in the fx object literal:

```
// Functions to manipulate the modal window
    fx = {

        // Checks for a modal window and returns it, or
        // else creates a new one and returns that
        "initModal" : function() {
                // If no elements are matched, the length
                // property will be 0
                if ( $(".modal-window").length==0 )
                {
                    // Creates a div, adds a class, and
                    // appends it to the body tag
                    return $("<div>")
                            .addClass("modal-window")
                            .appendTo("body");
                }
                else
                {
                    // Returns the modal window if one
                    // already exists in the DOM
                    return $(".modal-window");
                }
        },

        // Fades out the window and removes it from the DOM
        "boxout" : function(event) {
                // If an event was triggered by the element
                // that called this function, prevents the
                // default action from firing
                if ( event!=undefined )
                {
                    event.preventDefault();
                }

                // Removes the active class from all links
                $("a").removeClass("active");

                // Fades out the modal window, then removes
                // it from the DOM entirely
                $(".modal-window")
                    .fadeOut("slow", function() {
                            $(this).remove();
                        }
                    );
        }

    };
```

To incorporate this new function into the script, modify the click event handler for the Close button using the following bold code:

```
// Creates a button to close the window
$("<a>")
    .attr("href", "#")
    .addClass("modal-close-btn")
    .html("&times;")
    .click(function(event){
            // Removes modal window
            fx.boxout(event);
        })
    .appendTo(modal);
```

Save init.js and reload http://localhost/ in your browser. Click an event title to create a new modal window, and then click the Close button to watch the modal window fade out (see Figure 7-4).

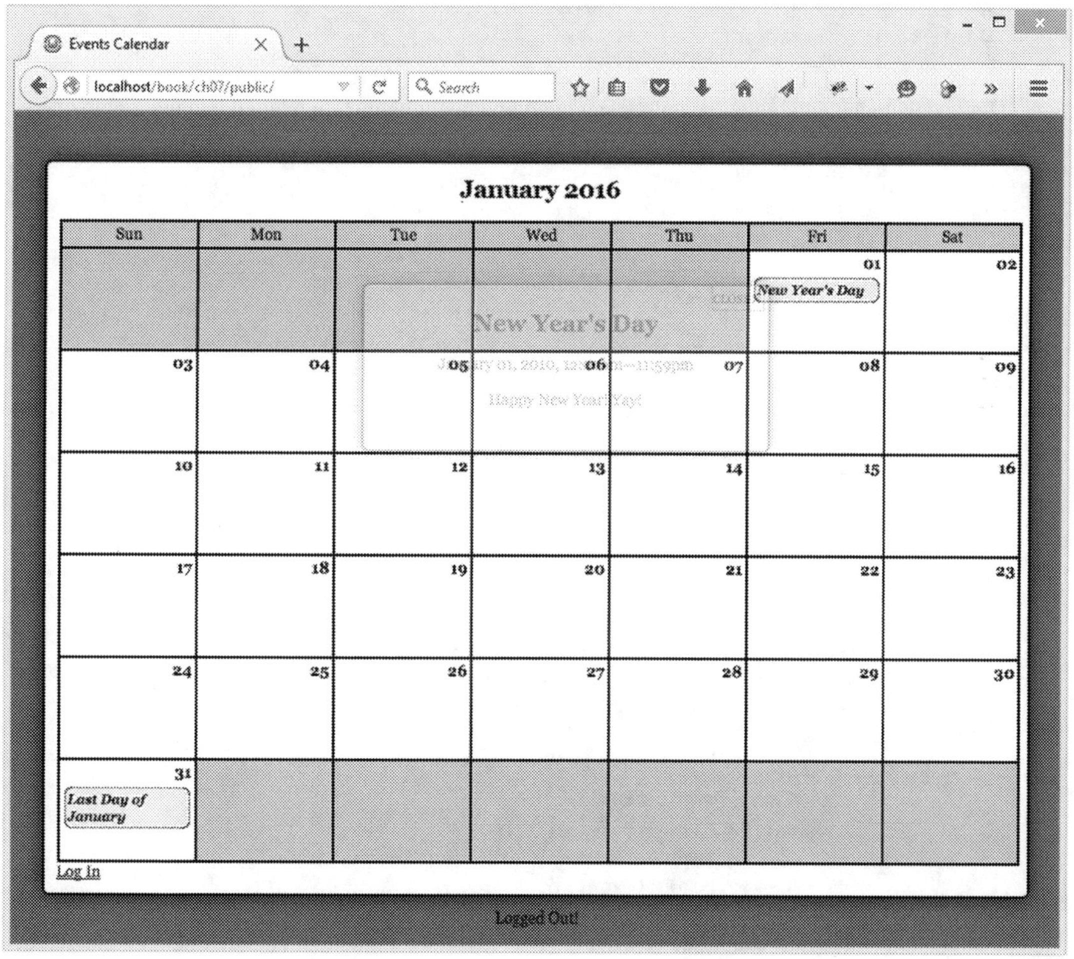

Figure 7-4. *The modal window mid-fade after the user clicks the Close button*

Adding an Overlay and Fade in the Modal Window

To add the overlay and fade in the modal window, you need to add another function to the fx object literal. It will be called boxin, and it will be called in the success callback of $.ajax() in the event title click handler. This function will accept two parameters: the data returned by ajax.inc.php (data) and the modal window object (modal).

First, the function will create a new div with a class of modal-overlay; next, it will hide the div and append it to the body element. To help usability, the overlay will also have a click handler attached to it that will remove the modal window when clicked by invoking fx.boxout().

Next, the function will hide the modal window and append the information stored in data to it. Finally, it will fade in both elements using .fadeIn().

You add this function to the fx object literal by inserting the code shown in bold:

```
// Functions to manipulate the modal window
    fx = {

        // Checks for a modal window and returns it, or
        // else creates a new one and returns that
        "initModal" : function() {
                // If no elements are matched, the length
                // property will be 0
                if ( $(".modal-window").length==0 )
                {
                    // Creates a div, adds a class, and
                    // appends it to the body tag
                    return $("<div>")
                            .addClass("modal-window")
                            .appendTo("body");
                }
                else
                {
                    // Returns the modal window if one
                    // already exists in the DOM
                    return $(".modal-window");
                }
        },

        // Adds the window to the markup and fades it in
        "boxin" : function(data, modal) {
                // Creates an overlay for the site, adds
                // a class and a click event handler, then
                // appends it to the body element
                $("<div>")
                    .hide()
                    .addClass("modal-overlay")
                    .click(function(event){
                            // Removes event
                            fx.boxout(event);
                    })
                    .appendTo("body");
```

```
    // Loads data into the modal window and
    // appends it to the body element
    modal
        .hide()
        .append(data)
        .appendTo("body");

    // Fades in the modal window and overlay
    $(".modal-window,.modal-overlay")
        .fadeIn("slow");
},

// Fades out the window and removes it from the DOM
"boxout" : function(event) {
    // If an event was triggered by the element
    // that called this function, prevents the
    // default action from firing
    if ( event!=undefined )
    {
        event.preventDefault();
    }

    // Removes the active class from all links
    $("a").removeClass("active");

    // Fades out the modal window, then removes
    // it from the DOM entirely
    $(".modal-window")
        .fadeOut("slow", function() {
                $(this).remove();
            }
        );
    }

};
```

Next, you need to modify the callback function that fires on a successful execution of $.ajax() when clicking an event title to call fx.boxin; you do so by adding the line of bold code that follows:

```
// Pulls up events in a modal window
$("body").on("click", "li>a", function(event){

    // Stops the link from loading view.php
    event.preventDefault();

    // Adds an "active" class to the link
    $(this).addClass("active");
```

```
        // Gets the query string from the link href
        var data = $(this)
                        .attr("href")
                        .replace(/.+?\?(.*)$/, "$1"),

        // Checks if the modal window exists and
        // selects it, or creates a new one
            modal = fx.initModal();

        // Creates a button to close the window
        $("<a>")
            .attr("href", "#")
            .addClass("modal-close-btn")
            .html("&times;")
            .click(function(event){
                        // Removes modal window
                        fx.boxout(event);
                })
            .appendTo(modal);

        // Loads the event data from the DB
        $.ajax({
                type: "POST",
                url: processFile,
                data: "action=event_view&" + data,
                success: function(data){
                        fx.boxin(data, modal);
                },
                error: function(msg) {
                        modal.append(msg);
                }
        });

    });
```

Save this code, reload `http://localhost/`, and click an event title to see the modal overlay and modal window fade in (see Figure 7-5).

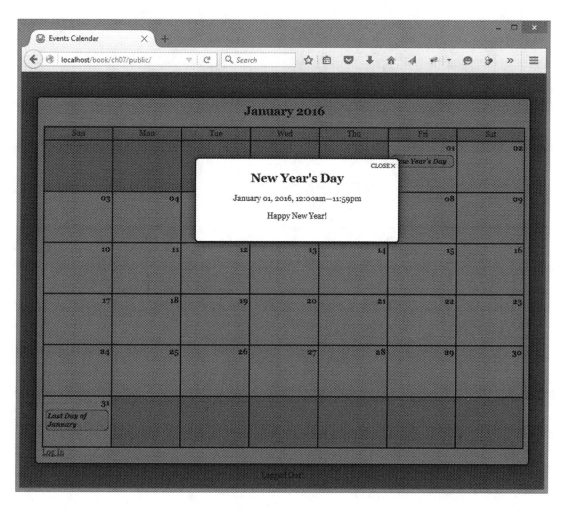

Figure 7-5. *The modal window with an overlay to help draw the focus*

You may have noticed that the modal window appears to flicker right as it's opened. This happens because fx.initModal() appends the modal window to the body element without hiding it. To correct this, add a call to .hide() in fx.initModal() using the following bold code:

```
// Functions to manipulate the modal window
    fx = {

        // Checks for a modal window and returns it, or
        // else creates a new one and returns that
        "initModal" : function() {
                // If no elements are matched, the length
                // property will be 0
```

```
          if ( $(".modal-window").length==0 )
          {
              // Creates a div, adds a class, and
              // appends it to the body tag
              return $("<div>")
                      .hide()
                      .addClass("modal-window")
                      .appendTo("body");
          }
          else
          {
              // Returns the modal window if one
              // already exists in the DOM
              return $(".modal-window");
          }
      },

  // Adds the window to the markup and fades it in
  "boxin" : function(data, modal) {
          // Code omitted for brevity
      },

  // Fades out the window and removes it from the DOM
  "boxout" : function(event) {
          // Code omitted for brevity
      }

};
```

Finally, clicking the Close button does not remove the overlay. To fade out and remove the overlay, simply modify the selector in fx.boxout() to include the class modal-overlay:

```
// Functions to manipulate the modal window
  fx = {

      // Checks for a modal window and returns it, or
      // else creates a new one and returns that
      "initModal" : function() {
              // Code omitted for brevity
          },

      // Adds the window to the markup and fades it in
      "boxin" : function(data, modal) {
              // Code omitted for brevity
          },

      // Fades out the window and removes it from the DOM
      "boxout" : function(event) {
              // If an event was triggered by the element
              // that called this function, prevents the
              // default action from firing
```

```
    if ( event!=undefined )
    {
        event.preventDefault();
    }

    // Removes the active class from all links
    $("a").removeClass("active");

    // Fades out the modal window and overlay,
    // then removes both from the DOM entirely
    $(".modal-window,.modal-overlay")
        .fadeOut("slow", function() {
                $(this).remove();
            }
        );
}

};
```

After making this change, reload `http://localhost/` and click an event title. The modal window and overlay will fade in, and clicking either the Close button or the overlay will cause the modal window and overlay to fade out.

Summary

In this chapter, you learned how to load event data dynamically with jQuery using the progressive enhancement technique. You also learned about event handling, basic effects, and even a little bit about regular expressions.

In the next chapter, you'll continue to add AJAX functionality by making the editing controls work via AJAX as well.

CHAPTER 8

■ ■ ■

Editing the Calendar with AJAX and jQuery

Now that your app can display event data without a page refresh, you can see the added convenience provided by AJAX in web applications. Historically, one of the biggest pitfalls of using web apps has been the fact that each action, no matter how small, usually required waiting for the page to refresh while the setting was saved. Web apps were convenient when a user needed access to his information on a shared computer, but the slow workflow was usually enough to make users lean toward desktop applications whenever possible.

However, with mainstream acceptance and use of AJAX, users can now make changes rapidly without constantly waiting for a page to reload. This makes web apps feel more like desktop apps, which also makes them much more appealing to users.

In this chapter, you'll learn to add scripts that make the editing controls for administrators function smoothly without requiring a page refresh for each action. The only action that will require a page refresh is the login, since this requires changes to the session.

■ **Note**   Before starting the exercises in this chapter, please log in to the calendar application. The default login relies on a username of `testuser` and a password of `admin`.

Opening the Event Creation Form

To start, you'll modify the script to let administrators add new events without a page refresh. Open `init.js` and select the button to add new events by its class (`admin`). Add a click event handler that prevents the default action and (for now) logs a message to confirm it fired properly:

```
"use strict";

jQuery(function($){

var processFile = "assets/inc/ajax.inc.php",
    fx = {
        "initModal" : function() {...},
        "boxin" : function(data, modal) {...},
        "boxout" : function(event) {...}
    }
```

261

```
// Pulls up events in a modal window
$("body").on("click", "li>a", function(event){...});

// Displays the edit form as a modal window
$("body").on("click", ".admin", function(event){

        // Prevents the form from submitting
        event.preventDefault();

        // Logs a message to prove the handler was triggered
        console.log( "Add a New Event button clicked!" );

    });

});
```

▓ **Note**   For the sake of brevity, all unchanged functions have been abbreviated, and comments have been omitted from code samples in this chapter. You can find the code at the book's Apress page, http://www.apress.com/9781484212318.

Save this code and refresh http://localhost/. Click the "Add a New Event" button, and you'll see the following result logged to the console:

```
Add a New Event button clicked!
```

Adding an AJAX Call to Load the Form

Next, create a variable to store an action that will be sent to the processing file. You're loading the editing and creation form, so set the action to event_edit.

Now you can call the $.ajax() function. This function is similar to the script for loading event data into the modal window; in fact, the only difference is in the data submitted and the way the return value is handled.

On a successful load, you hide the form and store a reference to it in the variable form. Next, you check for a modal window using fx.initModal() and fade it in using fx.boxin() with a null first argument. Finally, you append the form to the modal window, fade it in, and assign to it the class edit-form for easy selection later.

Add the following bold code to init.js to carry out these steps:

```
"use strict";

jQuery(function($){

var processFile = "assets/inc/ajax.inc.php",
    fx = {
        "initModal" : function() {...},
        "boxin" : function(data, modal) {...},
        "boxout" : function(event) {...}
    }
```

```
// Pulls up events in a modal window
$("body").on("click", "li>a", function(event){...});

// Displays the edit form as a modal window
$("body").on("click", ".admin", function(event){

        // Prevents the form from submitting
        event.preventDefault();

        // Loads the action for the processing file
        var action = "edit_event";

        // Loads the editing form and displays it
        $.ajax({
                type: "POST",
                url: processFile,
                data: "action="+action,
                success: function(data){
                        // Hides the form
                        var form = $(data).hide(),

                        // Make sure the modal window exists
                            modal = fx.initModal();

                        // Call the boxin function to create
                        // the modal overlay and fade it in
                        fx.boxin(null, modal);

                        // Load the form into the window,
                        // Fades in the content, and adds
                        // a class to the form
                        form
                            .appendTo(modal)
                            .addClass("edit-form")
                            .fadeIn("slow");
                },
                error: function(msg){
                    alert(msg);
                }
            });

    });

});
```

But you're not ready to run this code quite yet.

Modifying the AJAX Processing File to Load the Form

Before the preceding AJAX call will work, you need to modify the `ajax.inc.php` lookup array. Add a new array element that tells the script to create a new `Calendar` object, and then call the `displayForm()` method with the code shown in bold:

```php
<?php

declare(strict_types=1);

/*
 * Enable sessions if needed.
 * Avoid pesky warning if session already active.
 */
$status = session_status();
if ($status == PHP_SESSION_NONE){
    //There is no active session
    session_start();
}

/*
 * Include necessary files
 */
include_once '../../../sys/config/db-cred.inc.php';

/*
 * Define constants for config info
 */
foreach ( $C as $name => $val )
{
    define($name, $val);
}

/*
 * Create a lookup array for form actions
 */
define(ACTIONS, array(
        'event_view' => array(
                'object' => 'Calendar',
                'method' => 'displayEvent'
            ),
        'edit_event' => array(
                'object' => 'Calendar',
                'method' => 'displayForm'
            )
        )
    );
```

```
/*
 * Make sure the anti-CSRF token was passed and that the
 * requested action exists in the lookup array
 */
if ( isset(ACTIONS[$_POST['action']]) )
{
    $use_array = ACTIONS[$_POST['action']];
    $obj = new $use_array['object']($dbo);
    $method = $use_array['method'];

    /*
     * Check for an ID and sanitize it if found
     */
    if ( isset($_POST['event_id']) )
    {
        $id = (int) $_POST['event_id'];
    }
    else { $id = NULL; }

    echo $obj->$method($id);
}

function __autoload($class_name)
{
    $filename = '../../../sys/class/class.'
        . strtolower($class_name) . '.inc.php';
    if ( file_exists($filename) )
    {
        include_once $filename;
    }
}

?>
```

Now save the file, load http://localhost/, and click the "Add a New Event" button. A new modal window will fade in with the edit form inside (see Figure 8-1).

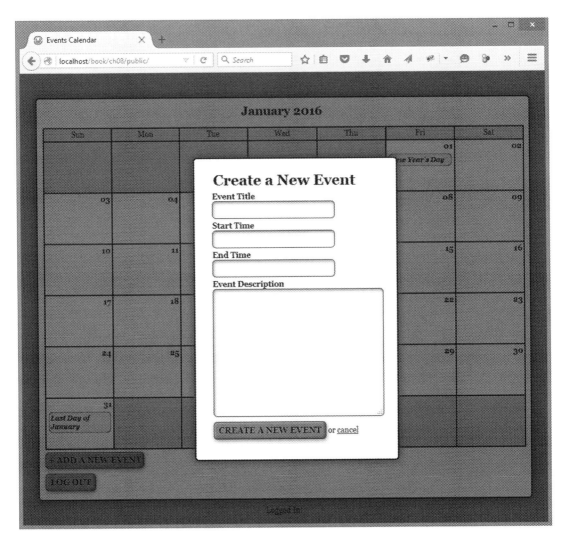

Figure 8-1. *The event creation form loaded in a modal window*

Making the Cancel Button Behave Like the Close Button

You may have noticed that the modal window doesn't contain a Close button when the form is displayed. However, the modal window does include a Cancel button that will refresh the page when clicked. Instead of adding more buttons to the window, you're simply going to make the Cancel button call the `fx.boxout()` method to close the window.

To accomplish this, use `.on()` to bind a click event handler to any link containing the word *cancel* inside a form with the `edit-form` class.

```
"use strict";

jQuery(function($){

var processFile = "assets/inc/ajax.inc.php",
    fx = {
        "initModal" : function() {...},
        "boxin" : function(data, modal) {...},
        "boxout" : function(event) {...}
    }

// Pulls up events in a modal window
$("body").on("click", "li>a", function(event){...});

// Displays the edit form as a modal window
$("body").on("click", ".admin", function(event){

// Make the cancel button on editing forms behave like the
// close button and fade out modal windows and overlays
$("body").on("click", ".edit-form a:contains(cancel)", function(event){
        fx.boxout(event);
    });

});
```

Save the file, reload http://localhost/, and click the "Add a New Event" button. After the modal window has loaded, click the Cancel link in the form. The modal window and overlay will fade out, just as they do when the Close button is clicked.

Saving New Events in the Database

To make the form work properly, you must now add a click event handler to the Submit button on the form. This handler will prevent the default form submission, and then it will use .serialize() to create a query string from the form inputs. It will then use the serialized data to submit the form via POST to ajax.inc.php.

Start by adding a new click handler to any inputs of type submit that exist in a form with the edit-form class. Using .on() ensures that dynamically created inputs will still be targeted by the handler. You can prevent the default action using event.preventDefault().

Do this by inserting the bold code into init.js:

```
"use strict";

jQuery(function($){

var processFile = "assets/inc/ajax.inc.php",
    fx = {
        "initModal" : function() {...},
        "boxin" : function(data, modal) {...},
        "boxout" : function(event) {...}
    }
```

```
// Pulls up events in a modal window
$("body").on("click", "li>a", function(event){...});

// Displays the edit form as a modal window
$("body").on("click", ".admin", function(event){

// Make the cancel button on editing forms behave like the
// close button and fade out modal windows and overlays
$("body").on("click", ".edit-form a:contains(cancel)", function(event){
        fx.boxout(event);
    });
```

```
// Edits events without reloading
$("body").on("click", ".edit-form input[type=submit]", function(event){

        // Prevents the default form action from executing
        event.preventDefault();

        // Logs a message to indicate the script is working
        console.log( "Form submission triggered!" );

    });

});
```

Next, save and reload the calendar in your browser. Click the "Add a New Event" button to bring up the modal window, and then click the "Create a New Event" button to submit the form. This outputs the following result to the console:

```
Form submission triggered!
```

Serializing the Form Data

To send the event data to the processing file, you need to convert the data to a query string. Fortunately, jQuery has a built-in method to do this called .serialize(). It will convert form inputs into a string of name-value pairs, separated by an ampersand (&).

Modify init.js to serialize the form data by selecting the parent form of the clicked input, and then serialize its data. Next, log the output to the console for now:

```
// Edits events without reloading
$("body").on("click", ".edit-form input[type=submit]", function(event){

        // Prevents the default form action from executing
        event.preventDefault();

        // Serializes the form data for use with $.ajax()
        var formData = $(this).parents("form").serialize();
```

```
// Logs a message to indicate the script is working
console.log( formData );
```

```
});
```

Save the preceding code and bring up the event creation form in your browser. Now enter the following test data:

- **Event Title:** Test Event

- **Event Start:** 2016-01-04 08:00:00

- **Event End:** 2016-01-04 10:00:00

- **Event Description:** This is a test description.

Click the "Create a New Event" button to submit the form and output the following to your console (the token value will vary):

```
event_title=Test+Event&event_start=2016-01-04+08%3A00%3A00&event_end=2016 ↩
-01-04+10%3A00%3A00&event_description=This+is+a+test+description.&event_id=&token= ↩
861e58daa0cfcf2c215f71d6f2bda1661e81c4c0&action=event_edit
```

Submitting the Serialized Form Data to the Processing File

Now that the form data is serialized, you're ready use $.ajax() to send the data to the processing file.

Use the POST method to submit the serialized data to ajax.inc.php, and then fade out the modal window and overlay using fx.boxout() on a successful submission. Also, log a confirmation message in the Firebug console and append the following bold code to init.js:

```
// Edits events without reloading
$("body").on("click", ".edit-form input[type=submit]", function(event){

        // Prevents the default form action from executing
        event.preventDefault();

        // Serializes the form data for use with $.ajax()
        var formData = $(this).parents("form").serialize();

        // Sends the data to the processing file
        $.ajax({
                type: "POST",
                url: processFile,
                data: formData,
                success: function(data) {
                    // Fades out the modal window
                    fx.boxout();

                    // Logs a message to the console
                    console.log( "Event saved!" );
                },
```

```
            error: function(msg) {
                alert(msg);
            }
        });

    });
```

At this point, the script is ready to save new events. But you're not ready to run this code quite yet. First, you need to modify ajax.inc.php to accept this data.

Modifying the AJAX Processing File to Handle New Submissions

Getting ajax.inc.php ready to accept submissions from the event editing form is as easy as adding a new element to the lookup array:

```php
<?php

declare(strict_types=1);

/*
 * Enable sessions if needed.
 * Avoid pesky warning if session already active.
 */
$status = session_status();
if ($status == PHP_SESSION_NONE){
    //There is no active session
    session_start();
}

/*
 * Include necessary files
 */
include_once '../../../sys/config/db-cred.inc.php';

/*
 * Define constants for config info
 */
foreach ( $C as $name => $val )
{
    define($name, $val);
}

/*
 * Create a lookup array for form actions
 */
define(ACTIONS, array(
        'event_view' => array(
                'object' => 'Calendar',
                'method' => 'displayEvent'
            ),
```

```
            'edit_event' => array(
                    'object' => 'Calendar',
                    'method' => 'displayForm'
                ),
            'event_edit' => array(
                    'object' => 'Calendar',
                    'method' => 'processForm'
                )
            )
        );

/*
 * Make sure the anti-CSRF token was passed and that the
 * requested action exists in the lookup array
 */
if ( isset(ACTIONS[$_POST['action']]) )
{
    $use_array = ACTIONS[$_POST['action']];
    $obj = new $use_array['object']($dbo);
    $method = $use_array['method'];

    /*
     * Check for an ID and sanitize it if found
     */
    if ( isset($_POST['event_id']) )
    {
        $id = (int) $_POST['event_id'];
    }
    else { $id = NULL; }

    echo $obj->$method($id);
}

function __autoload($class_name)
{
    $filename = '../../../sys/class/class.'
        . strtolower($class_name) . '.inc.php';
    if ( file_exists($filename) )
    {
        include_once $filename;
    }
}

?>
```

Save this file and reload http://localhost/. Next, click the "Add a New Event" button to bring up the form in a modal window, and then enter a new event with the following information:

- **Event Title:** Test Event

- **Event Start:** 2016-01-04 08:00:00

- **Event End:** 2016-01-04 10:00:00

- **Event Description:** This is a test description.

Now click the "Create a New Event" button; the modal window will fade out, and the following message will be logged into the console:

```
Event saved!
```

Note that the new event does not appear in the calendar unless the page is refreshed. This may confuse users, so in the next section you'll modify the app to add newly created events into the calendar after a successful save.

Adding Events Without Refreshing

Adding the new events to the calendar is fairly involved; after the event is saved, you need to take the following steps.

1. Deserialize the form data.

2. Create date objects for both the currently displayed month and the new event.

3. Make sure the month and year match up for the new event.

4. Get the new event's ID.

5. Determine on what day of the month the event falls.

6. Generate a new link with the proper event data and insert it into the corresponding calendar day.

This functionality will be enclosed in a new addition to the fx object literal called addevent, which will accept the returned data from ajax.inc.php (data), as well as the serialized form data (formData).

To begin, modify the fx object literal in init.js by inserting the following bold code:

```
"use strict";

jQuery(function($){

var processFile = "assets/inc/ajax.inc.php",
    fx = {
        "initModal" : function() {...},
        "boxin" : function(data, modal) {...},
        "boxout" : function(event) {...},

        // Adds a new event to the markup after saving
        "addevent" : function(data, formData){
            // Code to add the event goes here
        }
    };

$("body").on("click", "li>a", function(event){...});

$("body").on("click", ".admin", function(event){...});

$("body").on("click", ".edit-form a:contains(cancel)", function(event){...});

$("body").on("click", ".edit-form input[type=submit]", function(event){...});
```

Deserializing the Form Data

The first step when adding a new event is to deserialize the form data. Because this action can stand alone, you'll handle this step by creating an additional function in the fx object literal called deserialize that accepts a string (str):

```
fx = {
    "initModal" : function() {...},
    "boxin" : function(data, modal) {...},
    "boxout" : function(event) {...},

    // Adds a new event to the markup after saving
    "addevent" : function(data, formData){
            // Code to add the event goes here
        },

    // Deserializes the query string and returns
    // an event object
    "deserialize" : function(str){
            // Deserialize data here
        }
};
```

As you learned earlier in this book, a serialized string is a series of name-value pairs connected by an equals sign (=) and separated by ampersands (&). An example of two serialized name-value pairs might look like this:

```
name1=value1&name2=value2
```

To deserialize these values, start by splitting the string at each ampersand using the native JavaScript function, .split(). This function breaks the string into an array of name-value pairs:

```
Array
(
    0 => "name1=value1",
    1 => "name2=value2"
)
```

Next, you need to loop through the array of name-value pairs. Inside this loop, split the pairs at the equals sign and store the array in a variable called pairs. This means each name-value pair is split into an array, with the first index containing the name and the second index containing the value. The array follows this format:

```
Array
(
    0 => "name1",
    1 => "value1"
)
```

Store these values in variables called key and val, respectively, and then store them in a new object called entry as properties.

273

When the loop is completed, return the deserialized data object.

Next, add the following bold code inside fx.deserialize:

```
fx = {
    "initModal" : function() {...},
    "boxin" : function(data, modal) {...},
    "boxout" : function(event) {...},

    // Adds a new event to the markup after saving
    "addevent" : function(data, formData){
            // Code to add the event goes here
        },

    // Deserializes the query string and returns
    // an event object
    "deserialize" : function(str){
            // Breaks apart each name-value pair
            var data = str.split("&"),

            // Declares variables for use in the loop
                pairs=[], entry={}, key, val;

            // Loops through each name-value pair
            for (var x in data )
            {
                // Splits each pair into an array
                pairs = data[x].split("=");

                // The first element is the name
                key = pairs[0];

                // Second element is the value
                val = pairs[1];

                // Stores each value as an object property
                entry[key] = val;
            }
            return entry;
        }
};
```

Decoding Any URL-Encoded Characters in Form Values

Before fx.deserialize is officially ready for use, you must first modify it to decode any URL-encoded entities. When data is serialized, string values are encoded so that they can be passed in the query string. This means that the string "I'm testing & logging!" will be converted to the following when it is serialized:

```
I'm+testing+%26+logging!
```

To reverse this, replace all plus signs (+) with spaces using the regular expression /\+/g; this expression matches only plus signs. The g following the expression's closing delimiter makes the regular expression search globally, so more than one match will be replaced.

Next, you need to use the native, stand-alone JavaScript function, decodeURIComponent(). Create a new function in fx called urldecode and insert the following code:

```
fx = {
    "initModal" : function() {...},
    "boxin" : function(data, modal) {...},
    "boxout" : function(event) {...},

    // Adds a new event to the markup after saving
    "addevent" : function(data, formData){
            // Code to add the event goes here
        },

    // Deserializes the query string and returns
    // an event object
    "deserialize" : function(str){
            // Breaks apart each name-value pair
            var data = str.split("&"),

            // Declares variables for use in the loop
                pairs=[], entry={}, key, val;

            // Loops through each name-value pair
            for ( x in data )
            {
                // Splits each pair into an array
                pairs = data[x].split("=");

                // The first element is the name
                key = pairs[0];

                // Second element is the value
                val = pairs[1];

                // Stores each value as an object property
                entry[key] = val;
            }
            return entry;
        },

    // Decodes a query string value
    "urldecode" : function(str) {
            // Converts plus signs to spaces
            var converted = str.replace(/\+/g, ' ');

            // Converts any encoded entities back
            return decodeURIComponent(converted);
        }
};
```

Next, you implement fx.urldecode in fx.deserialize by adding the following code in bold:

```
fx = {
    "initModal" : function() {...},
    "boxin" : function(data, modal) {...},
    "boxout" : function(event) {...},

    // Adds a new event to the markup after saving
    "addevent" : function(data, formData){
            // Code to add the event goes here
        },

    // Deserializes the query string and returns
    // an event object
    "deserialize" : function(str){
            // Breaks apart each name-value pair
            var data = str.split("&"),

            // Declares variables for use in the loop
                pairs=[], entry={}, key, val;

            // Loops through each name-value pair
            for ( x in data )
            {
                // Splits each pair into an array
                pairs = data[x].split("=");

                // The first element is the name
                key = pairs[0];

                // Second element is the value
                val = pairs[1];

                // Reverses the URL encoding and stores
                // each value as an object property
                entry[key] = fx.urldecode(val);
            }
            return entry;
        },

    "urldecode" : function(str) {...}
};
```

Bringing It All Together

With fx.deserialize and fx.urldecode in place, you can now modify fx.addevent by adding a variable (entry) to store the deserialized event data:

```
fx = {
    "initModal" : function() {...},
    "boxin" : function(data, modal) {...},
    "boxout" : function(event) {...},
```

```
    // Adds a new event to the markup after saving
    "addevent" : function(data, formData){
            // Converts the query string to an object
            var entry = fx.deserialize(formData);
        },

    "deserialize" : function(str){...},
    "urldecode" : function(str) {...}
};
```

Creating Date Objects

Because only events created for the month being displayed should be added to the calendar, you need to determine what month and year is being displayed, as well as the month and year that the event occurs.

▒ **Note**   For this step you'll take advantage of JavaScript's built-in Date object, which provides methods to simplify many date-related operations. For a full explanation of all available methods associated with the Date object, visit http://w3schools.com/jsref/jsref_obj_date.asp.

Modifying the Calendar Class with an ID

To generate a Date object for the currently displayed month, you need to add an ID to the h2 element that displays the month above the calendar. To ensure cross-browser compatibility, modify the buildCalendar() method in the Calendar class with the following bold code:

```
public function buildCalendar()
{
    /*
     * Determine the calendar month and create an array of
     * weekday abbreviations to label the calendar columns
     */
    $cal_month = date('F Y', strtotime($this->_useDate));
    $cal_id = date('Y-m', strtotime($this->_useDate));
    define('WEEKDAYS', array('Sun', 'Mon', 'Tue',
            'Wed', 'Thu', 'Fri', 'Sat'));

    /*
     * Add a header to the calendar markup
     */
    $html = "\n\t<h2 id=\"month-$cal_id\">$cal_month</h2>";
    for ( $d=0, $labels=NULL; $d<7; ++$d )
    {
        $labels .= "\n\t\t<li>" . WEEKDAYS[$d] . "</li>";
    }
    $html .= "\n\t<ul class=\"weekdays\">"
        . $labels . "\n\t</ul>";

    // For brevity, the remainder of this method has been omitted
}
```

░ **Note**   Using the "month-" prefix for the ID means that you stay compliant with W3 standards, which state that element IDs must begin with a letter.

Building Date Objects in JavaScript

To ensure that the new event falls within the current month, create two empty Date objects: one for the current month and one for the new event.

To set the value of the current month's Date object, retrieve the ID attribute from the H2 element using the .attr() method, split it at the hyphens, and store it in the cdata variable.

For the new event, split the value of entry.event_start at the spaces and take the first array element (which is the date in the format of YYYY-MM-DD) and store it in a variable called date. Next, split the information at the hyphens and store the array in a variable called edata.

To set the Date objects, use the data from cdata and edata to set the date in cal and event, respectively. Finally, modify fx.addevent with the following bold code:

```
fx = {
    "initModal" : function() {...},
    "boxin" : function(data, modal) {...},
    "boxout" : function(event) {...},

    // Adds a new event to the markup after saving
    "addevent" : function(data, formData){
            // Converts the query string to an object
            var entry = fx.deserialize(formData),

            // Makes a date object for current month
                cal = new Date(NaN),

            // Makes a date object for the new event
                event = new Date(NaN),

            // Extracts the calendar month from the H2 ID
                cdata = $("h2").attr("id").split('-'),

            // Extracts the event day, month, and year
                date = entry.event_start.split(' ')[0],

            // Splits the event data into pieces
                edata = date.split('-');

            // Sets the date for the calendar date object
            cal.setFullYear(cdata[1], cdata[2], 1);

            // Sets the date for the event date object
            event.setFullYear(edata[0], edata[1], edata[2]);
        },

    "deserialize" : function(str){...},
    "urldecode" : function(str) {...}
};
```

Fixing Time Zone Inconsistencies

You aren't passing a time or time zone to the Date object, so that object will default to midnight Greenwich Mean Time (00:00:00 GMT). This can cause your dates to behave unexpectedly for users in different time zones. To address this problem, you need to adjust the date by the time zone offset using two built-in Date object methods: .setMinutes() and .getTimezoneOffset().

The return value of .getTimezoneOffset() is the difference in the number of minutes between GMT and the user's time zone. For instance, the return value of .getTimezoneOffset() in Mountain Standard Time (-0700) is 420.

Using .setMinutes(), you can add the value of the time zone offset to the Date object, which will return the date to midnight on the given day, no matter what time zone the user is in.

You can make this adjustment using the following bold code:

```
fx = {
    "initModal" : function() {...},
    "boxin" : function(data, modal) {...},
    "boxout" : function(event) {...},

    // Adds a new event to the markup after saving
    "addevent" : function(data, formData){
            // Converts the query string to an object
            var entry = fx.deserialize(formData),

            // Makes a date object for current month
                cal = new Date(NaN),

            // Makes a date object for the new event
                event = new Date(NaN),

            // Extracts the event day, month, and year
                date = entry.event_start.split(' ')[0],

            // Splits the event data into pieces
                edata = date.split('-'),

            // Extracts the calendar month from the H2 ID
                cdata = $("h2").attr("id").split('-');

            // Sets the date for the calendar date object
            cal.setFullYear(cdata[1], cdata[2], 1);

            // Sets the date for the event date object
            event.setFullYear(edata[0], edata[1], edata[2]);

            // Since the date object is created using
            // GMT, then adjusted for the local time zone,
            // adjust the offset to ensure a proper date
            event.setMinutes(event.getTimezoneOffset());
    },

    "deserialize" : function(str){...},
    "urldecode" : function(str) {...}
};
```

Ensuring the Event Occurs in the Current Month

Your next step is to set up a conditional statement that ensures that only events that belong on the calendar are appended. If both the year and month match between the current calendar month and the event date, you can extract the day of the month using the Date object's `.getDay()` method. To work properly with the next step, which adds leading zeroes to single-digit dates, you also need to convert this value to a string, which is accomplished by passing the value to `String()`.

The day of the month needs to have a leading zero to properly match the calendar. For example, if the returned date is only one digit, you prepend a leading zero to the date. Do this by inserting the following bold code:

```
fx = {
    "initModal" : function() {...},
    "boxin" : function(data, modal) {...},
    "boxout" : function(event) {...},

    // Adds a new event to the markup after saving
    "addevent" : function(data, formData){
            // Converts the query string to an object
            var entry = fx.deserialize(formData),

            // Makes a date object for current month
                cal = new Date(NaN),

            // Makes a date object for the new event
                event = new Date(NaN),

            // Extracts the event day, month, and year
                date = entry.event_start.split(' ')[0],

            // Splits the event data into pieces
                edata = date.split('-'),

            // Extracts the calendar month from the H2 ID
                cdata = $("h2").attr("id").split('-');

            // Sets the date for the calendar date object
            cal.setFullYear(cdata[1], cdata[2], 1);

            // Sets the date for the event date object
            event.setFullYear(edata[0], edata[1], edata[2]);

            // Since the date object is created using
            // GMT, then adjusted for the local timezone,
            // adjust the offset to ensure a proper date
            event.setMinutes(event.getTimezoneOffset());

            // If the year and month match, start the process
            // of adding the new event to the calendar
            if ( cal.getFullYear()==event.getFullYear()
                    && cal.getMonth()==event.getMonth() )
```

```
          {
              // Gets the day of the month for event
              var day = String(event.getDate());

              // Adds a leading zero to 1-digit days
              day = day.length==1 ? "0"+day : day;
          }
      },

    "deserialize" : function(str){...},
    "urldecode" : function(str) {...}
};
```

Appending the Event to the Calendar

You're finally ready to append the new event to the calendar. To do so, create a new anchor element, hide it, set its href attribute, and use the title of the event as the link text.

Next, set a one-second delay using .delay(1000) and fade in the new event.

You can implement this by adding the following code shown in bold:

```
fx = {
    "initModal" : function() {...},
    "boxin" : function(data, modal) {...},
    "boxout" : function(event) {...},

    // Adds a new event to the markup after saving
    "addevent" : function(data, formData){
            // Converts the query string to an object
            var entry = fx.deserialize(formData),

            // Makes a date object for current month
                cal = new Date(NaN),

            // Makes a date object for the new event
                event = new Date(NaN),

            // Extracts the event day, month, and year
                date = entry.event_start.split(' ')[0],

            // Splits the event data into pieces
                edata = date.split('-'),

            // Extracts the calendar month from the H2 ID
                cdata = $("h2").attr("id").split('-');

            // Sets the date for the calendar date object
            cal.setFullYear(cdata[1], cdata[2], 1);

            // Sets the date for the event date object
            event.setFullYear(edata[0], edata[1], edata[2]);
```

```
                    // Since the date object is created using
                    // GMT, then adjusted for the local timezone,
                    // adjust the offset to ensure a proper date
                    event.setMinutes(event.getTimezoneOffset());

                    // If the year and month match, start the process
                    // of adding the new event to the calendar
                    if ( cal.getFullYear()==event.getFullYear()
                            && cal.getMonth()==event.getMonth() )
                    {
                        // Gets the day of the month for event
                        var day = String(event.getDate());

                        // Adds a leading zero to 1-digit days
                        day = day.length==1 ? "0"+day : day;

                        // Adds the new date link
                        $("<a>")
                            .hide()
                            .attr("href", "view.php?event_id="+data)
                            .text(entry.event_title)
                            .insertAfter($("strong:contains("+day+")"))
                            .delay(1000)
                            .fadeIn("slow");
                    }
                },

        "deserialize" : function(str){...},
        "urldecode" : function(str) {...}
}
```

■ **Note**   The data variable is undefined as of right now. You'll remedy this in the next section.

Now, back in the click event handler for the Submit button, modify the success callback of the $.ajax()
function to execute fx.addevent() by using the following bold code:

```
// Edits events without reloading
$("body").on("click", ".edit-form input[type=submit]", function (event){

        // Prevents the default form action from executing
        event.preventDefault();

        // Serializes the form data for use with $.ajax()
        var formData = $(this).parents("form").serialize();
```

```
// Sends the data to the processing file
$.ajax({
        type: "POST",
        url: processFile,
        data: formData,
        success: function(data) {
            // Fades out the modal window
            fx.boxout();

            // Adds the event to the calendar
            fx.addevent(data, formData);
        },
        error: function(msg) {
            alert(msg);
        }
    });

});
```

Save this file and reload http://localhost/. Bring up the event creation form and create a new event with the following information:

- **Event Title:** Addition Test

- **Event Start:** 2016-01-09 12:00:00

- **Event End:** 2016-01-09 14:00:00

- **Event Description:** This is a test of the dynamic addition of new events to the calendar.

Submitting the form causes the modal window to fade out; a second later, the new event title will fade in on the calendar in the proper place (see Figure 8-2).

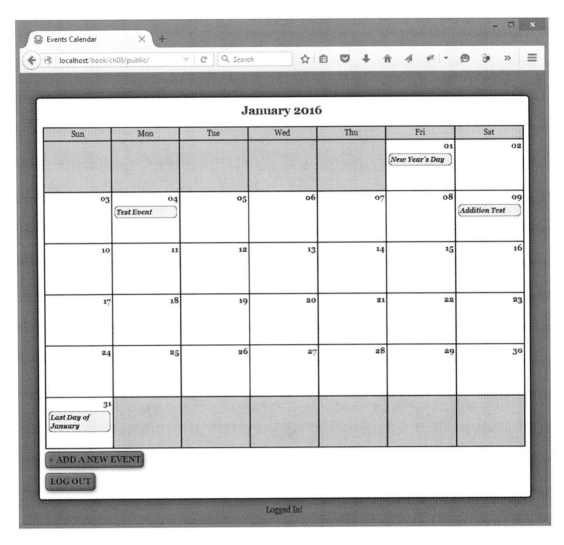

Figure 8-2. *The calendar after the new event is created*

Getting the New Event's Correct ID

Currently, a new event is not viewable without a page refresh after it is created. To see this, try immediately clicking the newly created "Addition Test" link you just added. If you have been following the development since Chapter 4, you will get the rather surprising result shown in Figure 8-3. (If you have not been following along, you may get a different result, such as an empty dialog box, or even a fatal error!)

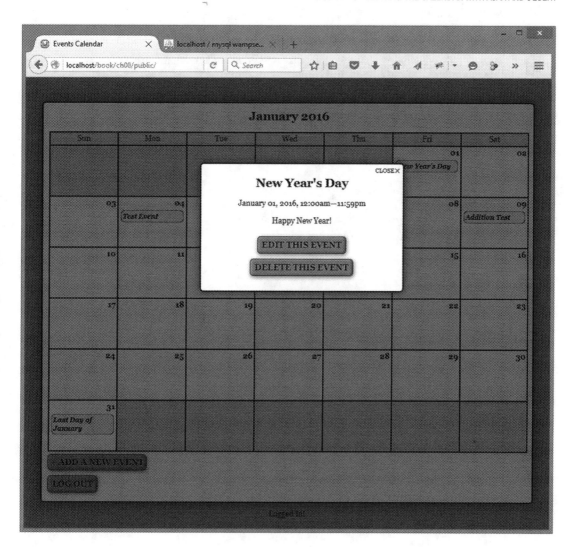

Figure 8-3. *Something has gone terribly wrong!*

You may very well ask what on Earth has gone wrong here. Well, no need to panic. If you open the file /sys/class/class.calendar.inc.php and examine the processForm() method, you'll notice that upon successful completion, it returns TRUE. Then TRUE was interpreted as an event ID, cast to the integer 1, and so New Year's Day was fetched. (If you've been following the development, this event will have ID equal to 1.)

Modifying the Event Creation Method to Return New Event IDs

To fix this new event ID problem, you only need to make one small adjustment in the processForm()
method. Inside this method, modify the return command to output the ID of the last inserted row using
PDO's lastInsertId() method:

```
public function processForm()
{
    /*
     * Exit if the action isn't set properly
     */
    if ( $_POST['action']!='event_edit' )
    {
        return "The method processForm was accessed incorrectly";
    }

    /*
     * Escape data from the form
     */
    $title = htmlentities($_POST['event_title'], ENT_QUOTES);
    $desc = htmlentities($_POST['event_description'], ENT_QUOTES);
    $start = htmlentities($_POST['event_start'], ENT_QUOTES);
    $end = htmlentities($_POST['event_end'], ENT_QUOTES);

    /*
     * If no event ID passed, create a new event
     */
    if ( empty($_POST['event_id']) )
    {
        $sql = "INSERT INTO `events`
                    (`event_title`, `event_desc`, `event_start`,
                        `event_end`)
                VALUES
                    (:title, :description, :start, :end)";
    }

    /*
     * Update the event if it's being edited
     */
    else
    {
        /*
         * Cast the event ID as an integer for security
         */
        $id = (int) $_POST['event_id'];
        $sql = "UPDATE `events`
                SET
                    `event_title`=:title,
                    `event_desc`=:description,
                    `event_start`=:start,
                    `event_end`=:end
                WHERE `event_id`=$id";
    }
```

```
    /*
     * Execute the create or edit query after binding the data
     */
    try
    {
        $stmt = $this->db->prepare($sql);
        $stmt->bindParam(":title", $title, PDO::PARAM_STR);
        $stmt->bindParam(":description", $desc, PDO::PARAM_STR);
        $stmt->bindParam(":start", $start, PDO::PARAM_STR);
        $stmt->bindParam(":end", $end, PDO::PARAM_STR);
        $stmt->execute();
        $stmt->closeCursor();

        /*
         * Returns the ID of the event
         */
        return $this->db->lastInsertId();
    }
    catch ( Exception $e )
    {
        return $e->getMessage();
    }
}
```

After making the preceding change, save this file and reload http://localhost/ in your browser. Next, create a new event with the following information:

- **Event Title:** ID Test

- **Event Start:** 2016-01-06 12:00:00

- **Event End:** 2016-01-06 16:00:00

- **Event Description:** This event should be immediately viewable after creation.

Now save the event, and the title will appear on the calendar. Click the title, and the event will load in a modal window (see Figure 8-4).

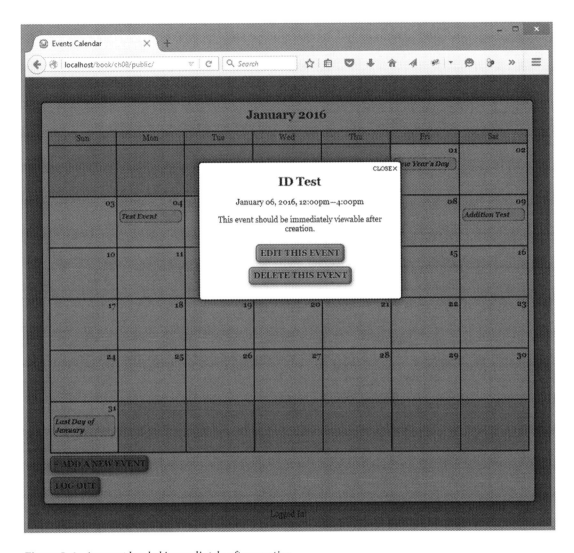

Figure 8-4. *An event loaded immediately after creation*

Editing Events in a Modal Window

In its current state, your app is only a short ways away from allowing users to edit events from the modal window as well. The existing click event handler for loading the event creation form will also work for event editing with only a little modification.

To start, expand the selector to include any element with a class admin; you can accomplish this by including the following bold code:

```
// Displays the edit form as a modal window
$("body").on("click", ".admin-options form,.admin", function(event){

        // Prevents the form from submitting
        event.preventDefault();
```

```
        // Loads the action for the processing file
        var action = "edit_event";

        // Loads the editing form and displays it
        $.ajax({
                type: "POST",
                url: processFile,
                data: "action="+action,
                success: function(data){
                        // Hides the form
                        var form = $(data).hide(),

                        // Make sure the modal window exists
                            modal = fx.initModal();

                        // Call the boxin function to create
                        // the modal overlay and fade it in
                        fx.boxin(null, modal);

                        // Load the form into the window,
                        // fades in the content, and adds
                        // a class to the form
                        form
                            .appendTo(modal)
                            .addClass("edit-form")
                            .fadeIn("slow");
                },
                error: function(msg){
                    alert(msg);
                }
        });
});
```

Determining the Form Action

In the editing controls displayed for individual events, the button names describe the action taken by the button (e.g., edit_event for the "Edit This Event" button and delete_event for the "Delete This Event" button). These buttons will be used by ajax.inc.php as the action for the submission.

Because the event creation button doesn't have a button name, you need to keep a default value (edit_event).

To access the name of the clicked button, you use a property of the event object called target. This property contains a reference to the element that triggered the event. Use jQuery to select the event target and use .attr() to retrieve its name.

Now modify the event handler using the following bold code:

```
// Displays the edit form as a modal window
$("body").on("click", ".admin-options form,.admin", function(event){

        // Prevents the form from submitting
        event.preventDefault();
```

```
// Sets the action for the form submission
var action = $(event.target).attr("name") || "edit_event";

// Loads the editing form and displays it
$.ajax({
        type: "POST",
        url: processFile,
        data: "action="+action,
        success: function(data){
                // Hides the form
                var form = $(data).hide(),

                // Make sure the modal window exists
                    modal = fx.initModal();

                // Call the boxin function to create
                // the modal overlay and fade it in
                fx.boxin(null, modal);

                // Load the form into the window,
                // fades in the content, and adds
                // a class to the form
                form
                    .appendTo(modal)
                    .addClass("edit-form")
                    .fadeIn("slow");
        },
        error: function(msg){
            alert(msg);
        }
    });
});
```

Storing the Event ID if One Exists

Next, the event ID needs to be extracted, assuming it's available. To find this value, use the event.target property again, but this time look for the sibling element with the name event_id, and then store the value of this in a variable called id. You add this to the event handler using the following bold code:

```
// Displays the edit form as a modal window
$("body").on("click", ".admin-options form,.admin", function(event){

        // Prevents the form from submitting
        event.preventDefault();

        // Sets the action for the form submission
        var action = $(event.target).attr("name") || "edit_event",
```

```
    // Saves the value of the event_id input
        id = $(event.target)
                .siblings("input[name=event_id]")
                    .val();

    // Loads the editing form and displays it
    $.ajax({
            type: "POST",
            url: processFile,
            data: "action="+action,
            success: function(data){
                    // Hides the form
                    var form = $(data).hide(),

                    // Make sure the modal window exists
                        modal = fx.initModal();

                    // Call the boxin function to create
                    // the modal overlay and fade it in
                    fx.boxin(null, modal);

                    // Load the form into the window,
                    // fades in the content, and adds
                    // a class to the form
                    form
                        .appendTo(modal)
                        .addClass("edit-form")
                        .fadeIn("slow");
            },
            error: function(msg){
                alert(msg);
            }
        });
});
```

Adding the Event ID to the Query String

With the ID stored in the `id` variable, you can now append the value to the query string for submission to `ajax.inc.php`.

Check whether `id` is undefined first, and then create an `event_id` name-value pair. Next, attach the data to the query string using the following bold code:

```
// Displays the edit form as a modal window
$("body").on("click", ".admin-options form,.admin", function(event){

    // Prevents the form from submitting
    event.preventDefault();

    // Sets the action for the form submission
    var action = $(event.target).attr("name") || "edit_event",
```

```
    // Saves the value of the event_id input
        id = $(event.target)
                .siblings("input[name=event_id]")
                    .val();

    // Creates an additional param for the ID if set
    id = ( id!=undefined ) ? "&event_id="+id : "";

    // Loads the editing form and displays it
    $.ajax({
            type: "POST",
            url: processFile,
            data: "action="+action+id,
            success: function(data){
                    // Hides the form
                    var form = $(data).hide(),

                    // Make sure the modal window exists
                        modal = fx.initModal();

                    // Call the boxin function to create
                    // the modal overlay and fade it in
                    fx.boxin(null, modal);

                    // Load the form into the window,
                    // fades in the content, and adds
                    // a class to the form
                    form
                        .appendTo(modal)
                        .addClass("edit-form")
                        .fadeIn("slow");
            },
            error: function(msg){
                alert(msg);
            }
        });
});
```

Removing Event Data from the Modal Window

To replace the content of the modal window with the editing form, you must first remove the event display information.

Where you've called fx.initModal() in the success handler, select all children that are not the Close button and remove them. After removing them, call .end() to revert back to the original selection of the modal window. (After calling children, the jQuery object only references the child elements you just removed.)

You can accomplish this by adding the following bold code:

```
// Displays the edit form as a modal window
$("body").on("click", ".admin-options form,.admin", function(event){
        // Prevents the form from submitting
        event.preventDefault();

        // Sets the action for the form submission
        var action = $(event.target).attr("name") || "edit_event",

        // Saves the value of the event_id input
            id = $(event.target)
                    .siblings("input[name=event_id]")
                        .val();

        // Creates an additional param for the ID if set
        id = ( id!=undefined ) ? "&event_id="+id : "";

        // Loads the editing form and displays it
        $.ajax({
                type: "POST",
                url: processFile,
                data: "action="+action+id,
                success: function(data){
                        // Hides the form
                        var form = $(data).hide(),

                        // Make sure the modal window exists
                            modal = fx.initModal()
                                .children(":not(.modal-close-btn)")
                                    .remove()
                                    .end();

                        // Call the boxin function to create
                        // the modal overlay and fade it in
                        fx.boxin(null, modal);

                        // Load the form into the window,
                        // fades in the content, and adds
                        // a class to the form
                        form
                            .appendTo(modal)
                            .addClass("edit-form")
                            .fadeIn("slow");
                },
                error: function(msg){
                    alert(msg);
                }
        });
    });
```

After saving this file and reloading `http://localhost/` in your browser, click the New Year's Day event title to bring up the event description. Inside the modal window, click the "Edit This Event" button; this causes the event description to disappear, and the editing form will fade in with the data for the entry loaded into the form for editing (see Figure 8-5).

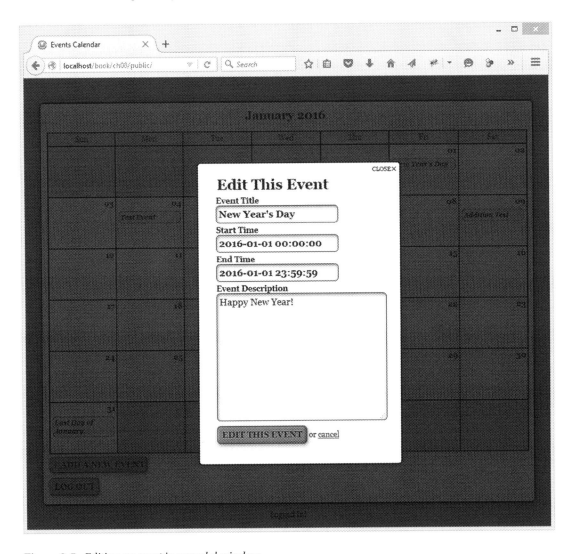

Figure 8-5. *Editing an event in a modal window*

Ensuring Only New Events Are Added to the Calendar

If you make an edit to the New Year's Day event and save it, an extra event title will be appended to the calendar (see Figure 8-6).

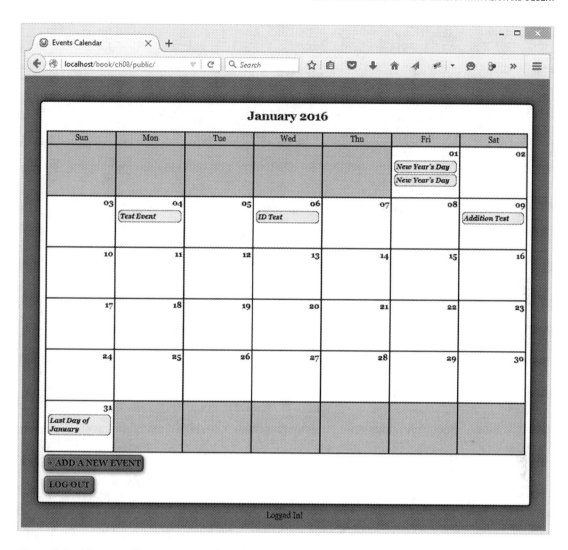

Figure 8-6. *After you edit an event, its title is duplicated*

If you refresh the page, you will eliminate the duplicate.

To prevent this duplicate problem, you need to add an additional tweak to the form submission click handler. Because events being edited will have their ID loaded in the editing form's hidden input named event_id, you can check for a length in the input's value. If the length is not zero, don't call fx.addevent(). Insert the following bold code to make this check:

```
// Edits events without reloading
$("body").on("click", ".edit-form input[type=submit]", function (event){

        // Prevents the default form action from executing
        event.preventDefault();
```

```
        // Serializes the form data for use with $.ajax()
        var formData = $(this).parents("form").serialize();

        // Sends the data to the processing file
        $.ajax({
                type: "POST",
                url: processFile,
                data: formData,
                success: function(data) {
                    // Fades out the modal window
                    fx.boxout();

                    // If this is a new event, adds it to
                    // the calendar
                    if ( $("[name=event_id]").val().length==0 )
                    {
                        fx.addevent(data, formData);
                    }
                },
                error: function(msg) {
                    alert(msg);
                }
        });

    });
```

You're very nearly done with the event editing functionality. However, you may have noticed one remaining issue. If the event *title* happens to be changed, then the new title does not appear without a page refresh. (Try this now if you haven't already.) Fortunately, you can fix this easily enough. You only need to compare the title appearing on the main calendar page with the (possibly) different title contained in the form at the time of submission.

Insert the following bold code to implement this logic:

```
// Edits events without reloading
$("body").on("click", ".edit-form input[type=submit]", function (event){

    // Prevents the default form action from executing
    event.preventDefault();

    // If editing an existing event, need to pay attention to title.
    if ( $(this).attr("name")=="event_submit" && $(".active").length > 0 )
    {
        // Need to check if the event title has been changed.
        // Here's the title that's on the main calendar page.
        var oldTitle = $(".active")[0].innerHTML;

        // Here we fish out the (possibly) different title from the form data.
        var formArray = $(this).parents("form").serializeArray();
        var titleArray = $.grep(formArray, function(elem) {
            return elem.name === 'event_title';
        });
```

```
    var newTitle = titleArray.length > 0 ? titleArray[0].value : "";

    if (newTitle !== oldTitle)
    {
        // The event title has been changed, so update the page.
        $(".active")[0].innerHTML = newTitle;
    }
}

// Serializes the form data for use with $.ajax()
var formData = $(this).parents("form").serialize();

// Sends the data to the processing file
$.ajax({
        type: "POST",
        url: processFile,
        data: formData,
        success: function(data) {
            // Fades out the modal window
            fx.boxout();

            // If this is a new event, adds it to
            // the calendar
            if ( $("[name=event_id]").val().length==0 )
            {
                fx.addevent(data, formData);
            }
        },
        error: function(msg) {
            alert(msg);
        }
    });

});
```

With these changes in place, your users can now edit events without seeing potentially confusing duplicate titles or stale titles appearing on the page.

Confirming Deletion in a Modal Window

To round out your application, you're also going to allow users to delete entries without a page refresh. A good portion of the script you need to do this is already in place, so adding this functionality will mostly require tweaks to your existing code.

Displaying the Confirmation Dialog

To display the confirmation dialog for event deletion when the "Delete This Event" button is clicked, you need to add an additional element to the lookup array in ajax.inc.php:

```php
<?php

declare(strict_types=1);

/*
 * Enable sessions if needed.
 * Avoid pesky warning if session already active.
 */
$status = session_status();
if ($status == PHP_SESSION_NONE){
    //There is no active session
    session_start();
}

/*
 * Include necessary files
 */
include_once '../../../sys/config/db-cred.inc.php';

/*
 * Define constants for config info
 */
foreach ( $C as $name => $val )
{
    define($name, $val);
}

/*
 * Create a lookup array for form actions
 */
define(ACTIONS, array((
        'event_view' => array(
                'object' => 'Calendar',
                'method' => 'displayEvent'
            ),
        'edit_event' => array(
                'object' => 'Calendar',
                'method' => 'displayForm'
            ),
        'event_edit' => array(
                'object' => 'Calendar',
                'method' => 'processForm'
            ),
```

```php
        'delete_event' => array(
                'object' => 'Calendar',
                'method' => 'confirmDelete'
            )
        )
    );

/*
 * Make sure the anti-CSRF token was passed and that the
 * requested action exists in the lookup array
 */
if ( isset(ACTIONS[$_POST['action']]) )
{
    $use_array = ACTIONS[$_POST['action']];
    $obj = new $use_array['object']($dbo);
    $method = $use_array['method'];

    /*
     * Check for an ID and sanitize it if found
     */
    if ( isset($_POST['event_id']) )
    {
        $id = (int) $_POST['event_id'];
    }
    else { $id = NULL; }

    echo $obj->$method($id);
}

function __autoload($class_name)
{
    $filename = '../../../sys/class/class.'
        . strtolower($class_name) . '.inc.php';
    if ( file_exists($filename) )
    {
        include_once $filename;
    }
}

?>
```

Clicking the "Delete This Event" button from a modal window at this point now causes the confirmation dialog to appear (see Figure 8-7).

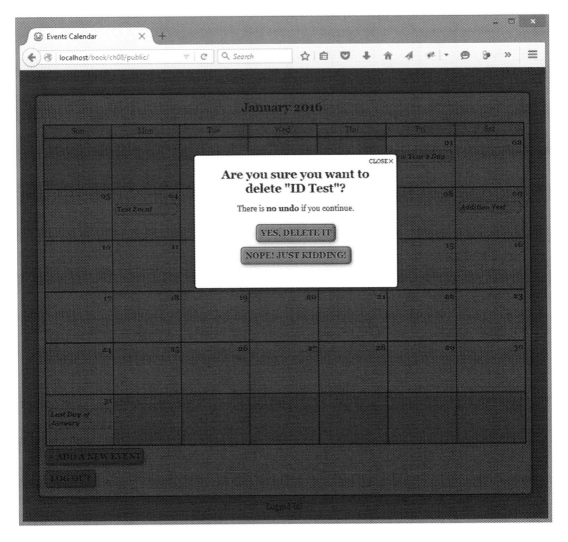

Figure 8-7. *The confirmation dialog to delete an event displayed in a modal window*

Configuring the Form Submission Event Handler for Deletion

Confirming event deletion requires a little more modification to init.js. To execute properly, the value of the Submit button needs to be stored and passed to the processing file. This is because the form can be submitted with either Yes, Delete It or Nope! Just Kidding! as values; the script checks which button was clicked to determine what action to take.

To store the button's value, use the this keyword as the jQuery selector, and then store the returned string from .val() as a variable called submitVal. Next, check whether the button's name attribute is confirm_delete. If so, append the action confirm_delete and the value of the button to the query string before submitting it.

Insert the following code shown in bold to accomplish this:

```
// Edits events without reloading
$("body").on("click", ".edit-form input[type=submit]", function (event){

        // Prevents the default form action from executing
        event.preventDefault();

        // If editing an existing event, need to pay attention to title.
        if ( $(this).attr("name")=="event_submit" && $(".active").length > 0 )
        {
            // Need to check if the event title has been changed.
            // Here's the title that's on the main calendar page.
            var oldTitle = $(".active")[0].innerHTML;

            // Here we fish out the (possibly) different title from the form data.
            var formArray = $(this).parents("form").serializeArray();
            var titleArray = $.grep(formArray, function(elem) {
                return elem.name === 'event_title';
            });
            var newTitle = titleArray.length > 0 ? titleArray[0].value : "";

            if (newTitle !== oldTitle)
            {
                // The event title has been changed, so update the page.
                $(".active")[0].innerHTML = newTitle;
            }
        }

        // Serializes the form data for use with $.ajax()
        var formData = $(this).parents("form").serialize(),

        // Stores the value of the submit button
            submitVal = $(this).val();

        // If this is the deletion form, appends an action
        if ( $(this).attr("name")=="confirm_delete" )
        {
            // Adds necessary info to the query string
            formData += "&action=confirm_delete"
                + "&confirm_delete="+submitVal;
        }

        // Sends the data to the processing file
        $.ajax({
                type: "POST",
                url: processFile,
                data: formData,
                success: function(data) {
                    // Fades out the modal window
                    fx.boxout();
```

```
                        // If this is a new event, adds it to
                        // the calendar
                        if ( $("[name=event_id]").val().length==0 )
                        {
                            fx.addevent(data, formData);
                        }
                    },
                    error: function(msg) {
                        alert(msg);
                    }
                });

        });
```

Modifying the Processing File to Confirm Deletion

Finally, you need to add an additional element to the lookup array in ajax.inc.php to make the Delete
button work:

```php
<?php

declare(strict_types=1);

/*
 * Enable sessions if needed.
 * Avoid pesky warning if session already active.
 */
$status = session_status();
if ($status == PHP_SESSION_NONE){
    //There is no active session
    session_start();
}

/*
 * Include necessary files
 */
include_once '../../../sys/config/db-cred.inc.php';

/*
 * Define constants for config info
 */
foreach ( $C as $name => $val )
{
    define($name, $val);
}

/*
 * Create a lookup array for form actions
 */
```

```php
    define(ACTIONS, array((
            'event_view' => array(
                    'object' => 'Calendar',
                    'method' => 'displayEvent'
                ),
            'edit_event' => array(
                    'object' => 'Calendar',
                    'method' => 'displayForm'
                ),
            'event_edit' => array(
                    'object' => 'Calendar',
                    'method' => 'processForm'
                ),
            'delete_event' => array(
                    'object' => 'Calendar',
                    'method' => 'confirmDelete'
                ),
            'confirm_delete' => array(
                    'object' => 'Calendar',
                    'method' => 'confirmDelete'
                )
            )
        );

/*
 * Make sure the anti-CSRF token was passed and that the
 * requested action exists in the lookup array
 */
if ( isset(ACTIONS[$_POST['action']]) )
{
    $use_array = ACTIONS[$_POST['action']];
    $obj = new $use_array['object']($dbo);
    $method = $use_array['method'];

    /*
     * Check for an ID and sanitize it if found
     */
    if ( isset($_POST['event_id']) )
    {
        $id = (int) $_POST['event_id'];
    }
    else { $id = NULL; }

    echo $obj->$method($id);
}

function __autoload($class_name)
{
    $filename = '../../../sys/class/class.'
        . strtolower($class_name) . '.inc.php';
```

```
    if ( file_exists($filename) )
    {
        include_once $filename;
    }
}

?>
```

You can test the preceding code by deleting the ID Test event from the calendar. After the modal window fades out, the event title is still present and clickable; however, if you try to view the event's details, its information is unavailable, and it doesn't make sense (see Figure 8-8).

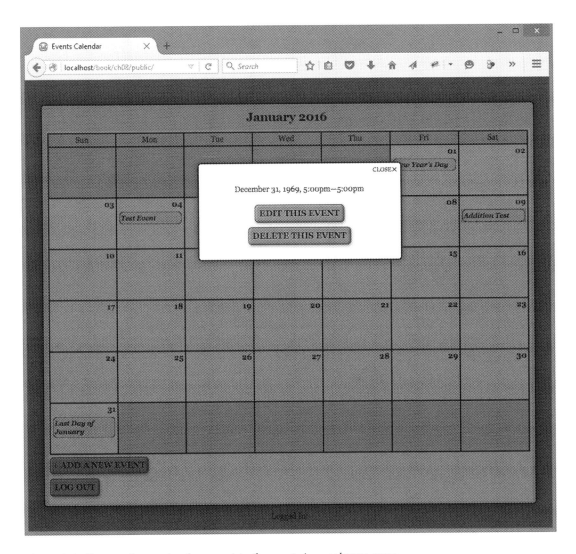

Figure 8-8. *Because the event no longer exists, the event view makes no sense*

Removing the Event from the Calendar After Deletion

You want to avoid the confusion caused by having non-existent events on the calendar after a user deletes them, so you need to add functionality to remove events from the calendar once this occurs.

To do this, add a new function to the fx object literal called removeevent. This function will use the active class applied to events when they're brought up in the modal window to fade them out and remove them from the DOM. You can add this function to fx using the following bold code:

```
fx = {
    "initModal" : function() {...},
    "boxin" : function(data, modal) {...},
    "boxout" : function(event) {...},
    "addevent" : function(data, formData){...},

    // Removes an event from the markup after deletion
    "removeevent" : function()
    {
            // Removes any event with the class "active"
            $(".active")
                .fadeOut("slow", function(){
                        $(this).remove();
                });
    },

    "deserialize" : function(str){...},
    "urldecode" : function(str) {...}
};
```

Modifying the Form Submission Handler to Remove Deleted Events

To remove events after they are deleted, add a new variable called remove to the form submission event handler. This will store a Boolean value that tells the script whether to remove an event. By default, this value will be set to false, which means the event should not be removed.

The only condition under which an event should be removed is if the "Yes, Delete It" button is clicked from the confirmation dialog. Add a check for this text in the Submit button and set remove to true if a match is made.

Inside the success handler, set up a conditional that checks whether remove is true and fires fx.removeevent() if it is.

Finally, to prevent empty elements from being added to the calendar, modify the conditional that fires fx.addevent() to ensure that remove is false before executing.

You can make these changes by adding the code shown in bold:

```
// Edits events without reloading
$("body").on("click", ".edit-form input[type=submit]", function (event){

        // Prevents the default form action from executing
        event.preventDefault();
```

```
    // If editing an existing event, need to pay attention to title.
    if ( $(this).attr("name")=="event_submit" && $(".active").length > 0 )
    {
        // Need to check if the event title has been changed.
        // Here's the title that's on the main calendar page.
        var oldTitle = $(".active")[0].innerHTML;

        // Here we fish out the (possibly) different title from the form data.
        var formArray = $(this).parents("form").serializeArray();
        var titleArray = $.grep(formArray, function(elem) {
            return elem.name === 'event_title';
        });
        var newTitle = titleArray.length > 0 ? titleArray[0].value : "";

        if (newTitle !== oldTitle)
        {
            // The event title has been changed, so update the page.
            $(".active")[0].innerHTML = newTitle;
        }
    }

    // Serializes the form data for use with $.ajax()
    var formData = $(this).parents("form").serialize(),

    // Stores the value of the submit button
        submitVal = $(this).val(),

    // Determines if the event should be removed
        remove = false;

    // If this is the deletion form, appends an action
    if ( $(this).attr("name")=="confirm_delete" )
    {
        // Adds necessary info to the query string
        formData += "&action=confirm_delete"
            + "&confirm_delete="+submitVal;

        // If the event is really being deleted, sets
        // a flag to remove it from the markup
        if ( submitVal=="Yes, Delete It" )
        {
            remove = true;
        }
    }

    // Sends the data to the processing file
    $.ajax({
            type: "POST",
            url: processFile,
            data: formData,
```

```
success: function(data) {
    // If this is a deleted event, removes
    // it from the markup
    if ( remove===true )
    {
        fx.removeevent();
    }

    // Fades out the modal window
    fx.boxout();

    // If this is a new event, adds it to
    // the calendar
    if ( $("[name=event_id]").val().length==0
        && remove===false )
    {
        fx.addevent(data, formData);
    }
},
error: function(msg) {
    alert(msg);
}
});

});
```

Save these changes, reload http://localhost/, and pull up the Test Event description. Delete the event; after you click the "Yes, Delete It" button, the modal box and event title will fade out, effectively eliminating the event from the calendar and eliminating any potential confusion for your users (see Figure 8-9).

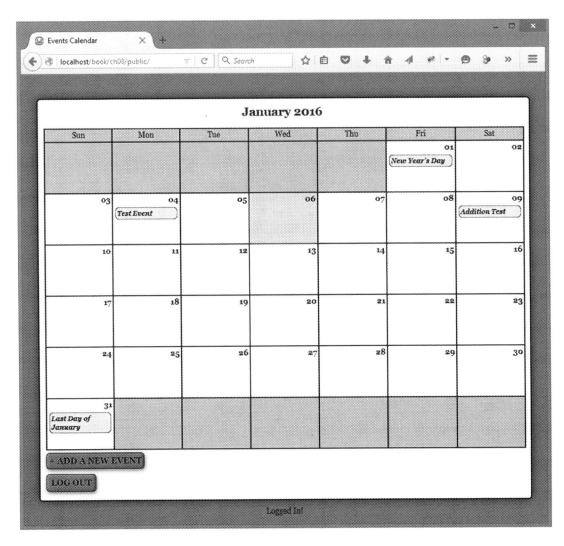

Figure 8-9. *After deleting Test Event, the event title is removed from the calendar*

Summary

In this chapter, you implemented controls that allow your users to quickly create, edit, and delete events without requiring a refresh of the page. This makes the application feel much more streamlined and user-friendly.

In the next chapter, you'll learn how to use regular expressions to confirm that the data entered in the editing forms is valid, ensuring that your app won't allow data that could potentially break it to be entered into the database.

PART 4

Advancing jQuery and PHP

At this point, you've got a functional calendar application. However, there are some things that you could add to improve the user experience, such as form validation. This part of the book will also cover advanced techniques such as validating user input with regular expressions and building custom jQuery plugins.

CHAPTER 9

∎ ∎ ∎

Performing Form Validation with Regular Expressions

It's your responsibility as a developer to ensure that your users' data is useful to your app, so you need to confirm that critical information is validated before storing it in your database.

In the case of the calendar application, the date format is critical: if the format isn't correct, the app will fail in several places. To verify that only valid dates are allowed into the database, you'll use **regular expressions** (regexes), which are powerful pattern-matching tools that allow developers much more control over data than a strict string comparison search.

Before you can get started with adding validation to your application, you need to get comfortable using regular expressions. In the first section of this chapter, you'll learn how to use the basic syntax of regexes. Then you'll put regexes to work doing server-side and client-side validation.

Getting Comfortable with Regular Expressions

Regular expressions are often perceived as intimidating, difficult tools. In fact, regexes have such a bad reputation among programmers that discussions about them are often peppered with this quote:

Some people, when confronted with a problem, think, "I know, I'll use regular expressions." Now they have two problems.

—Jamie Zawinski

This sentiment is not entirely unfounded because regular expressions come with a complex syntax and little margin for error. However, after overcoming the initial learning curve, regexes are an incredibly powerful tool with myriad applications in day-to-day programming.

Understanding Basic Regular Expression Syntax

In this book, you'll learn the Perl-Compatible Regular Expression (PCRE) syntax. This syntax is compatible with PHP and JavaScript, as well as most other programming languages.

∎ **Note**   You can read more about PCRE at `http://en.wikipedia.org/wiki/Perl_Compatible_Regular_Expressions`.

Setting Up a Test File

To learn how to use regexes, you'll need a file to use for testing. In the `public` folder, create a new file called `regex.php` and place the following code inside it:

```
<!DOCTYPE html
  PUBLIC "-//W3C//DTD XHTML 1.0 Strict//EN"
  "http://www.w3.org/TR/xhtml1/DTD/xhtml1-strict.dtd">

<html xmlns="http://www.w3.org/1999/xhtml" xml:lang="en" lang="en">

<head>
    <meta http-equiv="Content-Type"
          content="text/html;charset=utf-8" />
    <title>Regular Expression Demo</title>
    <style type="text/css">
        em {
            background-color: #FF0;
            border-top: 1px solid #000;
            border-bottom: 1px solid #000;
        }
    </style>
</head>

<body>
<?php

/*
 * Store the sample set of text to use for the examples of regex
 */
$string = <<<TEST_DATA

<h2>Regular Expression Testing</h2>
<p>
    In this document, there is a lot of text that can be matched
    using regex. The benefit of using a regular expression is much
    more flexible, albeit complex, syntax for text
    pattern matching.
</p>
<p>
    After you get the hang of regular expressions, also called
    regexes, they will become a powerful tool for pattern matching.
</p>
<hr />
TEST_DATA;
```

```
/*
 * Start by simply outputting the data
 */
echo $string;

?>

</body>

</html>
```

Save this file, and then load `http://localhost/regex.php` in your browser to view the sample script (see Figure 9-1).

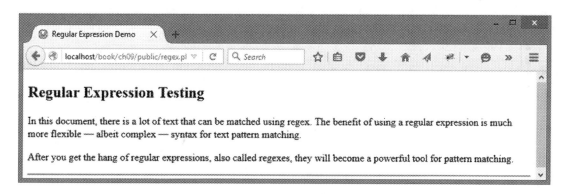

Figure 9-1. *The sample file for testing regular expressions*

Replacing Text with Regexes

To test regular expressions, you'll wrap matched patterns with `<em>` tags, which are styled in the test document to have top and bottom borders, as well as a yellow background.

Accomplishing this with regexes is similar using `str_replace()` in PHP with the `preg_replace()` function. A pattern to match is passed, followed by a string (or pattern) used to replace the matched pattern. Finally, the string within which the search is to be performed is passed:

```
preg_replace($pattern, $replacement, $string);
```

▨ **Note**   The *p* in `preg_replace()` signifies the use of PCRE. PHP also has `ereg_replace()`, which uses the slightly different POSIX regular expression syntax; however, the `ereg` family of functions has been deprecated since PHP 5.3.0.

The only difference between str_replace() and preg_replace() on a basic level is that the element passed to preg_replace() for the pattern must use *delimiters*, which let the function know which part of the regex is the pattern and which part consists of *modifiers*, or flags that affect how the pattern matches. You'll learn more about modifiers a little later in this section.

The delimiters for regex patterns in preg_replace() can be any non-alphanumeric, non-backslash, and non-whitespace characters placed at the beginning and end of the pattern. Most commonly, forward slashes (/) or hash signs (#) are used. For instance, if you want to search for the letters *cat* in a string, the pattern would be /cat/ (or #cat#, %cat%, @cat@, and so on).

Choosing Regexes vs. Regular String Replacement

To explore the differences between str_replace() and preg_replace(), try using both functions to wrap any occurrence of the word *regular* with <em> tags. Make the following modifications to regex.php:

```
<!DOCTYPE html
   PUBLIC "-//W3C//DTD XHTML 1.0 Strict//EN"
   "http://www.w3.org/TR/xhtml1/DTD/xhtml1-strict.dtd">

<html xmlns="http://www.w3.org/1999/xhtml" xml:lang="en" lang="en">

<head>
    <meta http-equiv="Content-Type"
        content="text/html;charset=utf-8" />
    <title>Regular Expression Demo</title>
    <style type="text/css">
        em {
            background-color: #FF0;
            border-top: 1px solid #000;
            border-bottom: 1px solid #000;
        }
    </style>
</head>

<body>
<?php

/*
 * Store the sample set of text to use for the examples of regex
 */
$string = <<<TEST_DATA

<h2>Regular Expression Testing</h2>
<p>
    In this document, there is a lot of text that can be matched
    using regex. The benefit of using a regular expression is much
    more flexible, albeit complex, syntax for text
    pattern matching.
</p>
```

```
<p>
    After you get the hang of regular expressions, also called
    regexes, they will become a powerful tool for pattern matching.
</p>
<hr />
TEST_DATA;

/*
 * Use str_replace() to highlight any occurrence of the word
 * "regular"
 */
echo str_replace("regular", "<em>regular</em>", $string);

/*
 * Use preg_replace() to highlight any occurrence of the word
 * "regular"
 */
echo preg_replace("/regular/", "<em>regular</em>", $string);

?>

</body>

</html>
```

Executing this script in your browser outputs the test information twice, with identical results (see Figure 9-2).

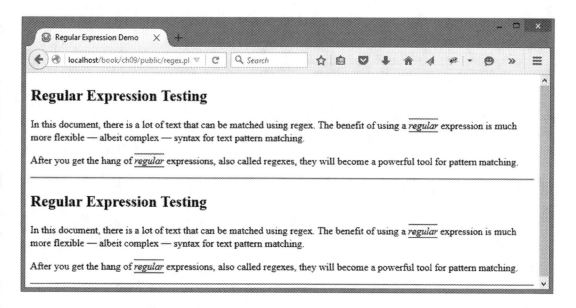

Figure 9-2. *The word regular highlighted with both regexes and regular string replacement*

Drilling Down on the Basics of Pattern Modifiers

You may have noticed that the word *regular* in the title is not highlighted. This is because the previous example is case sensitive.

To solve this problem with simple string replacement, you can opt to use the str_ireplace() function, which is nearly identical to str_replace(), except that it is case insensitive.

With regular expressions, you still use preg_replace(), but you need a modifier to signify case insensitivity. A modifier is a letter that follows the pattern delimiter, providing additional information to the regex about how it should handle patterns. For case insensitivity, the modifier i should be applied.

Modify regex.php to use case-insensitive replacement functions by making the modifications shown in bold:

```
<!DOCTYPE html
  PUBLIC "-//W3C//DTD XHTML 1.0 Strict//EN"
  "http://www.w3.org/TR/xhtml1/DTD/xhtml1-strict.dtd">

<html xmlns="http://www.w3.org/1999/xhtml" xml:lang="en" lang="en">

<head>
    <meta http-equiv="Content-Type"
        content="text/html;charset=utf-8" />
    <title>Regular Expression Demo</title>
    <style type="text/css">
        em {
            background-color: #FF0;
            border-top: 1px solid #000;
            border-bottom: 1px solid #000;
        }
    </style>
</head>

<body>
<?php

/*
 * Store the sample set of text to use for the examples of regex
 */
$string = <<<TEST_DATA

<h2>Regular Expression Testing</h2>
<p>
    In this document, there is a lot of text that can be matched
    using regex. The benefit of using a regular expression is much
    more flexible, albeit complex, syntax for text
    pattern matching.
</p>
<p>
    After you get the hang of regular expressions, also called
    regexes, they will become a powerful tool for pattern matching.
</p>
<hr />
TEST_DATA;
```

316

```
/*
 * Use str_ireplace() to highlight any occurrence of the word
 * "regular"
 */
echo str_ireplace("regular", "<em>regular</em>", $string);

/*
 * Use preg_replace() to highlight any occurrence of the word
 * "regular"
 */
echo preg_replace("/regular/i", "<em>regular</em>", $string);

?>

</body>

</html>
```

Now loading the file in your browser will highlight all occurrences of the word *regular*, regardless of case (see Figure 9-3).

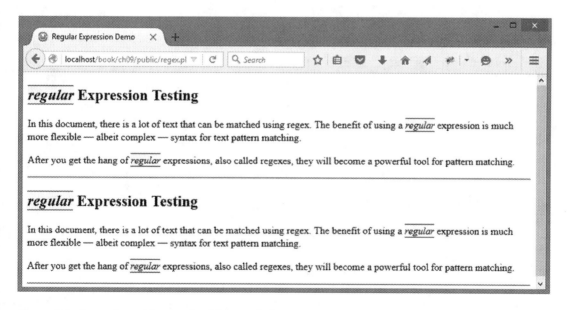

Figure 9-3. *A case-insensitive search of the sample data*

As you can see, this approach has a drawback: the capitalized *regular* in the title is changed to lowercase when it is replaced. In the next section, you'll learn how to avoid this issue by using groups in regexes.

Getting Fancy with Backreferences

The power of regexes starts to appear when you apply one of their most useful features: grouping and backreferences. A group is any part of a pattern that is enclosed in parentheses. A group can be used in the replacement string (or later in the pattern) with a *backreference*, a numbered reference to a named group.

This all sounds confusing, but in practice it's quite simple. Each set of parentheses from left to right in a regex is stored with a numeric backreference, which can be accessed using a backslash and the number of the backreference (\1) or by using a dollar sign and the number of the backreference ($1).

The benefit of this is that it gives regexes the ability to *use the matched value in the replacement*, instead of a predetermined value as in str_replace() and its ilk.

To keep the replacement contents in your previous example in the proper case, you need to use two occurrences of str_replace(); however, you can achieve the same effect by using a backreference in preg_replace() with just one function call.

Make the following modifications to regex.php to see the power of backreferences in regexes:

```
<!DOCTYPE html
  PUBLIC "-//W3C//DTD XHTML 1.0 Strict//EN"
  "http://www.w3.org/TR/xhtml1/DTD/xhtml1-strict.dtd">

<html xmlns="http://www.w3.org/1999/xhtml" xml:lang="en" lang="en">

<head>
    <meta http-equiv="Content-Type"
          content="text/html;charset=utf-8" />
    <title>Regular Expression Demo</title>
    <style type="text/css">
        em {
            background-color: #FF0;
            border-top: 1px solid #000;
            border-bottom: 1px solid #000;
        }
    </style>
</head>

<body>
<?php

/*
 * Store the sample set of text to use for the examples of regex
 */
$string = <<<TEST_DATA

<h2>Regular Expression Testing</h2>
<p>
    In this document, there is a lot of text that can be matched
    using regex. The benefit of using a regular expression is much
    more flexible, albeit complex, syntax for text
    pattern matching.
</p>
```

```
<p>
    After you get the hang of regular expressions, also called
    regexes, they will become a powerful tool for pattern matching.
</p>
<hr />
TEST_DATA;

/*
 * Use str_replace() to highlight any occurrence of the word
 * "regular"
 */
$check1 = str_replace("regular", "<em>regular</em>", $string);

/*
 * Use str_replace() again to highlight any capitalized occurrence
 * of the word "Regular"
 */
echo str_replace("Regular", "<em>Regular</em>", $check1);

/*
 * Use preg_replace() to highlight any occurrence of the word
 * "regular", case-insensitive
 */
echo preg_replace("/(regular)/i", "<em>$1</em>", $string);

?>

</body>

</html>
```

As the preceding code illustrates, it's already becoming cumbersome to use str_replace() for any kind of complex string matching. After saving the preceding changes and reloading your browser, however, you can achieve the desired outcome using both regexes and standard string replacement (see Figure 9-4).

319

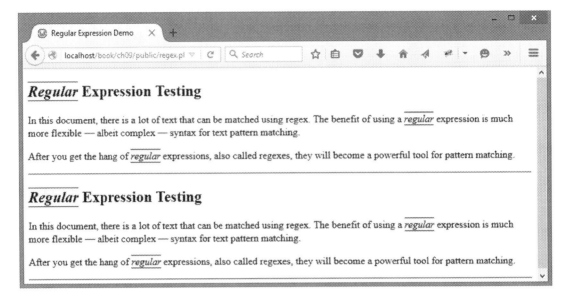

Figure 9-4. *A more complex replacement*

▨ **Note**   The remaining examples in this section will use only regexes.

Matching Character Classes

In some cases, it's desirable to match more than just a word. For instance, sometimes you want to verify that only a certain range of characters was used (i.e., to make sure only numbers were supplied for a phone number or that no special characters were used in a username field).

Regexes allow you to specify a character class, which is a set of characters enclosed in square brackets. For instance, to match any character between the letter *a* and the letter *c*, you use [a-c] in your pattern.

You can modify regex.php to highlight any character from A-C. Additionally, you can move the pattern into a variable and output it at the bottom of the sample data; this helps you see what pattern is being used when the script is loaded. Add the code shown in bold to accomplish this:

```
<!DOCTYPE html
  PUBLIC "-//W3C//DTD XHTML 1.0 Strict//EN"
  "http://www.w3.org/TR/xhtml1/DTD/xhtml1-strict.dtd">

<html xmlns="http://www.w3.org/1999/xhtml" xml:lang="en" lang="en">

<head>
    <meta http-equiv="Content-Type"
        content="text/html;charset=utf-8" />
    <title>Regular Expression Demo</title>
```

```
    <style type="text/css">
        em {
            background-color: #FF0;
            border-top: 1px solid #000;
            border-bottom: 1px solid #000;
        }
    </style>
</head>

<body>
<?php

/*
 * Store the sample set of text to use for the examples of regex
 */
$string = <<<TEST_DATA

<h2>Regular Expression Testing</h2>
<p>
    In this document, there is a lot of text that can be matched
    using regex. The benefit of using a regular expression is much
    more flexible, albeit complex, syntax for text
    pattern matching.
</p>
<p>
    After you get the hang of regular expressions, also called
    regexes, they will become a powerful tool for pattern matching.
</p>
<hr />
TEST_DATA;

/*
 * Use regex to highlight any occurence of the letters a-c
 */
$pattern = "/([a-c])/i";
echo preg_replace($pattern, "<em>$1</em>", $string);

/*
 * Output the pattern you just used
 */
echo "\n<p>Pattern used: <strong>$pattern</strong></p>";

?>

</body>

</html>
```

321

After reloading the page, you'll see the characters highlighted (see Figure 9-5). You can achieve identical results using [abc], [bac], or any other combination of the characters because the class will match any one character from the class. Also, because you're using the case-insensitive modifier (i), you don't need to include both uppercase and lowercase versions of the letters. Without the modifier, you would need to use [A-Ca-c] to match either case of the three letters.

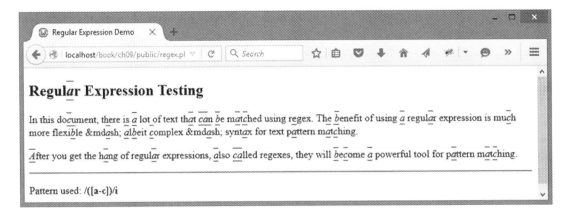

Figure 9-5. Any character from A-C is highlighted

Matching Any Character Except. . .

To match any character except those in a class, prefix the character class with a caret (^). To highlight any characters *except* A-C, use the pattern /([^a-c])/i (see Figure 9-6).

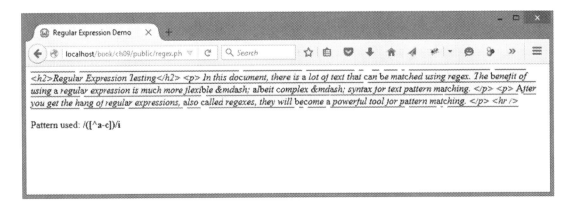

Figure 9-6. Highlighting all characters, except letters A-C

▓ **Note** It's important to mention that the preceding patterns enclose the character class *within parentheses*. Character classes do not store backreferences, so parentheses still must be used to reference the matched text later.

Using Character Class Shorthand

Certain character classes have a shorthand character. For example, there is a shorthand class for every word, digit, or space character:

- *Word character class shorthand* (\w): Matches patterns like [A-Za-z0-9_]

- *Digit character class shorthand* (\d): Matches patterns like [0-9]

- *Whitespace character class shorthand* (\s): Matches patterns like [\t\r\n]

Using these three shorthand classes can improve the readability of your regexes, which is extremely convenient when you're dealing with more complex patterns.

You can exclude a particular type of character by capitalizing the shorthand character:

- *Non-word character class shorthand* (\W): Matches patterns like [^A-Za-z0-9_]

- *Non-digit character class shorthand* (\D): Matches patterns like [^0-9]

- *Non-whitespace character class shorthand* (\S): Matches patterns like [^ \t\r\n]

■ **Note** \t, \r, and \n are special characters that represent tabs and newlines; a space is represented by a regular space character ( ).

Finding Word Boundaries

Another special symbol to be aware of is the word boundary symbol (\b). By placing this before and/or after a pattern, you can ensure that the pattern isn't contained *within* another word. For instance, if you want to match the word *stat*, but not *thermostat*, *statistic*, or *ecstatic*, you would use this pattern: /\bstat\b/.

Using Repetition Operators

When you use character classes, only one character out of the set is matched, unless the pattern specifies a different number of characters. Regular expressions give you several ways to specify a number of characters to match:

- The star operator (*) matches zero or more occurrences of a character.

- The plus operator (+) matches one or more occurrences of a character.

- The special repetition operator ({min,max}) allows you to specify a range of character matches.

Matching zero or more characters is useful when using a string that may or may not have a certain piece of a pattern in it. For example, if you want to match all occurrences of either *John* or *John Doe*, you can use this pattern to match both instances: /John(Doe)*/.

Matching one or more characters is good for verifying that at least one character was entered. For instance, if you want to verify that a user enters at least one character into a form input and that the character is a valid word character, you can use this pattern to validate the input: /\w+/.

Finally, matching a specific range of characters is especially useful when matching numeric ranges. For instance, you can use this pattern to ensure a value is between 0 and 99: /\b\d{1,2}\b/.

In your example file, use this regex pattern to find any words consisting of exactly four letters: /(\b\w{4}\b)/. You can see the results in Figure 9-7.

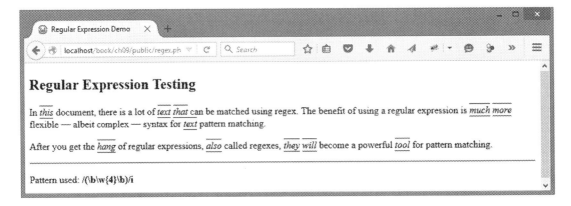

Figure 9-7. *Matching only words that consist of exactly four letters*

Detecting the Beginning or End of a String

Additionally, you can force the pattern to match from the beginning or end of the string (or both). If the pattern starts with a caret (^), the regex will only match if the pattern starts with a matching character. If it ends with a dollar sign ($), the regex will match only if the string ends with the preceding matching character.

You can combine these different symbols to make sure an entire string matches a pattern. This is useful when validating input because you can verify that the user only submitted valid information. For instance, you can use this regex pattern to verify that a username contains only the letters A-Z, the numbers 0-9, and the underscore character: /^\w+$/.

Using Alternation

In some cases, it's desirable to use either one pattern or another. This is called **alternation**, and it's accomplished using a pipe character (|). This approach allows you to define two or more possibilities for a match. For instance, you can use this pattern to match either three-, six-, or seven-letter words in regex.php: /\b(\w{3}|\w{6,7})\b/. Figure 9-8 shows the results.

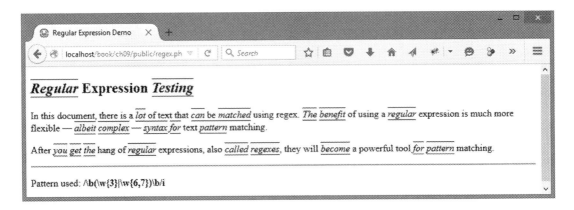

Figure 9-8. *Using alternation to match only three-, six-, and seven-letter words*

Using Optional Items

In some cases, it becomes necessary to allow certain items to be optional. For instance, to match both single and plural forms of a word like *expression*, you need to make the *s* optional.

To do this, place a question mark (?) after the optional item. If the optional part of the pattern is longer than one character, it needs to be captured in a group (you'll use this technique in the next section).

For now, use this pattern to highlight all occurrences of the word *expression* or *expressions*: /(expressions?)/i. Figure 9-9 shows the results.

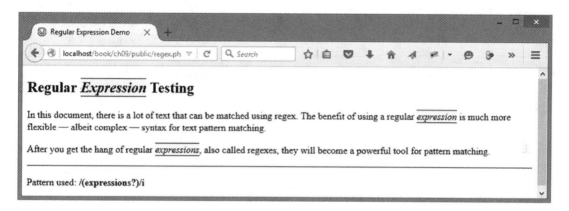

Figure 9-9. *Matching a pattern with an optional s at the end*

Putting It All Together

Now that you've got a general understanding of regular expressions, it's time to use your new knowledge to write a regex pattern that will match any occurrence of the phrases *regular expression* or *regex*, including the plural forms.

To start, look for the phrase *regex*: **/(regex)/i** (see Figure 9-10).

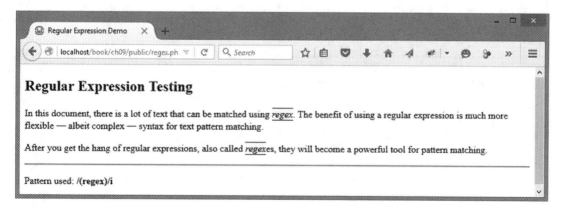

Figure 9-10. *Matching the word regex*

Next, add the ability for the phrase to be plural by inserting an optional *es* at the end: /(regex**(es)?**)/i (see Figure 9-11).

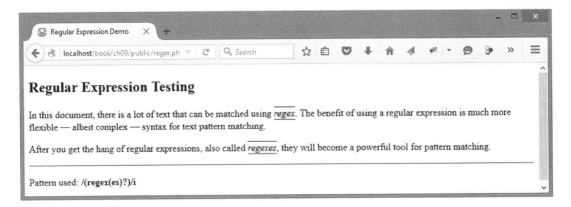

Figure 9-11. *Adding the optional match for the plural form of regex*

Next, add to the pattern so that it also matches the word *regular* with a space after it, and make the match optional: /(reg**(ular\s)?**ex(es)?)/i (see Figure 9-12).

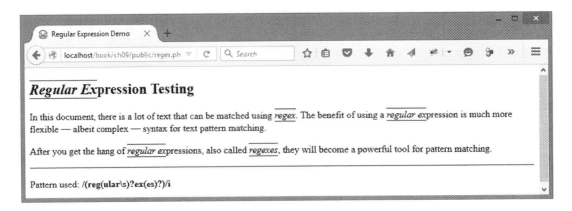

Figure 9-12. *Adding an optional check for the word regular*

Now expand the pattern to match the word *expression* as an alternative to *es*: /(reg(ular\s)?ex(**pression**|es)?)/i (see Figure 9-13).

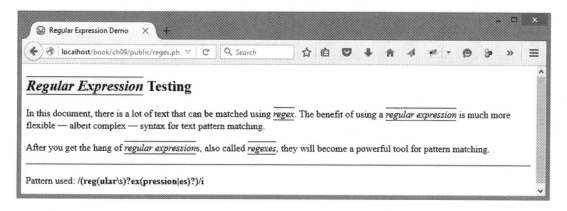

Figure 9-13. *Adding alternation to match expression*

Finally, add an optional *s* to the end of the match for *expression*: /(reg(ular\s)?ex(pression**s?**|es)?)/i (see Figure 9-14).

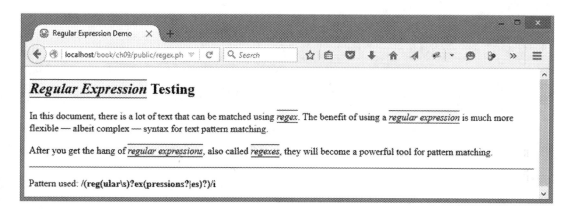

Figure 9-14. *The completed regular expression*

___

■ **Tip**   The examples in this chapter go over the most common features of regular expressions, but they don't cover everything that regexes have to offer. Jan Goyvaerts has put together a fantastic resource for learning all of the ins-and-outs of regexes, as well as some tools for testing them, at `www.regular-expressions.info/`.

___

Adding Server-Side Date Validation

Now that you have a basic understanding of regexes, you're ready to start validating user input. For this app, you need to ensure that the date format is correct, so that the app doesn't crash by attempting to parse a date that it can't understand.

You'll begin by adding server-side validation. This is more of a fallback because later you'll add validation with jQuery. However, you should *never* rely solely on JavaScript to validate user input because the user can easily turn off JavaScript support and therefore completely disable your JavaScript validation efforts.

Defining the Regex Pattern to Validate Dates

The first step toward implementing date validation is to define a regex pattern to match the desired format. The format the calendar app uses is YYYY-MM-DD HH:MM:SS.

Setting up Test Data

You need to modify regex.php with a valid date format and a few invalid formats so you can test your pattern. Start by matching zero or more numeric characters with your regex pattern. Do this by making the following changes shown in bold:

```
<!DOCTYPE html
  PUBLIC "-//W3C//DTD XHTML 1.0 Strict//EN"
  "http://www.w3.org/TR/xhtml1/DTD/xhtml1-strict.dtd">

<html xmlns="http://www.w3.org/1999/xhtml" xml:lang="en" lang="en">

<head>
    <meta http-equiv="Content-Type"
          content="text/html;charset=utf-8" />
    <title>Regular Expression Demo</title>
    <style type="text/css">
        em {
            background-color: #FF0;
            border-top: 1px solid #000;
            border-bottom: 1px solid #000;
        }
    </style>
</head>

<body>
<?php

/*
 * Set up several test date strings to ensure validation is working
 */
$date[] = '2016-01-14 12:00:00';
$date[] = 'Saturday, May 14th at 7pm';
$date[] = '02/03/10 10:00pm';
$date[] = '2016-01-14 102:00:00';

/*
 * Date validation pattern
 */
$pattern = "/(\d*)/";

foreach ( $date as $d )
{
    echo "<p>", preg_replace($pattern, "<em>$1</em>", $d), "</p>";
}
```

```
/*
 * Output the pattern you just used
 */
echo "\n<p>Pattern used: <strong>$pattern</strong></p>";

?>

</body>

</html>
```

After saving the preceding code, reload `http://localhost/regex.php` in your browser to see all numeric characters highlighted (see Figure 9-15).

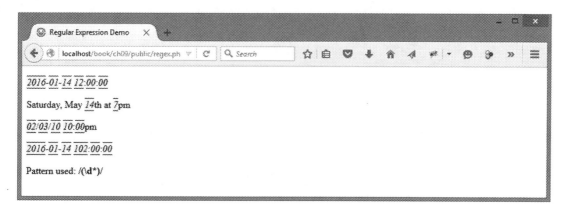

Figure 9-15. *Matching any numeric character*

Matching the Date Format

To match the date format, start by matching exactly four digits at the beginning of the string to validate the year: **/^(\d{4})/** (see Figure 9-16).

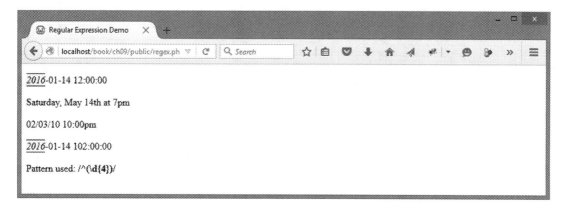

Figure 9-16. *Validating the year section of the date string*

Next, you need to validate the month by matching the hyphen and two more digits:
/^(\d{4}**(-\d{2})**)/ (see Figure 9-17).

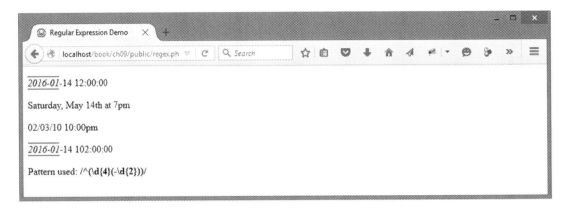

Figure 9-17. *Expanding the validate month section of the date string*

Notice that the month and date sections are identical: a hyphen followed by two digits. This means you can simply repeat the month-matching pattern to validate the day using a repetition operator after the group: /^(\d{4}(-\d{2})**{2}**)/ (see Figure 9-18).

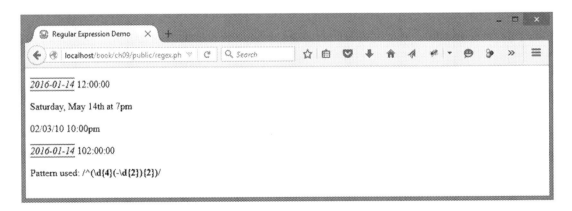

Figure 9-18. *Adding the day part of the date string to the pattern*

Now match a single space and the hour section: /^(\d{4}(-\d{2}){2} **(\d{2})**)/ (see Figure 9-19).

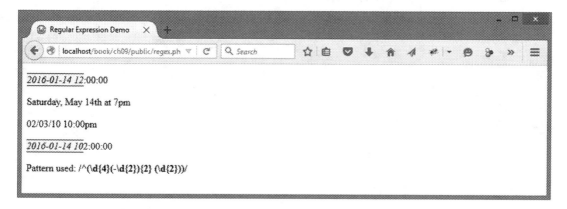

Figure 9-19. *Validating the hour section of the date string*

■ **Note**　Make sure that you include the space character. The shorthand class (\s) shouldn't be used because new lines and tabs should not match in this instance.

To validate the minutes, you match a colon and exactly two digits:
/^(\d{4}(-\d{2}){2} (\d{2})**(:\d{2})**)/ (see Figure 9-20).

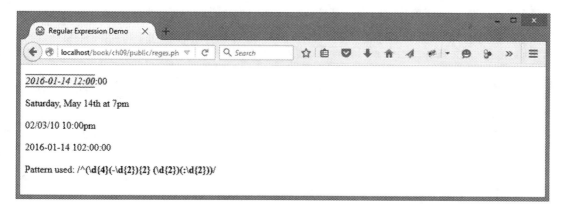

Figure 9-20. *Validating the minutes section of the date string*

Finally, repeat the pattern for the minutes to match the seconds, and then use the dollar sign modifier to match the end of the string: `/^(\d{4}(-\d{2}){2} (\d{2})(:\d{2})`**`{2}`**`)`**`$`**`/` (see Figure 9-21).

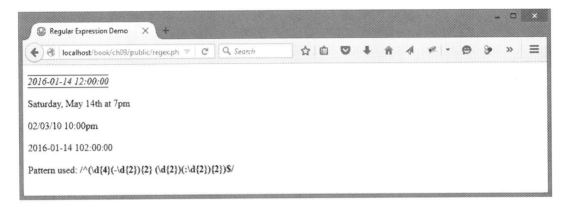

Figure 9-21. *Validating the seconds section of the date string and completing the pattern*

Armed with this regex pattern, you can now validate the date input in your application.

Adding a Validation Method to the Calendar Class

To validate the date string, you will add a new private method to the `Calendar` class called `_validDate()`. This method will accept the date string to be validated and then compare it to the validation pattern using `preg_match()`, which returns the number of matches found in the given string. Because this particular pattern will only match if the entire string conforms to the pattern, a valid date will return 1, while an invalid date will return 0. If the date is valid, the method will return TRUE; otherwise, it will return FALSE.

Add this method to the `Calendar` class by inserting the following bold code into `class.calendar.inc.php`:

```php
<?php

declare(strict_types=1);

class Calendar extends DB_Connect
{

    private $_useDate;

    private $_m;

    private $_y;

    private $_daysInMonth;

    private $_startDay;

    public function __construct($dbo=NULL, $useDate=NULL) {...}
```

```php
    public function buildCalendar() {...}

    public function displayEvent($id) {...}

    public function displayForm() {...}

    public function processForm() {...}

    public function confirmDelete($id) {...}

    /**
     * Validates a date string
     *
     * @param string $date the date string to validate
     * @return bool TRUE on success, FALSE on failure
     */
    private function _validDate($date)
    {
        /*
         * Define a regex pattern to check the date format
         */
        $pattern = '/^(\d{4}(-\d{2}){2} (\d{2})(:\d{2}){2})$/';

        /*
         * If a match is found, return TRUE. FALSE otherwise.
         */
        return preg_match($pattern, $date)==1 ? TRUE : FALSE;
    }

    private function _loadEventData($id=NULL) {...}

    private function _createEventObj() {...}

    private function _loadEventById($id) {...}

    private function _adminGeneralOptions() {...}

    private function _adminEntryOptions($id) {...}

}

?>
```

Returning an Error if the Dates Don't Validate

Your next step is to modify the processForm() method so it calls the _validDate() method on both the start and end times for new entries. If the validation fails, simply return an error message.

Add the following bold code to processForm() to implement the validation:

```php
<?php

declare(strict_types=1);

class Calendar extends DB_Connect
{
    private $_useDate;

    private $_m;

    private $_y;

    private $_daysInMonth;

    private $_startDay;

    public function __construct($dbo=NULL, $useDate=NULL) {...}

    public function buildCalendar() {...}

    public function displayEvent($id) {...}

    public function displayForm() {...}

    /**
     * Validates the form and saves/edits the event
     *
     * @return mixed TRUE on success, an error message on failure
     */
    public function processForm()
    {
        /*
         * Exit if the action isn't set properly
         */
        if ( $_POST['action']!='event_edit' )
        {
            return "The method processForm was accessed incorrectly";
        }

        /*
         * Escape data from the form
         */
        $title = htmlentities($_POST['event_title'], ENT_QUOTES);
        $desc = htmlentities($_POST['event_description'], ENT_QUOTES);
```

```php
$start = htmlentities($_POST['event_start'], ENT_QUOTES);
$end = htmlentities($_POST['event_end'], ENT_QUOTES);

/*
 * If the start or end dates aren't in a valid format, exit
 * the script with an error
 */
if ( !$this->_validDate($start)
        || !$this->_validDate($end) )
{
    return "Invalid date format! Use YYYY-MM-DD HH:MM:SS";
}

/*
 * If no event ID passed, create a new event
 */
if ( empty($_POST['event_id']) )
{
    $sql = "INSERT INTO `events`
                (`event_title`, `event_desc`, `event_start`,
                    `event_end`)
            VALUES
                (:title, :description, :start, :end)";
}

/*
 * Update the event if it's being edited
 */
else
{
    /*
     * Cast the event ID as an integer for security
     */
    $id = (int) $_POST['event_id'];
    $sql = "UPDATE `events`
            SET
                `event_title`=:title,
                `event_desc`=:description,
                `event_start`=:start,
                `event_end`=:end
            WHERE `event_id`=$id";
}

/*
 * Execute the create or edit query after binding the data
 */
try
{
    $stmt = $this->db->prepare($sql);
    $stmt->bindParam(":title", $title, PDO::PARAM_STR);
    $stmt->bindParam(":description", $desc, PDO::PARAM_STR);
```

```
            $stmt->bindParam(":start", $start, PDO::PARAM_STR);
            $stmt->bindParam(":end", $end, PDO::PARAM_STR);
            $stmt->execute();
            $stmt->closeCursor();

            /*
             * Returns the ID of the event
             */
            return $this->db->lastInsertId();
        }
        catch ( Exception $e )
        {
            return $e->getMessage();
        }
    }

    public function confirmDelete($id) {...}

    private function _validDate($date) {...}

    private function _loadEventData($id=NULL) {...}

    private function _createEventObj() {...}

    private function _loadEventById($id) {...}

    private function _adminGeneralOptions() {...}

    private function _adminEntryOptions($id) {...}
}

?>
```

You can test the validation by entering a bad entry into the form at `http://localhost/admin.php` (see Figure 9-22).

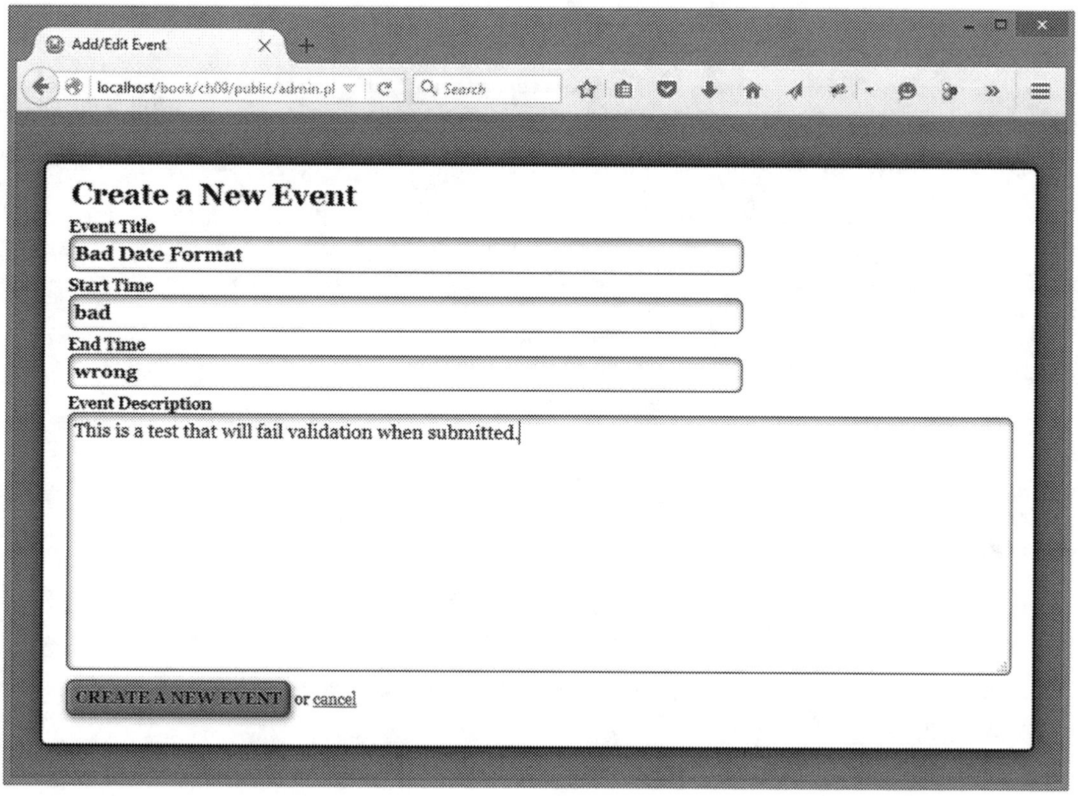

Figure 9-22. *An entry with bad date values that should fail validation*

▓ **Note**   You use http://localhost/admin.php because the only reason your server-side validation will be
invoked is if the user has JavaScript disabled. In that case, the modal windows would not function, and the user
would be brought to this form. In situations where JavaScript is enabled, the server-side acts as a double-check
and an additional security measure against mischievous users.

After this form is submitted, the app will simply output the error message and die (see Figure 9-23). The
calendar application is designed for users with JavaScript enabled; you use this approach to prevent the app
from displaying errors.

Invalid date format! Use YYYY-MM-DD HH:MM:SS

Figure 9-23. *The error message displayed when invalid dates are supplied*

Adding Client-Side Date Validation

For most users, JavaScript will be enabled. It's far more convenient as a user to get instant feedback on the form, so you will add new jQuery functionality to validate date strings on the client side.

Creating a New JavaScript File to Validate the Date String

Because you're going to continue to work with this script in the next chapter, you should put it in a separate file in the js folder called valid-date.js. This file will contain a function that is functionally equivalent to the _validDate() method in the Calendar class.

It will accept a date to validate, check it against the date-matching regex pattern you wrote previously using match(), and then return true if a match is found or false if match() returns null.

You build this function by inserting the following code into valid-date.js:

```
"use strict";

// Checks for a valid date string (YYYY-MM-DD HH:MM:SS)
function validDate(date)
{
    // Define the regex pattern to validate the format
    var pattern = /^(\d{4}(-\d{2}){2} (\d{2})(:\d{2}){2})$/;

    // Returns true if the date matches, false if it doesn't
    return date.match(pattern)!=null;
}
```

▓ **Note**   The regex pattern is not enclosed in quotes. If you used quotes, the pattern would be stored as a string and interpreted accordingly. This would result in the script looking for an exact character match, rather than interpreting the regex pattern properly.

Including the New File in the Footer

To use the validDate() function, you need to include the new JavaScript file *before* init.js, so that the function is available to be called. Do this by opening footer.inc.php in the common folder and inserting the following bold code:

```
    <script src="https://ajax.googleapis.com/ajax/libs/jquery/2.1.4/jquery.min.js">
    </script>
    <script src="assets/js/valid-date.js"></script>
    <script src="assets/js/init.js"></script>
</body>

</html>
```

Preventing the Form Submission if Validation Fails

Now that validDate() is available in init.js, you need to add date validation before the form can be submitted. Store the start and end dates in variables (start and end, respectively), and then check them using validDate() before allowing the form to be submitted.

Next, modify the click handler to the Submit button on the form that edits or creates events, and then trigger an alert with a helpful error message if either date input has an invalid value. You need to prevent the form from being submitted as well, so the user doesn't have to repopulate the other form fields.

You accomplish this by inserting the following bold code into init.js:

```
// Makes sure the document is ready before executing scripts
jQuery(function($){

var processFile = "assets/inc/ajax.inc.php",
    fx = {...}

$("body").on("click", "li>a", function(event){...});

$("body").on("click", ".admin-options form,.admin", function(event){...});

$("body").on("click", ".edit-form a:contains(cancel)", function(event){...});

// Edits events without reloading
$("body").on("click", ".edit-form input[type=submit]", function(event){

        // Prevents the default form action from executing
        event.preventDefault();

        // Serializes the form data for use with $.ajax()
        var formData = $(this).parents("form").serialize(),

        // Stores the value of the submit button
            submitVal = $(this).val(),

        // Determines if the event should be removed
            remove = false,

        // Saves the start date input string
            start = $(this).siblings("[name=event_start]").val(),

        // Saves the end date input string
            end = $(this).siblings("[name=event_end]").val();

        // If this is the deletion form, appends an action
        if ( $(this).attr("name")=="confirm_delete" )
        {
            // Adds necessary info to the query string
            formData += "&action=confirm_delete"
                + "&confirm_delete="+submitVal;
```

```
        // If the event is really being deleted, sets
        // a flag to remove it from the markup
        if ( submitVal=="Yes, Delete It" )
        {
            remove = true;
        }
    }

    // If creating/editing an event, checks for valid dates
    if ( $(this).siblings("[name=action]").val()=="event_edit" )
    {
        if ( !validDate(start) || !validDate(end) )
        {
            alert("Valid dates only! (YYYY-MM-DD HH:MM:SS)");
            return false;
        }
    }

    // Sends the data to the processing file
    $.ajax({
            type: "POST",
            url: processFile,
            data: formData,
            success: function(data) {
                // If this is a deleted event, removes
                // it from the markup
                if ( remove===true )
                {
                    fx.removeevent();
                }

                // Fades out the modal window
                fx.boxout();

                // If this is a new event, adds it to
                // the calendar
                if ( $("[name=event_id]").val().length==0
                    && remove===false )
                {
                    fx.addevent(data, formData);
                }
            },
            error: function(msg) {
                alert(msg);
            }
        });

});
```

Now save these changes, load `http://localhost/` in your browser, and then create a new event with bad parameters using the modal window form (see Figure 9-24).

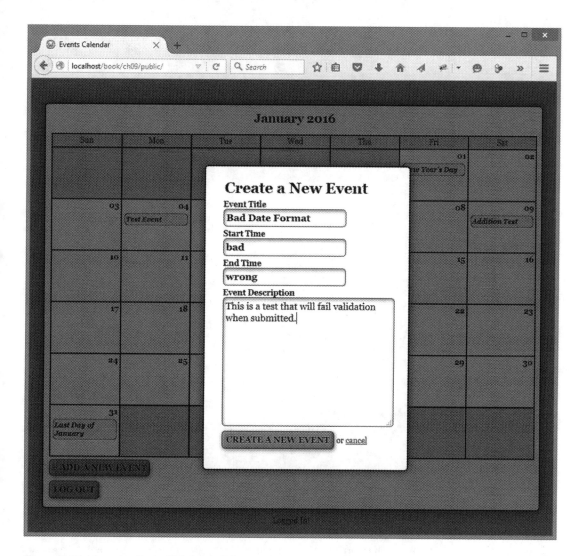

Figure 9-24. *An entry that will fail to validate*

If you click the Submit button at this point, the validation will fail, and the app will show an alert box with the error message about the date format (see Figure 9-25).

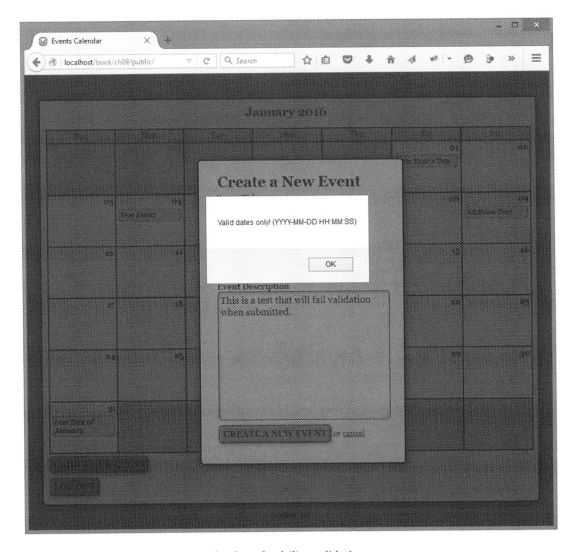

Figure 9-25. *The error message in an alert box after failing validation*

After clicking the OK button in the alert box, the user will be able to edit her entry without having to repopulate any fields.

Summary

In this chapter, you tackled using regular expressions for form validation. The concepts you learned can be applied to validating any type of data, and they will greatly aid you in making sure the information supplied in forms is usable by your applications.

In the next chapter, you'll learn how to extend the jQuery object, both by directly extending the jQuery core and by developing a custom plug-in for jQuery.

CHAPTER 10

Extending jQuery

jQuery's easy-to-use syntax led developers to begin writing scripts to achieve custom effects and other tasks. To make these scripts configurable and reusable, these developers constructed them as *plug-ins*, or scripts that extend jQuery by adding new methods to the library. In this chapter, you'll learn how to add your own plug-ins to jQuery.

Adding Functions to jQuery

In some cases, it may be desirable to add a function directly to the jQuery object, which means you would be able to call it like so:

```
$.yourFunction();
```

Adding functions to jQuery can help you keep your scripts organized and ensure that your function calls follow a consistent format. However, it's important to note that adding a function to jQuery *does not* allow you to chain it with a set of selected DOM elements; for this, you must use a method, which you'll learn how to do in this chapter.

Adding Your Date Validation Function to jQuery

In your first extending jQuery example, you will add the date validation function you wrote in the last chapter to the jQuery object. Specifically, you'll leverage valid-date.js.

Allowing Custom Aliases in jQuery Plug-ins

One thing you should consider is allowing custom aliases in your jQuery plug-ins. While this isn't strictly necessary, it is *strongly* encouraged because it can help you keep your plug-in from breaking if the $ shortcut is given up by jQuery.noConflict(). Better still, this feature is so simple to implement that it's actually a little silly not to include it.

When building a new plug-in, you should put the plug-in code within a function that is executed immediately when the script is loaded. At its outset, the script should look like this:

```
(function(){
    // plug-in code here...
})();
```

The second set of parentheses causes the preceding code to be executed immediately as a function, which is where the custom alias comes in. If you pass the jQuery object to the second set of parentheses and the $ shortcut to the internal function, then the code will work properly with the $ shortcut, even if it's given back to the global namespace using jQuery.noConflict():

```
(function($){
    // plug-in code here...
})(jQuery);
```

You could use any valid JavaScript variable name in place of the $, and the script would still execute properly with this method:

```
(function(custom){
    // Adds a background color to any paragraph
    // element using a custom alias
    custom("p").css("background-color","yellow");
})(jQuery);
```

Attaching the Function to the jQuery Object

To attach the function to jQuery, add the following code to valid-date.js:

```
(function($){

    // Extends the jQuery object to validate date strings
    $.validDate = function()
    {
        // code here
    };

})(jQuery);
```

Using this format, you now call the validDate() function like this:

```
$.validDate();
```

Allowing Configurable Options

Just as in the original validDate() function, a date string will be passed into the function. However, to make this function more configurable, you can pass in an object containing configuration options (if necessary) to modify the regex pattern used to match the date string:

```
(function($){

    // Extends the jQuery object to validate date strings
    $.validDate = function(date, options)
    {
        // code here
    };

})(jQuery);
```

The options object will only have one property: the pattern to be used for validation. Because you want the options object to be optional, you define a default value for the pattern in the function by inserting the following bold code:

```
(function($){

    // Extends the jQuery object to validate date strings
    $.validDate = function(date, options)
    {
        // Sets up default values for the method
        var defaults = {
            "pattern" : /^(\d{4}(-\d{2}){2} (\d{2})(:\d{2}){2})$/
        };
    };

})(jQuery);
```

Extending Default Options with User-Supplied Options

You can extend the default object using the $.extend() function, which will create a new object by combining the default options with the user-supplied options. If there are three options available and the user passes an object with only two of them defined, using $.extend() will only replace the two properties redefined by the user.

Insert the code shown in bold to extend the default object:

```
(function($){

    // Extends the jQuery object to validate date strings
    $.validDate = function(date, options)
    {
        // Sets up default values for the method
        var defaults = {
            "pattern" : /^(\d{4}(-\d{2}){2} (\d{2})(:\d{2}){2})$/
        },

        // Extends the defaults with user-supplied options
            opts = $.extend(defaults, options);
    };

})(jQuery);
```

Performing Validation and Returning a Value

The step to perform validation and return a value is nearly identical to one in the original function, except you access the pattern here through the opts object:

```
(function($){

    // Extends the jQuery object to validate date strings
    $.validDate = function(date, options)
```

```
    {
        // Sets up default values for the method
        var defaults = {
            "pattern" : /^(\d{4}(-\d{2}){2} (\d{2})(:\d{2}){2})$/
        },

        // Extends the defaults with user-supplied options
            opts = $.extend(defaults, options);

        // Returns true if a match is found, false otherwise
        return date.match(opts.pattern)!=null;
    };

})(jQuery);
```

Conforming to jQuery Plug-in File Naming Conventions

To officially call a plug-in a plug-in, you must use the jQuery naming conventions for your plug-in files. The accepted format is jquery.[name of plug-in].js. To meet this guideline, change the name of valid-date.js to jquery.validDate.js.

Modifying the Include Script

Now that the file name has changed, you need to update footer.inc.php to include it. Make the changes shown in bold to load the correct file:

```
    <script src="https://ajax.googleapis.com/ajax/libs/jquery/2.1.4/jquery.min.js">
    </script>
    <script src="assets/js/jquery.validDate.js"></script>
    <script src="assets/js/init.js"></script>
</body>

</html>
```

Modifying the Initialization Script

Finally, adjust init.js to call the new jQuery function you've just added by making the adjustments shown in bold:

```
jQuery(function($){

var processFile = "assets/inc/ajax.inc.php",
    fx = {...}

$("body").on("click", "li>a", function(event){...});

$("body").on("click", ".admin-options form,.admin", function(event)(event){...});

$("body").on("click", ".edit-form a:contains(cancel)", function(event){...});
```

```
// Edits events without reloading
$("body").on("click", ".edit-form input[type=submit]", function(event){

        // Prevents the default form action from executing
        event.preventDefault();

        // Serializes the form data for use with $.ajax()
        var formData = $(this).parents("form").serialize(),

        // Stores the value of the submit button
            submitVal = $(this).val(),

        // Determines if the event should be removed
            remove = false,

        // Saves the start date input string
            start = $(this).siblings("[name=event_start]").val(),

        // Saves the end date input string
            end = $(this).siblings("[name=event_end]").val();

        // If this is the deletion form, appends an action
        if ( $(this).attr("name")=="confirm_delete" )
        {
            // Adds necessary info to the query string
            formData += "&action=confirm_delete"
                + "&confirm_delete="+submitVal;

            // If the event is really being deleted, sets
            // a flag to remove it from the markup
            if ( submitVal=="Yes, Delete It" )
            {
                remove = true;
            }
        }

        // If creating/editing an event, checks for valid dates
        if ( $(this).siblings("[name=action]").val()=="event_edit" )
        {
            if ( !$.validDate(start) || !$.validDate(end) )
            {
                alert("Valid dates only! (YYYY-MM-DD HH:MM:SS)");
                return false;
            }
        }

        // Sends the data to the processing file
        $.ajax({
                type: "POST",
                url: processFile,
                data: formData,
```

```
            success: function(data) {
                // If this is a deleted event, removes
                // it from the markup
                if ( remove===true )
                {
                    fx.removeevent();
                }

                // Fades out the modal window
                fx.boxout();

                // If this is a new event, adds it to
                // the calendar
                if ( $("[name=event_id]").val().length==0
                    && remove===false )
                {
                    fx.addevent(data, formData);
                }
            },
            error: function(msg) {
                alert(msg);
            }
        });

    });

});
```

After saving the preceding code, you can reload `http://localhost/` and try to submit a new event with bad date values. The result is identical to the result obtained when using the original `validDate()` function.

Adding Methods to jQuery

To add a chainable method to the jQuery object, you have to attach it to the `fn` object of jQuery. This allows you to call the method on a set of selected elements:

```
$(".class").yourPlug-in();
```

░ **Note** The `fn` object of jQuery is actually just an alias for the jQuery object's `prototype` object. Modifying the prototype of an object will affect all future instances of that object, rather than just the current instance. For more information on this, check out the brief and simple explanation of the `prototype` object in JavaScript at `www.javascriptkit.com/javatutors/proto.shtml`.

Building Your Plug-in

The plug-in you'll build in this section will rely on a simple method to enlarge the event titles when a user hovers over them, and then return them to their original size when the user moves his mouse off the title.

This plug-in will be called `dateZoom`, and it will allow the user to configure the size, speed, and easing equation used for the animation.

Creating a Properly Named Plug-in File

Your first order of business when creating this plug-in is to give it a name. Create a new file in the `js` folder called `jquery.dateZoom.js` and insert the custom alias function:

```
(function($){
    // plug-in code here
})(jQuery);
```

Inside this function, attach the new method to the `fn` object by inserting the following bold code:

```
(function($){

    // A plug-in that enlarges the text of an element when moused
    // over, then returns it to its original size on mouse out
    $.fn.dateZoom = function(options)
    {
        // code here
    };

})(jQuery);
```

Providing Publicly Accessible Default Options

In your `validDate()` plug-in, the function's default options are stored in a private object. This can be undesirable, especially in instances where a user might apply the plug-in method to multiple sets of elements and then want to modify the defaults for all instances.

To make default options publicly accessible, you can store them in the `dateZoom` namespace. For your `dateZoom` plug-in, create a publicly accessible `defaults` object that contains six custom properties:

- `fontsize`: The size to which the font will expand. Set this to 110% by default.

- `easing`: The easing function to use for the animation. Set this to `swing` by default.

- `duration`: The number of milliseconds the animation should last. Set this to 600 by default.

- `selector`: The CSS selector of the element(s) to bind to. Set this to `li>a` by default.

- `match`: The property to match with the element(s) to bind to. Set this to `href` by default.

- `callback`: A function that fires upon completion of the animation. Set this to `null` by default.

Now add the default options to the dateZoom plug-in by inserting the following bold code:

```
(function($){

    // A plug-in that enlarges the text of an element when moused
    // over, then returns it to its original size on mouse out
    $.fn.dateZoom = function(options)
    {
        // code here
    };

    // Defines default values for the plug-in
    $.fn.dateZoom.defaults = {
            "fontsize" : "110%",
            "easing" : "swing",
            "duration" : "600",
            "selector" : "li>a",
            "match" : "href",
            "callback" : null
        };

})(jQuery);
```

At this point, a user can change the defaults for all calls to the dateZoom plug-in using syntax something like this:

```
$.fn.dateZoom.defaults.fontsize = "120%";
```

To override default options, a user can pass an object with new values for one or more of the default options, as in the validDate plug-in. You can use $.extend() to create a new object that contains values for the current invocation of the plug-in when it is created.

The following bold code adds this functionality to the dateZoom plug-in:

```
(function($){

    // A plug-in that enlarges the text of an element when moused
    // over, then returns it to its original size on mouse out
    $.fn.dateZoom = function(options)
    {
        // Only overwrites values that were explicitly passed by
        // the user in options
        var opts = $.extend($.fn.dateZoom.defaults, options);

        // more code here
    };

    // Defines default values for the plug-in
    $.fn.dateZoom.defaults = {
            "fontsize" : "110%",
            "easing" : "swing",
            "duration" : "600",
```

```
        "selector" : "li>a",
        "match" : "href",
        "callback" : null
    };

})(jQuery);
```

Maintaining Chainability

To keep plug-in methods chainable, the method must return the modified jQuery object. Fortunately, this is easy to accomplish with jQuery: all you need to do is run the .each() method on the this object to iterate over each selected element, and then return the this object.

In the dateZoom plug-in, you can make your method chainable by inserting the code shown in bold:

```
(function($){

    // A plug-in that enlarges the text of an element when moused
    // over, then returns it to its original size on mouse out
    $.fn.dateZoom = function(options)
    {
        // Only overwrites values that were explicitly passed by
        // the user in options
        var opts = $.extend($.fn.dateZoom.defaults, options);

        // Loops through each matched element and returns the
        // modified jQuery object to maintain chainability
        return this.each(function(){
            // more code here
        });
    };

    // Defines default values for the plug-in
    $.fn.dateZoom.defaults = {
            "fontsize" : "110%",
            "easing" : "swing",
            "duration" : "600",
            "selector" : "li>a",
            "match" : "href",
            "callback" : null
    };

})(jQuery);
```

Creating a Publicly Accessible Helper Method

To keep your plug-in code clean and organized, you will place the actual animation of the elements in a helper method called zoom.

This method, like the defaults object, will be publicly accessible under the dateZoom namespace. Making this method public means that a user can potentially redefine the method before calling the plug-in or even call the method outside of the plug-in, if she so desires.

351

You create the zoom method by inserting the following bold code into the dateZoom plug-in:

```
(function($){

    // A plug-in that enlarges the text of an element when moused
    // over, then returns it to its original size on mouse out
    $.fn.dateZoom = function(options)
    {
        // Only overwrites values that were explicitly passed by
        // the user in options
        var opts = $.extend($.fn.dateZoom.defaults, options);

        // Loops through each matched element and returns the
        // modified jQuery object to maintain chainability
        return this.each(function(){
            // more code here
        });
    };

    // Defines default values for the plug-in
    $.fn.dateZoom.defaults = {
            "fontsize" : "110%",
            "easing" : "swing",
            "duration" : "600",
            "selector" : "li>a",
            "match" : "href",
            "callback" : null
        };

    // Defines a utility function that is available outside of the
    // plug-in if a user is so inclined to use it
    $.fn.dateZoom.zoom = function(element, size, opts)
    {
        // zoom the elements
    };

})(jQuery);
```

This method accepts the element to animate, the size to which it should be animated, and an object containing options.

▓ **Note**   You're keeping the size separate from the rest of the options because the element's original font size will be used for returning the element to its original state and that value is not available in the options object.

Inside this method, you will use the .animate(), .dequeue(), and .clearQueue() methods to animate the object and prevent animation queue buildup; add the code shown in bold to accomplish this:

```
(function($){

    // A plug-in that enlarges the text of an element when moused
    // over, then returns it to its original size on mouse out
    $.fn.dateZoom = function(options)
    {
        // Only overwrites values that were explicitly passed by
        // the user in options
        var opts = $.extend($.fn.dateZoom.defaults, options);

        // Loops through each matched element and returns the
        // modified jQuery object to maintain chainability
        return this.each(function(){
            // more code here
        });
    };

    // Defines default values for the plug-in
    $.fn.dateZoom.defaults = {
            "fontsize" : "110%",
            "easing" : "swing",
            "duration" : "600",
            "selector" : "li>a",
            "match" : "href",
            "callback" : null
        };

    // Defines a utility function that is available outside of the
    // plug-in if a user is so inclined to use it
    $.fn.dateZoom.zoom = function(element, size, opts)
    {
        // Limit zoom effect to currently hovered element.
        if (opts.match)
        {
            element = $.grep($(element), function(elem) {
                return elem[opts.match] === $('a:hover')[0][opts.match];
            });
        }

        $(element).animate({
                "font-size" : size
            },{
                "duration" : opts.duration,
                "easing" : opts.easing,
                "complete" : opts.callback
            })
            .dequeue()      // Prevents jumpy animation
            .clearQueue(); // Ensures only one animation occurs
    };

})(jQuery);
```

▓ **Note** The .dequeue() method takes the current animation out of the animation queue, preventing the animation from jumping to the end when the queue is cleared with .clearQueue(). Allowing the queue to build up can cause the animated element to look jumpy or to perform the animation many times in rapid succession, which is definitely an undesirable effect.

Modifying Each Matched Element

Because the .each() method accepts a callback, you can easily modify each matched element in the jQuery object being processed. For the dateZoom plug-in, you'll add hover event handlers to each selected element.

When a user hovers her mouse over an element to which dateZoom has been applied, the zoom method will run. This method relies on the selector property of the defaults object to specify the type of element to which the effect is applied.

The optional match property of the defaults object is provided to further narrow the element(s) affected if desired. If this option is specified, note that it uses the jQuery $.grep function to filter the initially selected elements further based on a successful match to the currently moused-over element ($('a:hover')[0][opts.match]).

The fontsize property resizes the text accordingly. When the user stops hovering, the original text size will be passed to zoom, and the element's text will return to its original size. To store the original size, use the .css() method and place the original font size in a private variable.

You use the .hover() method to implement this functionality by inserting the following bold code into the dateZoom plug-in:

```
(function($){

    // A plug-in that enlarges the text of an element when moused
    // over, then returns it to its original size on mouse out
    $.fn.dateZoom = function(options)
    {
        // Only overwrites values that were explicitly passed by
        // the user in options
        var opts = $.extend($.fn.dateZoom.defaults, options);

        // Loops through each matched element and returns the
        // modified jQuery object to maintain chainability
        return this.each(function(){
            // Stores the original font size of the element
            var originalsize = $(opts.selector).css("font-size");

            // Binds functions to the hover event. The first is
            // triggered when the user hovers over the element, and
            // the second when the user stops hovering
            $(this).hover(function(){
                    $.fn.dateZoom.zoom(opts.selector, opts.fontsize, opts);
                },
                function(){
                    $.fn.dateZoom.zoom(opts.selector, originalsize, opts);
                });
        });
    };
```

```
        // Defines default values for the plug-in
        $.fn.dateZoom.defaults = {
                "fontsize" : "110%",
                "easing" : "swing",
                "duration" : "600",
                "selector" : "li>a",
                "match" : "href",
                "callback" : null
        };

        // Defines a utility function that is available outside of the
        // plug-in if a user is so inclined to use it
        $.fn.dateZoom.zoom = function(element, size, opts)
        {
            // Limit zoom effect to currently hovered element.
            if (opts.match)
            {
                element = $.grep($(element), function(elem) {
                    return elem[opts.match] === $('a:hover')[0][opts.match];
                });
            }

            $(element).animate({
                    "font-size" : size
                },{
                    "duration" : opts.duration,
                    "easing" : opts.easing,
                    "complete" : opts.callback
                })
            .dequeue()      // Prevents jumpy animation
            .clearQueue(); // Ensures only one animation occurs
        };

})(jQuery);
```

Implementing Your Plug-in

At this point, your plug-in is ready to implement. All that remains is to include the file and select a set of elements to run it on.

Including the Plug-in File

To include the plug-in file, you need to modify footer.inc.php and add a new script tag. As with the validDate plug-in, the dateZoom plug-in needs to be included *before* init.js, so that the method is available to be called:

```
    <script src="https://ajax.googleapis.com/ajax/libs/jquery/2.1.4/jquery.min.js">
    </script>
    <script src="assets/js/jquery.validDate.js"></script>
    <script src="assets/js/jquery.dateZoom.js"></script>
    <script src="assets/js/init.js"></script>
</body>

</html>
```

Initializing the Plug-in on a Set of Elements

The plug-in is now included in the application, so you can call the .dateZoom() method on a set of elements. The next set of changes requires that you modify init.js, so open that file now.

Begin by changing the default fontsize value to 13px, and then add the .dateZoom() method to the chain of methods on the set of elements selected with the selector property ("li>a" in this application). As already indicated, you implement these changes by modifying init.js, as shown in the bold code that follows:

```
jQuery(function($){

var processFile = "assets/inc/ajax.inc.php",
    fx = {...}

// Set a default font-size value for dateZoom
$.fn.dateZoom.defaults.fontsize = "13px";

// Pulls up events in a modal window and attaches a zoom effect
$("body")
    .dateZoom()
    .on("click", "li>a", function(event){

            // Stops the link from loading view.php
            event.preventDefault();

            // Adds an "active" class to the link
            $(this).addClass("active");

            // Gets the query string from the link href
            var data = $(this)
                        .attr("href")
                        .replace(/.+?\?(.*)$/, "$1"),
```

```
            // Checks if the modal window exists and
            // selects it, or creates a new one
                modal = fx.checkmodal();

            // Creates a button to close the window
            $("<a>")
                .attr("href", "#")
                .addClass("modal-close-btn")
                .html("&times;")
                .click(function(event){
                            // Removes event
                            fx.boxout(event);
                        })
                .appendTo(modal);

            // Loads the event data from the DB
            $.ajax({
                    type: "POST",
                    url: processFile,
                    data: "action=event_view&"+data,
                    success: function(data){
                            // Displays event data
                            fx.boxin(data, modal);
                        },
                    error: function(msg) {
                            alert(msg);
                        }
                });

        });

$("body").on("click", ".admin-options form,.admin", function(event)(event){...});

$("body").on("click", ".edit-form a:contains(cancel)", function(event){...});

// Edits events without reloading
$("body").on("click", ".edit-form input[type=submit]", function(event){...});

});
```

Save these changes, reload http://localhost/ in your browser, and then hover over an event title to see the dateZoom plug-in in action (see Figure 10-1).

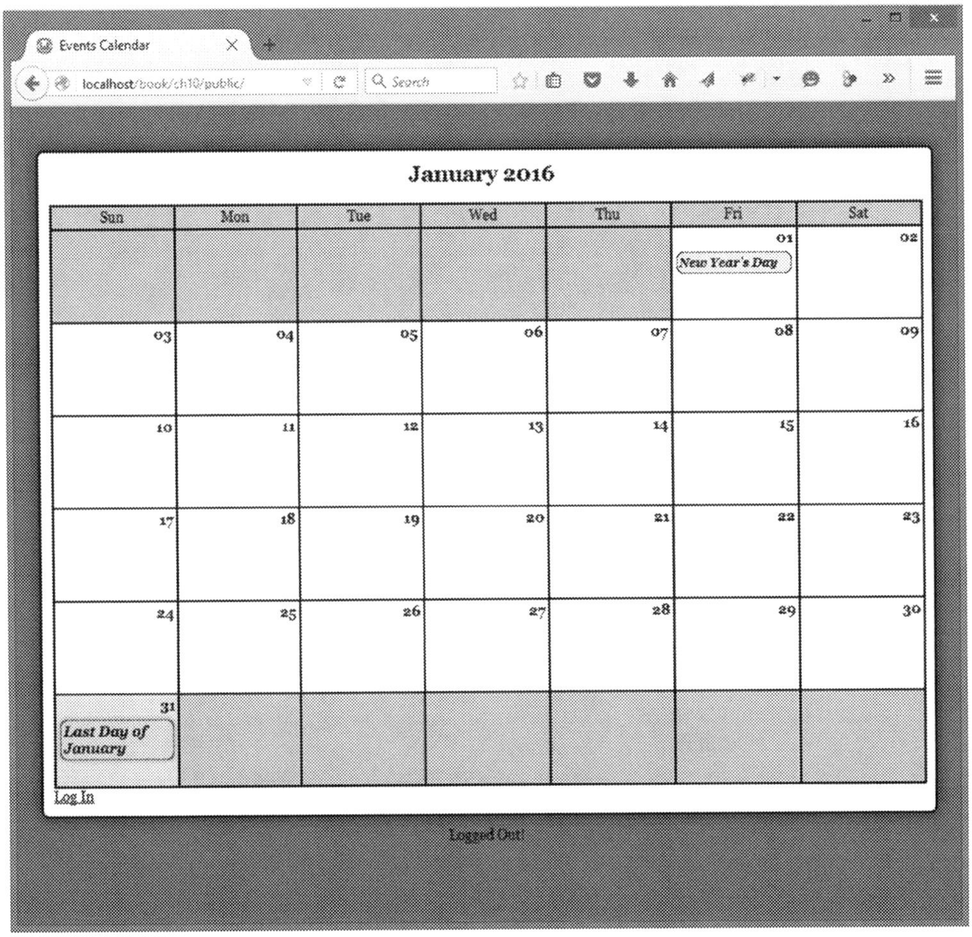

Figure 10-1. *The event title enlarges when hovered over*

It is also an instructive experiment to temporarily disable the `match` property of the `defaults` object, by setting it to the empty string `""`, and then reloading. If you do this, you'll notice that *all* the `selector` elements (`"li>a"` in this application) will get the zoom effect whenever *any* one of them is moused over. This shows the variety and power, but also the possible complexity, that comes with jQuery's (CSS-derived) methods for accessing elements in the DOM.

Summary

You should now feel comfortable building custom plug-ins in jQuery, both as chainable methods and as functions. This chapter is fairly short, but that brevity stands as a testament to the ease with which you can extend the jQuery library with your own custom scripts.

Congratulations! You've now learned how to use PHP and jQuery together to build custom applications with a desktop app-like feel. Now you're ready to bring all your great ideas to life on the Web!

APPENDIX A

Brief Notes on PHP 7

In this appendix, we briefly examine some of the changes made in version 7 of the PHP language.

The majority of legacy code will run unchanged (as did all the code in the previous edition of this book), but here we take a look at those new features that are most useful for your purposes.

Note For further reading on all of the changes for PHP 7, see the official migration guide at http://php.net/manual/en/migration70.php.

Strict Typing

For those who prefer structure and discipline in their coding practices, a welcome addition in PHP 7 is the optional per-file directive `strict_types`, which subjects all function calls and return statements within a file to "strict" type checking for scalar types. And in addition to the already existing `callable` and `array` types, PHP 7 has added `string`, `int`, `float`, and `bool` variable types. Parameter types are specified in the argument list, and the return type is specified with a colon after the argument list.

Here are strict types in action:

```php
<?php

declare(strict_types=1);

function doStuff(int $int=0, string $str="", float $flt=0.0, bool $b=False): string
{
    echo $int . "<br/>";
    echo $flt . "<br/>";
    echo $b . "<br/>";
    return $str;
}

$output = doStuff(1, "hi there", "2.34", True); // Oops! 2.34 should not have quotes!
echo $output . "<br/>";

?>
```

When you load this script in your browser, you will see something like the following:

Fatal error: Uncaught TypeError: Argument 3 passed to doStuff() must be of the type ↵
float, string given, called in C:\wamp\www\book\appendix\test.php on line 13 and ↵
defined in C:\wamp\www\book\appendix\test.php:5 Stack trace: #0 ↵
C:\wamp\www\book\appendix\test.php(13): doStuff(1, 'hi there', '2.34', true) ↵
#1 {main} thrown in **C:\wamp\www\book\appendix\test.php** on line **5**

This is actually a good thing! It is generally better for your code to fail early and noisily. Silent bugs are essentially land mines that you (or worse, a user) will set off, usually at rather inconvenient times. The argument type declaration in the definition of doStuff() specified a float for its third argument, but instead a string was passed (because of the quotes).

Let's fix that argument type bug by removing the quotes around 2.34, and then introduce another, different bug–a return type error. Here is the code:

```php
<?php

declare(strict_types=1);

function doStuff(int $int=0, string $str="", float $flt=0.0, bool $b=False): string
{
    echo $int . "<br/>";
    echo $flt . "<br/>";
    echo $b . "<br/>";
    return $flt; // Oops! Supposed to be a string (such as $str).
}

$output = doStuff(1, "hi there", 2.34, True);
echo $output . "<br/>";

?>
```

When you load this script in your browser, you will see

```
1
2.34
1
```

Fatal error: Uncaught TypeError: Return value of doStuff() must be of the type ↵
string, float returned in C:\wamp\www\book\appendix\test.php:10 Stack trace: ↵
#0 C:\wamp\www\book\appendix\test.php(13): doStuff(1, 'hi there', 2.34, true) #1 ↵
{main} thrown in **C:\wamp\www\book\appendix\test.php** on line **10**

This time, you "drew the foul" by using the wrong return type: a float instead of the promised string.

Although it is ultimately a matter of personal (or team) preference, we believe that the strict typing introduced in PHP 7 is very worthwhile, and possibly the most useful of the newly added features.

New Exceptions

With the addition of strict typing discussed above, PHP 7 provides a corresponding exception: `TypeError`.
Here is the above code wrapped in a `try` block using this new exception type:

```php
<?php

declare(strict_types=1);

function doStuff(int $int=0, string $str="", float $flt=0.0, bool $b=False): string
{
    echo $int . "<br/>";
    echo $flt . "<br/>";
    echo $b . "<br/>";
    return $flt; // Oops! Supposed to be a string (such as $str).
}

try {
    $output = doStuff(1, "hi there", 2.34, True);
    echo $output . "<br/>";
} catch(TypeError $e) {
    echo $e;
}

?>
```

You can choose how best to handle the exception, but the point is the error is no longer fatal. The above
code dumps all the information about the exception:

```
1
2.34
1
TypeError: Return value of doStuff() must be of the type string, float returned ↵
in C:\wamp\www\book\appendix\test.php:10 Stack trace: #0 ↵
C:\wamp\www\book\appendix\test.php(14): doStuff(1, 'hi there', 2.34, true) #1 {main}
```

Also included in PHP 7 are `ArithmeticError`, `AssertionError`, `DivisionByZeroError`, and `ParseError`
exceptions. Refer to the link given above for more information.

Constant Arrays

Another welcome addition is the ability to define constant (read only) arrays. This protects lookup tables and other such data that are not intended to change during program execution. The array can be as deeply nested as desired.

Unlike with normal variables, there is no preceding $ with array constants, and it is customary (though not required) to name them using all uppercase letters. Otherwise, the syntax is familiar:

```php
<?php

declare(strict_types=1);

define('ACTIONS', array(
        'user_login' => array(
                'object' => 'Admin',
                'method' => 'processLoginForm',
                'header' => 'Location: ../../'
            ),
        'user_logout' => array(
                'object' => 'Admin',
                'method' => 'processLogout',
                'header' => 'Location: ../../'
            )
        )
    );

echo ACTIONS['user_logout']['method'];

?>
```

Here is the result:

---

processLogout

If any attempt is made to alter a constant array, either by adding a new value or reassigning an existing value like this:

```php
<?php

declare(strict_types=1);

define('ACTIONS', array(
        'user_login' => array(
                'object' => 'Admin',
                'method' => 'processLoginForm',
                'header' => 'Location: ../../'
            ),
```

```
        'user_logout' => array(
                'object' => 'Admin',
                'method' => 'processLogout',
                'header' => 'Location: ../../'
            )
        )
    );

ACTIONS['user_logout']['method'] = 'somethingElse'; // Not allowed!

?>
```

Then, happily, when your code runs you will find out immediately with a message like:

Fatal error: Cannot use temporary expression in write context in ↵
C:\wamp\www\appendix\test.php on line **24**

This again is a boon to those who prefer added structure and safety in their coding practices.

Argument Unpacking

Another handy feature that's been added is argument unpacking, in which the elements of an array variable can be expanded as individual arguments to a function that expects a list of scalars rather than an array as its input. This allows you more flexibility in how you invoke a given function, without having to rewrite the parameter list in its definition (and in the case of a library function, you may not even have that option).

This operator, often called the "splat" operator (in particular by the Ruby community) consists of three dots (periods) and is used like this:

```
<?php

declare(strict_types=1);

function add($a, $b, $c) {
    return $a + $b + $c;
}

$two_more = [2, 5];

echo add(1, ...$two_more); // Unpack the elements of $two_more.
?>
```

You get the expected sum:

8

Note that while the ... operator unpacks all the elements in the array to which it is applied, the function call still uses only those arguments listed in its definition. In other words, if the array to be unpacked contained more than two elements (in this example), then all the additional elements would simply be ignored. (You can try yourself, and see that something like $two_more = [2, 5, 77, -13]; still gives the same sum of 8 above.) This is consistent with existing PHP behavior.

Integer Division

An integer division function, intdiv(), has been added to make integer division convenient and explicit. It works just how you'd expect:

```php
<?php

declare(strict_types=1);

$num = 11;
$den = 3;
$result = intdiv($num, $den);

echo $result;

?>
```

The truncated integer value is returned:

3

Syntactic Sugar

As of this writing, the final PHP 7 release is still pending, and you are encouraged to check the latest documentation, but here we mention a couple more goodies that have already made it in.

A special conditional operator, called the "null coalesce" operator, denoted by a double question mark, has been added, and it expands on the functionality of the ternary conditional operator. The null coalesce operator checks for a non-null value before falling through to a final value. In addition, this new operator is chainable.

A code snippet says it all:

```php
<?php

declare(strict_types=1);

$alpha = null;
$beta = null;
$gamma = "I'm not null!";

echo $alpha ?? 'this value' . "<br/>";
echo $alpha ?? $beta ?? $gamma ?? 'that value' . "<br/>"; // chainable

?>
```

And the output is

```
this value
I'm not null!
```

The last feature we'll look at was no doubt inspired by the Perl community, and it concerns sorting. Consider the following routine, albeit clunky, code that performs a case-insensitive alphabetical sort:

```php
<?php

declare(strict_types=1);

$values = ['Zebra', 'zed', 'apple', 'baseball', 'Angel'];

usort($values, function($a, $b) {
    $x = strtolower($a);
    $y = strtolower($b);
    return ($x < $y) ? -1 : (($x > $y) ? 1 : 0);
});

var_dump($values);

?>
```

This code does get the job done:

```
array(5) { [0]=> string(5) "Angel" [1]=> string(5) "apple" [2]=> string(8) "baseball" ↵
[3]=> string(5) "Zebra" [4]=> string(3) "zed" }
```

But with the new PHP 7 "spaceship" operator, <=>, the same result can be achieved much more elegantly, as the following code demonstrates:

```php
<?php

declare(strict_types=1);

$values = ['Zebra', 'zed', 'apple', 'baseball', 'Angel'];

usort($values, function($a, $b) {
    return strtolower($a) <=> strtolower($b); // spaceship!
});

var_dump($values);

?>
```

And you can check that the output is exactly the same as before, but was achieved with much cleaner code.

Again, keep checking the latest PHP 7 documentation online for an exhaustive treatment of all language features and a detailed migration guide.

Index

■ L, M, N

■ O

■ P, Q

Get the eBook for only $5!

Why limit yourself?

Now you can take the weightless companion with you wherever you go and access your content on your PC, phone, tablet, or reader.

Since you've purchased this print book, we're happy to offer you the eBook in all 3 formats for just $5.

Convenient and fully searchable, the PDF version enables you to easily find and copy code—or perform examples by quickly toggling between instructions and applications. The MOBI format is ideal for your Kindle, while the ePUB can be utilized on a variety of mobile devices.

To learn more, go to www.apress.com/companion or contact support@apress.com.

Printed in the United States
By Bookmasters